WALKING OVER EGGSHELLS

by

LUCINDA E CLARKE

Walking over Eggshells

Umhlanga Press

Editor: Poppy Reid
Purplesage.editing@gmail.com

Front Cover artist:
SelfPubBookCovers.com/FrinaArt

Book cover compiled by
D.H.

This book is dedicated to my wonderful husband
and all those who have had a positive
impact on my life and given me help
and encouragement along the way

Also by Lucinda E Clarke:

Truth, Lies and Propaganda
More Truth, Lies and Propaganda
Amie an African Adventure
Amie and the Child of Africa
Unhappily Ever After

Contents

FOREWORD

I wrote this book for several reasons. Should my brain begin to disintegrate as I get older, I want to be able to revisit my life and some of the mad and crazy things I have done a sort of self-introduction if you like! I can sit in my rocking chair and recall who I was and, at least, some of the experiences from my past. Everything you read is true, and although other characters in the story may have quite different memories, this is how I saw and experienced the events. I have changed names and locations to protect the guilty and the innocent.

My story is primarily about mental abuse, not as obvious and accepted as other forms of abuse, but often much more damaging in the long-term. It leaves you with a low self-image and takes away the confidence you need to leave home and make your way in the world. I would like to raise awareness of this type of abuse, as little has been written about it.

No narrative is all doom and gloom, so I have included many lighter moments, for I have no wish to present a depressing and self-pitying account of my life. It has been quite amazing at times and also a little bizarre with lots of hilarious moments.

Most importantly, I sincerely hope that my experiences and the final revelation will help others. By this, I mean other people who have been caught in the same spiral of misery and despair. Maybe my story will give them hope that life is for living, and that they too can rise above the mental abuse they suffered in childhood.

Spain 2013 ©

1 DUBLIN EARLY CHILDHOOD

The first time I tried to leave home I was three years old. Not that I could have told you that at the time, but many years later, while looking at some childhood photos, I asked my mother what age I was when I wore the red hat and coat. "Three," she replied and I remember quite clearly putting them on for my first intended escape into the outside world.

It was a cold, overcast day in a quiet suburb of Dublin at the beginning of the fifties. We were in the lounge, and my mother was sitting by the fire listening to the radio. I walked quietly to the door, hoping she wouldn't notice, but as I reached up towards the door handle, she reminded me in her cold, hard voice, not to let the cold air in from the hallway. I opened the door just wide enough to squeeze through and pulled it shut behind me.

I dived under my bed and pulled out a small brown, cardboard suitcase. I'd thought about this departure for some time and had already made a mental list of what I would need on the journey to my new life. I packed three Noddy books, my favourite doll, a comb and a clean pair of underpants. I struggled into my coat and hat and I was ready to run away.

Quietly I crept back along the hallway to the front door and gazed up at the door latch, it was way above my head.

"And where do you think you're going?" My mother stood in the lounge doorway, her arms folded across her chest and she looked furious. Having got this far, there was no turning back.

"I'm leaving home," I squeaked.

"Oh, really, and where are you going?"

"I'm, uh….." I knew exactly where I was going. I'd thought about it very carefully, but I was not about to tell my mother. She would know where I was and maybe, just maybe, come and try to bring me back.

"Little girls who want to leave home should be tall enough to reach the door knob. If you go, then don't bother coming back, I never want to see you again. I don't want you. You're nothing but a nuisance. I wanted a good little girl who would do as she was told, not a bad, bad little girl like you." My mother went back into the lounge and slammed the door.

I blinked back the tears, why couldn't my mother love me? I tried so hard to be good. Earlier that morning I had broken a glass full of milk. It slipped out of my hands and crashed to the floor.

"Look what you've done now!" screamed my mother.

"I'm sorry Mummy, it fell," I burst into tears.

"Clear it up right now!"

"Yes, yes, but please don't be cross with me, please. I'm sorry, I'm sorry." I was shaking as I looked at the mess on the floor. The milk was slowly disappearing under the stove.

"You never give me any reason to like you. You're always saying 'sorry.' If you really meant it you wouldn't do the same thing again and again and again. You said 'sorry' when you broke my best cup. I suppose that just fell too? Don't say 'sorry.' 'Sorry' doesn't mean anything to you."

As soon as my mother had gone back into the lounge, I dragged a chair from the kitchen, climbed up and opened the front door. I jammed the suitcase in the gap and returned the chair to its place in the kitchen. Then as quickly as I could, I grabbed the case and ran down the front driveway.

I was petrified of my mother. She was so cold and always so very, very angry, I could never, ever please her. The slightest thing I did upset her, and then I knew I would get a hiding and that hurt a lot. Not surprisingly I cried when the slipper was applied to my little legs, but the more I cried the more she hit me, "to give you something to cry about."

I wanted it all to stop and I wanted a kind, loving mummy. The only solution I could think of was to leave home, get away from her, and find a new mummy.

Five houses along the road lived Aunty Gladys and Uncle Douglas, they didn't have any children, and I knew they had a spare room I could have. They were always cheerful, always smiling and very kind. Sometimes Aunty Gladys would even give me a cuddle, so I'd decided that I was going to live with them. We would laugh a lot, they would hug me every day and be nice to me and I would be happy.

I had to stand on my suitcase to reach their doorbell, and it took several attempts before I finally heard the echoing chimes from the other side of the door. It never occurred to me that they might be out, that there wouldn't be anyone there to welcome me in.

I was just about to climb on my case again and ring a second time when the door opened. Aunty Gladys looked puzzled. She knew I was not allowed out of the garden by myself.

"I've run away from home and I've come to live with you," I blurted out. Uncle Douglas appeared in the doorway.

"What's this all about?" he asked.

"Lucinda has run away from home and wants to come and live with us," repeated Aunty Gladys.

It was getting chilly on the doorstep and I couldn't understand why they didn't sweep me into their arms and carry me inside. I had imagined that Aunty Gladys would take me into the kitchen, offer me some hot chocolate and then we would make plans for all the wonderful things we were going to do together.

But that didn't happen. They just stared at me. What was wrong? This wasn't the way I'd planned it or dreamed about it. Why weren't they pleased to see me?

Uncle Douglas broke the silence. "You can't come and live here," he said.

"You must go home," added Aunty Gladys.

"But..." I couldn't think of anything to say. If I was not going to live here, *where was I going to live*?

Large tears ran down my cheeks as I just stood there. I could never go home, I knew what would happen, the slipper, Mummy screaming and shouting. I would be sent to bed with no supper, and then would come the silence and that was the worst punishment of all.

Of course I was dragged home after they telephoned my mother and told her to come and collect her daughter. It didn't take too long for the pain on my legs to wear off, no matter how hard she used the slipper, but the silence could last for days and days. When I look back, I think the record was just over a month. Not one word spoken directly to me. There were plenty of asides, and remarks made to the dog, about how ungrateful the younger generation was, how badly behaved it was, and how disrespectful it was to the older generation.

At first I would beg for forgiveness. I was sorry, I would never, ever do anything wrong ever again. Please, please talk to me. Please let everything be all right. I would throw my arms around her and try to climb up on her lap to kiss and make up, but she always pushed me away.

After several days, I would get frustrated and angry and then of course, I would say or do something wrong again, and the whole cycle would start over. There were very small islands of calm among the oceans of misery, but they only lasted a day or two and then I would, often without realizing it, upset her again in some way and the beating, the anger and the silence would begin all over again.

I was born long before the days when children had rights, before children were considered real people. Then, they were regarded as the property of their parents and you were either a good child or a bad child. It was also long before the advent of Child Line, and the terms physical, sexual or emotional abuse were not everyday terms.

To the outside world, all appeared normal and content. We lived in a three bedroom bungalow on the outskirts of Dublin. We had all the modern amenities, the indoor bathroom, the telephone and the car. I'm sure there were millions of children worldwide who would have envied me my standard of living, my pretty clothes, my books and toys. I was given adequate food and I was seldom cold. But no material possessions could make up for the lack of love and the constant recriminations. Had I known there were beggars on the streets, or starving refugees with loving, caring families, I would happily have exchanged places with them.

But I had little knowledge of the outside world, mine was confined to the house and garden, with occasional trips to go shopping in the city. Even that sometimes led to disaster. I remember one particular occasion when we had met up with one of my mother's friends and her son. We had gone for coffee in one of the smartest department stores in the city. Too young to drink coffee or tea, I was handed a fizzy drink. In those days we were not asked what we would like, that was decided for us. Gordon, two years older than me, challenged me to a race as to who could finish first. I had no idea it wasn't wise to drink fizzy drinks quickly, so I not only lost the race, I also brought it all back up over my new outfit. My mother was apoplectic and I was hauled unceremoniously out of the shop, thrown into the car, and taken home for a good hiding. Once the slippers were back on, I knew I faced several more days of silence.

In later years, I have tried to understand my mother and the way she behaved, and if I'm honest, her life had not been idyllic either.

Born to rich, colonial parents, her father was an important businessman living overseas. He owned large tracts of land, office blocks in the city, and an estate up in the hills to escape the summer heat.

My grandmother was quite a socialite in her day, and with an army of servants to care for the houses and gardens, she had little to do but play bridge and plan evening entertainments. Then of course, there was the colonial club, the races and a host of other functions to attend.

My grandfather owned and ran a widely read English language newspaper, and he was also a stringer for the Daily Mail and The Telegraph in London. He told me he hated writing, but he'd inherited the business. His family originally came from Scotland, but my great, great, grandfather was sent to China as a missionary, and soon lost his religious zeal in pursuit of commerce and journalism. His father was very successful, and while my grandfather professed to hate journalism, he certainly seemed to make a success of it.

My mother Margaret was the only surviving child, after her younger brother died at the age of two from yellow fever. I don't think she was lonely, and I don't know how much or how little affection she received from her parents, but they obviously cared for her and gave her the best of the material world.

She had her own full time nanny, and I was told that she did not even visit the toilet by herself until she was seven years old. I believe she was very spoiled, had a high opinion of herself, and she would throw big temper tantrums when it was time for her to leave the adults and go home to bed. She had friends her own age to play with, sons and daughters of other colonials, and there are albums full of pictures showing picnics and outings in the hot sunshine.

But war clouds were gathering on the horizon, and it was thought suitable that my mother should return to England to continue her education. My grandmother brought her back to England and Margaret was left with the Bath branch of the family, and sent to an exclusive private school. Granny returned abroad soon after.

In those days, people closed ranks on discussing anything with the youngsters that was critical about the older generation, and I only guessed from the odd remark I overheard, that my mother created chaos in the household. She expected everyone to wait on her, and she complained bitterly about their harsh treatment. She was not used to being a member of an ordinary family with several other children, and she certainly didn't like to wait her turn for anything.

She once told me that her father had sent money to buy her a new bicycle and they only got her one that was secondhand. She kissed a boy, and was petrified she would get pregnant, she complained they had never told her the facts of life. However, apart from these two complaints, she never told me anything else about her time in Bath.

But even if the family loved her, it must have been hard, as she didn't see her parents again for seven years. In those days, it wasn't possible to hop on a plane and visit offspring in the school holidays. The voyage by sea took six weeks each way and it's unlikely that my Grandfather could take that amount of time away from the business.

My mother was a very average student, moving on to an equally exclusive private high school for the daughters of gentlemen farmers, where the main subjects would seem to be how to catch and keep a husband. At some point my mother learned how to type and do Pitman's shorthand, but I don't believe she ever saw herself working.

Overseas things were going from bad to worse. My grandmother was sent home to England for her own safety, and my grandfather was interned as a prisoner of war by the Japanese after they invaded China. My grandmother was reunited with her daughter just before the outbreak of World War II.

It was 1939, my mother was just 18 years old and was keen to join up. She enlisted in the Army and was in the Fanny's, first learning to drive and then becoming an instructor and eventually an instructor's instructor. They drove vehicles of all kinds, lorries, ambulances and trucks.

When it was decided that Princess Elizabeth should also join the forces, the Army put together a unit based near Windsor, which would allow the Princess to return home each night to sleep at the castle. There are photographs of the unit taken in 1945, with Her Royal Highness sitting in the same group as my mother.

Even in the army, my mother must have wielded influence, as she often boasted how she would get the other girls to bring her breakfast in bed every morning. How she got away with this I have never figured out, but she always hated early rising.

Through personal intervention by Winston Churchill, my grandfather was eventually exchanged for a Japanese prisoner and was repatriated to England. He arrived in London, with half a crown in the pocket of a borrowed suit. After a spell in hospital, he was released, and because he talked in his sleep, my grandmother discovered he had been working for MI 6, the British Secret Service.

I worshipped my grandfather. There were whispered tales of brave deeds and secret meetings. He, along with others, had informed the Americans and the British of the imminent bombings of Pearl Harbour and as we now know, these warnings were ignored with the objective of bringing America into the war. My grandfather had met and interviewed Lawrence of Arabia and he was friends with Chaing Kai-shek. As such, he was not a favourite of Mao Tse-tung who ousted the former leader, exiling him to Formosa, now known as Taiwan.

Grandfather had been kept in solitary confinement by the Japanese for over two years and been tortured, they suspected he was a spy. He was taken out into the yard several times to face a firing squad. The soldiers fired blanks at him. The only reason he survived was the attention of the local people who had once worked for him, and who slipped him extra food and blankets. In prison, he kept his mind agile by reciting everything from times tables to chemical formulae. He drew imaginary pictures on his cell wall and never gave up hope that one day he would be released.

I wish I could expand on his life, but I know only those facts I have written. Had I been older or more aware, I would have asked him numerous questions and perhaps written about his life instead of my own.

His arrival back in England upset my mother, who had formed a close bond with my grandmother, a quiet, gentle soul. But now my grandfather was back, all that changed and my mother was forced to take a back seat. She was very bitter about the loss of wealth, the servants and their privileged position in society. There was no recompense for the loss of all their property overseas, much of it destroyed, nor for the newspaper empire. The British Secret Service, neither then nor now, publicly welcomes or acknowledges any of their employees.

My grandparents moved into a small flat on the outskirts of London, and as my grandfather recovered, he took a job in Baker Street working at the head office of Marks and Spencer.

In the meantime, my mother had met a young Irishman, they became engaged, and the wedding took place in 1946, in Sutton, Surrey, after which they left England to settle in Dublin, where my father went to work for a major international insurance group.

I made my appearance in 1948, in a private Dublin nursing home and full of enthusiasm, my father rushed off to register me as Lucinda Elizabeth, much to my mother's horror. She planned to name me Pita, Russian for girl.

Several months later, the three of us moved to Cork and there was talk of my father being sent to Cape Town to help spearhead an insurance company in South Africa. Maybe that's another stranger than fiction fact, as fate was to prove much later.

By now, my father was already ill and they moved back to Dublin to be closer to the rest of the family, although my mother was at war with every single one of them. I did hear that the transfer to Cork in the first place, was because of the rows between my mother and her in-laws. She complained about their interference, their insensitiveness and their lack of respect towards her.

I don't remember my father at all. I was only two years old when he died quietly at his parents' home one evening, from cancer. It was unfortunate that his parents happened to be out at a party that evening, something for which my mother never forgave them.

We moved into a bungalow, three doors away from my father's younger sister. It proves that we were not close to the other members of the family, as it never occurred to me to run away to live with my real aunty who lived even closer than my mother's friends 'Aunty' Gladys and 'Uncle' Douglas.

Each Sunday I would peep from behind the net curtains and watch my paternal grandfather park his car just down the road and visit his daughter, son in law and grandchildren. He never visited our house. Occasionally, one of my cousins would come over later with a toy, or some sweets left for me by my grandparents, all of which my mother put straight into the dustbin.

At some point, there must have been some reconciliation within the family as I do remember the odd visit to their house on the other side of Dublin. I was fascinated by the tall pampas grass that grew on the back lawn, the tortoises that hid away in winter, the real elephant's foot stool and the glass bead curtain.

My paternal grandfather was a successful insurance broker, and a member of all the right clubs and societies. After my father died, the Masons offered to help with my education. My mother refused. She had never come to terms with that part of my father's life which she had been unable to dominate. The secrets surrounding the Freemasons were an insult to her and a part of my father's life that excluded her.

I was sent to the best private Protestant school in Dublin, but I remember being unhappy at school and I was not very popular. On one occasion I was the only child in the class not invited to the most popular girl's birthday party. Since I was still in kindergarten at the time, I may not have been totally aware of this, but my mother found out, explained the situation and told me how awful I was, who would want me at their birthday party?

For birthday or Christmas my mother would have a party for me and invite the cousins and a few of the children from school of whom she approved. She would dress me up beautifully and warn me beforehand that I must behave and not get my clothes dirty, and was not to eat too much and have nice manners and not to snatch the presents and so on. I never remember enjoying any of the parties.

Christmas was especially difficult as I was to open each present slowly, peel off the Sellotape, and not tear the paper so that it could be folded neatly for re-use. Once the present was identified, and I had learned to write, there was the thank you note to compose. If I made one mistake, I had to start all over again, it had to be perfect. This was very difficult for a six year old and always ended in tears. By the time I was free to play with the new acquisitions, it was well past Christmas.

Was I a difficult child? No more than any other I guess, but my only real memories of those days were misery, fear and a very low self-esteem. I started to bite my nails, and nibbled them down to the quick. Mother covered my fingers with bitter aloes, which tasted foul to begin with, but I got used to the taste and it was only in my late teens that I finally let my nails grow.

The one bright light in my life was my fifth birthday present. My mother had dog-sat for a friend and she was so impressed with the Cairn Terrier, that she ordered a puppy from the next litter. I was enchanted with the little ball of rough fur. I suggested the usual childish names, but my mother announced that his name would be Boko, after one of the famous Siamese twins who had been successfully separated, and so I now had a dog named Boko. Who was I to question this rather strange name?

Sadly, Cairns are not affectionate dogs and at every opportunity, Boko made a furious bid to run away from home, even if the gate was only left open for a minute, and at regular intervals I also attempted to run away from home. On one occasion I left with no idea of where to go, so I just kept walking and walking and walking. It didn't matter where I was going, I only knew that I had to get away. I don't think my mother ever called the police, but she found me that day and remarked that she didn't think that anyone so small could have travelled so far.

Much is written about physical and sexual abuse, but mental abuse is not so obvious and many children suffer as the victims of cruel behavior from their parents. It leaves them with a low self-image, a nervous disposition and the inability to make confident decisions. In short it erodes you as a functioning person and you seldom reach your full potential. While I had all the outward trappings of a well cared for, middle class child, I was trapped in a living hell. It's such a strong belief in all cultures that mothers love their children even more than they love themselves. In the animal world mothers will put their lives at risk to protect their young. Tell anyone that your mother doesn't love you, and they will believe there is something radically wrong with you. I was told incessantly that there was definitely something wrong with me. I was bad, wicked and evil.

I began ballet lessons at the age of two and appeared on stage when I was only three smiling bravely while dreading the end of the performance and the criticism and silences that would follow. It was after one ballet lesson that my mother examined my legs, there was something wrong, but she couldn't figure out what. We went to the doctor and I was to go to hospital and stay there for several months. I had no idea what was the matter with me and no one thought to tell me. By getting ill, I had shamed her. This was very unfair, but it was almost two decades later before I discovered the truth.

Mother did tell me that she would never be able to kiss or cuddle me, as she was afraid for my health. She didn't explain why and refused to answer any of my questions. I'm not sure to this day if my mother truly believed this, but I will try to give her the benefit of the doubt.

I was only six years old when I went into the sanatorium. The required treatment to make me better was lots of rest and lots of fresh air and streptomycin, the new wonder drug. I was there for almost a year. I tried to be good, but I remember wetting the bed and the nurses being very angry with me. My mother didn't help. She made herself unpopular with everyone. When I was admitted into hospital, the pretty nighties she had made for me were returned to her. She created a terrible scene at the reception desk and I remember a lot of shouting and screaming.

We were all given a white night shirt with a red jersey to wear over it. A nurse would bring piles of these into the ward and leave them on the end of one of the beds. Those children who were able to get out of bed and walk, dived into the piles, choosing the largest shirts and jerseys for themselves. They would take the next size down to give to their friends. I was bed bound with a long, heavy iron splint attached to my left leg. When the clothing arrived, I could never reach it, so I always ended up with shirts and jerseys that were far too small for me. Often, the shirt only came half way down my chest and left my lower back exposed. All the beds were on an open verandah and I remember shivering, especially in the winter. There was nothing to stop the wind and rain blowing in, and we had to huddle under the thin bedding to try and keep warm. Even today I have a particular fear of being cold.

As if being open to the elements at the front wasn't enough, the wall behind was peppered with open grills to let in extra fresh air. The hospital backed on to a low-cost housing area and the young boys would often amuse themselves by posting a variety of rubbish through the vents. Then they waited to hear the screams and I certainly gave them value for effort, especially the day a bicycle tyre landed on top of me. I was petrified. I sat rigid in bed looking at the black rubber circular tube, I had no idea what it was.

I mentioned earlier that I went to a Protestant school, now I was in a Catholic hospital, the only non-Catholic in the place. Once the other children found out, they informed me that I would go straight to hell for not worshipping the right god. If I could, I would have converted and become a Roman Catholic there and then, but I didn't know how. I was left in solitary isolation every Sunday as each bed was wheeled off so that everyone could attend mass.

On Good Friday, we were all warned not to utter a word between the hours of twelve and three, the time that Christ was on the cross. I sat quietly playing with my dolls, until I suddenly realized with horror that I had been talking to them. I looked round, and sure enough other children were watching me. I was discovered. A minute after the clock struck three, everyone assured me that my chances of going to hell had been doubled. It was a certainty, so I might as well face it.

The nursing staff was totally fed up with my mother, she bucked the system on every occasion. Sunday was visiting day and ropes were strung along the ends of each bed, to avoid spreading whatever it was we had. All visitors were to stand at the end of the bed and remain behind the ropes. My mother refused to obey the rules and crossed the line. Not to give me a kiss or a cuddle, but just on principle, no one was going to tell her what she could and couldn't do. One Sunday she even brought Boko in and what a scene that caused.

My grandparents in London sent me regular parcels of sweets, colouring books, and the Children's Newspaper. Any parcels were dumped at the end of the bed and again, I couldn't reach them. I was seldom left with anything, as the other patients descended in hoards, ripping open the brown paper parcel.

"Can I have this?"

"Can I have that?"

I could only nod and let them divide the contents of my parcel and take it all away. I was left with the Children's Newspaper and no one wanted to read that, least of all me. I didn't have the confidence to say "no" to anyone.

At last, they decided to discharge me from hospital and send me home. It must have been summertime, as I remember lying on the camp bed in the garden, watching Boko race around the flowerbeds and across the lawn, while I paid scant attention to my lessons. I had a series of private tutors all of whom found me difficult to teach. I honestly don't remember any of them now. I only know that I had taught myself to read before I was four and that all I wanted to do was read, especially about Noddy and any other Enid Blyton book I could get my hands on.

Altogether, I was a year in bed and at the age of seven I had to learn to walk again. This was a frustrating time, as like all seven year olds, why walk when you can run? Understandably, everyone wanted to protect me from falling. I heard my mother tell everyone that I suffered from 'water on the knee' and I will never forget the painful hot poultices that were applied to my leg every day.

Since the doctor told my mother that she must feed me well and give me nourishing food, we had cooked meat three times a week. It wasn't good quality meat, but the stringy stuff, with a layer of fat on the one side you simply can't cut off. I remember trying very hard to eat it, but my stomach just rebelled, and I would heave just looking at the stew. But I had to eat it, my mother was determined, and the more I rebelled, the sterner she became. What I did not eat at lunchtime was presented cold at suppertime and the following morning for breakfast. Do you remember, "You don't get pudding if you don't finish your first course?" I never remember having pudding and I would look longingly at the sliced banana with milk and strawberry jam that I seldom, if ever, got to eat.

I returned to school and life continued much the way it had before, until one day, when I was ten, I came home to find that we were leaving Ireland.

"We're going to live in England," my mother told me. This was exciting news and I looked forward to the move. Maybe a new country meant a new life? Maybe Mummy would be happy and loving in a new country?

2 ENGLAND, THE COTSWOLDS

At first we stayed briefly with my mother's parents in their small flat outside London. I was sent to the local primary school, very different from my smart private school in Dublin.

There were constant rows between my mother and her parents. She wanted to live with them and they said no, she must make her own home for herself and her child. My mother screamed and cried and blamed my grandfather for losing everything overseas because of his selfish principles and bringing all this misery on the family. But my grandfather stood firm.

In hindsight, there certainly wasn't enough space for us in the flat and eventually my mother dragged me off to stay with a friend of hers in the Cotswolds. At that time, the local council was offering good mortgage rates on bungalows being built on the outskirts of town. I guess they were trying to encourage immigration to the rural areas, even in those days, the youth couldn't wait to escape to the nearby cities.

My mother paid the deposit and took out a mortgage and towards the end of 1958, we finally moved in.

Again, I was sent to private school, and I quite enjoyed going there and made good friends. What I did *not* enjoy, was going home. Nothing had changed. I was still on the receiving end of the slipper at least four times a week and the silences went on and on and on. There were frequent threats about sending me away. I was told that I should have died and my father lived, and that I was a child of the devil.

But, if anyone rang the doorbell, my mother suddenly switched into loving mode and spoke to me so nicely. For a few glorious minutes, I could relax and I would run off with a smile to make tea or coffee for the visitors. However, the moment the door closed on the retreating guests, my mother snapped back into freeze mode again. This did not happen very often however, as my mother had few friends and even fewer callers.

There was always this heavy atmosphere in the house. There were no happy vibes, and in every verbal response I was tip toeing on eggshells. I was always waiting for the next explosion, and most times it took me by surprise, since so often I did something terribly wrong without realizing it.

It's always possible to find faults if you look for them, and my dreadful behaviour was one fault after another. I'd not hung a dress up quite straight, I'd let the dog run in with muddy feet, or I'd not moved quickly enough in response to a demand for tea or coffee. I was in trouble if I was two minutes late from school because I had stopped to talk to someone, or if the supper wasn't on hot plates, or I didn't get the coal in before the fireside scuttle was empty. I was at fault if I left creases in the newspaper or read it too loudly letting the pages rustle, or maybe I spilled sugar on the floor. There were so many things I could do wrong, and I did all of them at one time or another.

My mother had no real social life. She never went out in the evenings, and had only one real friend, May. They would talk for hours and hours on the phone, and May was told continually what a difficult and awful child I was.

I was quite friendly with May's daughter Christine and I loved visiting their house. Her dad was fun too and would tease me and make me laugh. This was the only time I did get out, if I was sent on an errand to Christine's house.

I was not allowed out to play on the estate with the other children and when eventually my mother gave up taking me to and from school and I got my first bicycle, I was to go straight to school in the morning and straight home in the afternoon.

There was little time left for me to play. For as long as I could remember, I had helped my mother clean the house. As I grew older, I did more and more and she did less and less. She liked to sit by the fire, read the newspaper and do the daily crossword. Later, from 1960, when we got our first television, she watched that the rest of the time.

Like an idiot, when I was about ten years old, I tried to gain favour by cooking breakfast and taking it to her in bed. From then on, it was breakfast in bed every morning, week in and week out.

Saturday was cleaning day, and my first job was to tidy the house before we could even start. Unlike me, my mother was never tidy, and it was a big job to hang up and put away all the clothes that she had worn the previous week. In primary school we did the washing on Saturdays, in high school, it was my job every Wednesday afternoon when I got home from school. Looking back now, I spent a lot of my time doing housework and I hated it. I still do!

There was yet another medical scare in my final year of primary school. I had worn glasses from the age of two, and paid regular visits to the hospital to have my eyes tested. Apparently they were a bit strange because I didn't use them together and the ophthalmologist told my mother that I would have to have an eye operation.

I was not unduly alarmed about this until my mother told me that they removed your eye from the socket and left it dangling on your cheek while they worked on it, and all this while you were awake!! I was panic stricken and got little cheer from my mother who seemed rather pleased by my terror, but grumbled about possible cost and the inconvenience. Any excuse to assure me what a bother I was, was not to be missed. She did nothing to dispel my fears of the operation, and I had nightmares thinking about my eyes rolling off my cheeks and disappearing onto the floor under the operating table.

I did the only thing I could think of. I stopped reading under the bedclothes at night. While all my friends went to bed at a reasonable time, in primary school, six o'clock was my bedtime. It was far too early, and I was seldom sleepy enough by then. This was compounded in summer when it did not get dark early and I could hear the sounds of kids my age playing outside my window. My mother's answer was to put heavy black-out curtains on the window that darkened the room but this still didn't make me sleepy. I solved this by reading under the bed clothes, always on the alert for footsteps outside the door. If I was caught, it was another thrashing, the silent treatment, and worst of all, confiscation of the book. But try as I would, I couldn't wish myself to sleep when I wasn't tired. When I didn't get caught reading, I felt it was one small victory over the tyranny.

However, after I stopped reading under the bedclothes, my eyes miraculously improved and the operation was not mentioned again. To replace the reading, I began to invent another world for myself which I constructed down to the last detail. Previously I had simply wished to be other people, promising myself that when I woke I would be miles away and belong in another family. Or, my real parents would arrive on the doorstep to claim me.

They were always just ordinary people, I didn't want to be a lost princess or anything grand, I knew those were just fairy tales. Of course, no one ever came for me.

I discovered a new world that was totally under my control, and from lying awake in bed living my fantasy existence, I began to take it into everyday life and spent many hours daydreaming. I daydreamed at school, I daydreamed on the way to and from school, I day dreamed while I did the washing up. Every time, and it was most of the time, the silent treatment was in effect, I escaped into my world which was calm and ordered where I had brothers and sisters and loving parents. In retrospect, I always knew the difference between the real and the imagined, but often there was the passage between the two worlds, where for a few seconds, I wondered just who and where I was.

I started writing stories, but my mother found some and sneered and giggled over my first attempts. I stopped writing.

I'm not sure how my mother coped financially. I know she had a war widow's pension, and a pension from the insurance company, but there was never any spare money. This isn't a problem if you're not trying to impress everyone with how much you 'do' have, but we had to keep up appearances at all costs. So, when it came to taking food to school for the starving babies in Africa, I would be forced to make up one fatuous excuse after the other as to why I arrived empty handed, yet, at the same time, my private ballet lessons continued. A weekly hour of torture which I loathed. I begged my mother to let me go horse riding instead.

"Oh, and just how am I supposed to pay for that, along with everything else? You seem to think money grows on trees," was the answer.

"But if I stopped ballet, then you could use that money to pay for riding lessons."

"Ballet is the only thing that might help turn you into a lady. Personally I don't think you'll ever be a lady, but it won't be because I haven't done my best. You're certainly not going horse riding, you can forget that idea right now."

"I promise I will be really good if you let me go horse riding."

"You promise! Your promises are like pie crusts, made to be broken."

"Please can I give up ballet? I hate it, even if you won't let me go horse riding instead?"

"No!! Why do you have to be so difficult Lucinda? I said no and I mean it. I don't want to hear another word about it. I give you enough as it is, but you're always asking for more. When you've taken everything from me, and I'm left with nothing, what happens then? Oh yes, you'll just go off and leave me without so much as a thank you. You've always been ungrateful, no wonder no one likes you and you don't have any friends."

I tried to stand up for myself, what she was saying was untrue and it was so unfair. "But I do have friends, there's Elizabeth and Pauline and…"

My mother didn't let me finish. "They won't last, not when they find out what you're *really* like, the lies you tell, how you're so deceitful. No one wants to be friends with you. I have a good mind to tell their mothers what you're like and they will be told not to play with you."

But I wasn't her daughter for nothing and in this instance I was just as determined. I had a friend at school that had a pony, and, what was even better, another friend with a pony he was bored with. I organized for Melanie to get her mother to ask me over to play, knowing that it would be hard for my mother to refuse without a really good excuse. From the moment I arrived, until the moment I heard my mother's car approaching, I was on and off those ponies all day.

I was allowed to play with Melanie on the farm occasionally during the holidays and I looked forward to those days when we were free to run and play with the ponies. I nearly came to grief on one occasion, it was possibly the last time I ever went there. I scraped my foot going through a gate on the pony and drew blood. It needed a tetanus jab, but unfortunately it was discovered at the hospital that I was allergic to the antidote, and they had to inject me with it very, very slowly. Sadly, this coincided with Princess Margaret's wedding which my mother wanted to watch on TV. Instead we were stuck in casualty for hours and this threw her into such a funk that it lasted for weeks.

I had lied to her about how I cut my foot, not daring to mention the horses, and when I blurted out the truth to the nurse, I begged her not to tell my mother. To my amazement and relief, she laughed and promised not to.

I lied a lot, though my mother had explained that if I told the truth about my numerous misdemeanors, she would not get the slipper out and she would not be angry. I tried it. It didn't work. She got just as angry and she took the slipper off just as often. So, if I lied, there was just the odd time she believed me and I escaped punishment.

I took the dreaded 11 plus exam at the end of primary school and although I found it very easy, I was still amazed to learn that I had passed among the top fifteen girls in the county of Gloucestershire. When the letter arrived, my mother opened it and gave me the news. At last, proof I was a daughter worth having.

"Are you proud of me?"

"It only proves that miracles still happen."

"Can I have a hug?"

"No, I'm busy. This is all going to cost a fortune with all the uniform and equipment, as if I haven't had to spend enough on you already. It's the least we could expect after I sent you to private school. Hurry up with that ironing." My mother walked off grumbling to herself.

Years later, I learned that she boasted to all the neighbours about how well I had done, but I never heard a whisper of it and she certainly never said anything positive to me.

It didn't occur to me then, but if the uniform and equipment for the Grammar School was expensive, the local Secondary Modern School also had a uniform which was probably around the same price.

My mother had taken work three half days a week, collecting insurance premiums from clients at home. I often asked if I could either stay at home or go visit and play with a friend. She preferred me to come and sit in the car. It was deadly boring, but I always had a book, so I could lose myself in another world for most of the day. I didn't want to get out and walk about in the villages. Having settled into my book, I preferred to stay there and live the experience from beginning to end. This lack of enthusiasm on my part became another bone of contention between us. I don't believe that the money collecting trips were particularly exhausting, but it was yet another excuse for my mother to allow me to take over the running of the house completely.

I waited excitedly for the new term to begin that September of 1960. My mother expressed some doubts about letting me attend a state run school, but she was re-assured since this Grammar School had recently celebrated its quincentenary, having been founded in 1460 by John Chedworth, Bishop of Lincoln. Why he should found a school on the other side of the country, escapes me, but, my godmother's daughter was doing very well there, and, to give it status in mother's eyes, the headmaster was a product of the public school system and ran the school along the same lines.

All went well to start with. I was put into the top class in the first year and was really enjoying it when, three weeks into term, after complaining of a bad headache, the doctor pronounced I had glandular fever. This resulted in a minimum of three weeks in bed and then taking it easy for up to six months after that.

When I returned to school, I had missed most of the groundwork in most of the subjects. I was not allowed to play sports, but huddled on the edge of the hockey pitch and lurked by the wall bars at gym. My new sports gear was hardly worn and to add to my woes, most of the other kids had already formed firm friendships and I was left on the sidelines.

I can't say I blame them for not making friends with me. I was always so miserable! I had very little to talk about regarding family life, no brothers or sisters to laugh and joke about and I wasn't about to tell them how mean my mother was. After all, she was fine, it was me who was the problem. Most mothers are not mean, no one understood the concept. I would be seen as a liar if they met my mother who switched on the charm like a tap and left them thinking how fabulous she was.

I was possibly the most unpopular girl in the whole school. At the square dancing club on Thursday afternoon, there were twenty two boys and twenty three girls, and guess who sat out the whole session? And not just one session, but week after week after week. I should have given up and changed activity, but I persisted, at least I could listen to the music and study the walls, chairs and potted plants. Even that was better than being at home.

My mother thought young people were growing up much too fast. She resented the new upsurge in 'the young', and there were many examples of what she would not allow me to do. I wasn't permitted to read comics, so I borrowed them from other kids at school and read them in the bathroom. I got myself a pen friend in America, and that proved unpopular as my mother had a deep, abiding hatred for those on the other side of the Atlantic left over from the war years, 'overpaid, over loud and over here.' I was not permitted to wear young, fashionable clothes, I had to wear classical styles, so as hemlines rose by the day, mine remained firmly well below the knee.

I begged for a pair of stockings, I was approaching sixteen and still in ankle socks. My mother refused, saying they were a waste of money as I would only ladder them and ask for more. So, I engineered for my American pen friend to send me some. She did even better than that, she sent me two pairs and I treasured them. Sadly, they were extra fine and I spent hours trying to mend the runs that appeared as if by magic every time I put them on. As each hole appeared, I would carefully sew it up, but once they were beyond repair, it was back into the socks.

I was given permission to attend a school dance at the local community hall, but the humiliation of wearing the twin set and a tight tweed skirt (miniskirts were getting shorter) with my round-toed shoes and white ankle socks (while winkle pickers and points were all the rage) was just too much. The boys gave me one look and moved away.

There were also battles once I started domestic science classes at school. We were always given a list of ingredients to bring the following week. We seldom had any of these in the house, since my mother didn't cook. I did the cooking and I could assemble most of the ready prepared meals to come out of the local supermarket, but things like flour, icing sugar and baking powder were strangers to our larder. Since mother couldn't afford to buy all this extra food, she decided that whatever I cooked in school should be our main meal that night. So I always arrived with a different set of ingredients to everyone else. This did not endear me to the domestic science teacher, who was usually quite sweet and adored by all the other girls in the class.

Why didn't I tell her the truth? I have no idea, except that I was either ashamed or too shy. I often deliberately left the ingredients at home, knowing I would get into trouble, but preferred this to the embarrassment of arriving yet again with the wrong foods. The pancakes were a particular bone of contention, because my mother bought flour especially for the occasion. They are not particularly nice cold, but my mother declared they would do for supper. My pancakes did not turn out all that well and I was fiercely envious of the others as they ate theirs fresh and hot at the end of the lesson. I wrapped mine carefully in paper and they spent the rest of the day in my satchel where they got very squashed! I cooked pancakes week after week in my domestic science classes until all the flour was used up. Frankly my pancake manufacturing never got any better despite repeated attempts, and they didn't impress my mother either as we chewed our way through them every Tuesday night.

The years went by and nothing much changed, nothing got any

better. I remember two particularly awful occasions. In general I am very patient, but it all ran out one day and I flung one of the windows wide open and screamed at the top of my lungs about just how awful my mother was, I wanted all the neighbours to know. I didn't care any longer. Unfortunately, the window broke and if I had been in trouble before, it was now doubly compounded. First came the beating, then I had to pay for the new glass, which was fair enough, I had little control over my pocket money anyway, but I was also sent round to see a policeman who lived nearby, to confess my sins. I was shaking as I walked up the path and rang the doorbell, but to my amazement, he was really quite nice and not at all the monster I was expecting. I had been told to confess my latest wicked deed as well, allowing the porridge to burn, which was the start of yet another row. I honestly thought that perhaps I could be arrested for such terrible misdeeds or I would be sent away 'into care'.

On the second occasion, I also lost control, and threw the teapot against the wall. It missed my mother by miles, although I don't think I was really aiming at her. I watched in horror as the tea turned the cream wallpaper, dark brown. Although I got the silent treatment and had to forfeit months of pocket money for new wallpaper, that time I was not beaten. For once I think my mother was lost for words. I'm not sure what made me explode on those two occasions, maybe just too much pressure and my frustrations coming to the boil.

There were many more instances when I held my temper, but even going to my room didn't work. My mother followed me and continued to shout and harangue me, or rather continue her verbal asides as if I did not exist. She would grab my tennis racquet and bash the bedclothes and scream at me to get up so I could go back into the lounge and listen to a long list of my sins, yet again.

Despite being in high school, my bedtime was now only an hour later at 7 o'clock. I could stay up on a Tuesday until eight as a very special treat if I had been very, very good, to watch 'Whacko' with Jimmy Edwards on the TV. However I missed this more often than I saw it, always due to some minor transgression. It was yet another weapon my mother had to make my life miserable, she would send me to bed on the slightest pretext just as I was settling down to watch.

By the time I was fifteen years old, my bedtime was officially 8 o'clock, a time I was not going to admit to my schoolmates. When they discussed television programmes they had watched the night before, I was never able to join in the conversation. I either pretended to agree, or I made the excuse I was doing something else.

It seemed that everything I wanted to do or have was forbidden. Could I keep a baby mouse? No. A friend gave me one and I kept it in my pocket and on the top of the wardrobe for weeks, until one morning

I found it dead. I was heartbroken, but that was one transgression I managed to keep secret.

I had also started smoking in a desperate effort to make and keep friends. I was one of the group who regularly disappeared to the far end of the rugby pitch every lunch hour in the fond belief that the staff didn't know exactly what we were up to. I also admit to stealing occasionally from my mother's purse, buying sweets and offering them to other children to try and buy friendship.

I wanted to join the church choir and passed the audition which I managed to attend by pretending to go to the library. Again, permission was refused, because my mother didn't want to be tied down at specific times every Sunday. We did attend church every week, and I became quite confused during divinity lessons before confirmation, about one's proper state of mind before taking communion.

When she was sick after having me, my mother had made a pact with God. If she survived, then she would go to church each and every week until she died. The divinity lessons said that before taking communion, you had to forgive others their sins and be in a peaceful and happy state of mind. If not, then you violated the whole meaning of the holy sacrament. Obviously, this didn't apply to my mother. She was the ice cold anger machine as far as the lychgate, then all smiles and charm, as we walked up the path. The behaviour reversed as we left the church grounds and were on our own. I was stupid enough to mention this and wished I never had. She said that living with me made it impossible for anyone, even a saint, to feel calm and forgiving at any time at all.

I made another attempt to gain my mother's love. I had noticed that her Bible that she read every night in bed was very worn and shabby and some of the pages were loose. So I decided that I would buy her a new one. She would think it was thoughtful of me. I saved hard for weeks and weeks and then spent a long time in the local book shop deciding on the very best one I could afford. I wrapped it the night before Christmas and then watched with bated breath the next day as she took the paper off.

"What's this?" she enquired squinting at me.

"It's a new Bible, I was going to write in the front, but I didn't know if you should write in a Bible, but I noticed that your old one was getting…"

"How dare you!" she screamed, interrupting my explanation. "Your father gave me that Bible and I certainly don't want another one, certainly not from you!" She flung it across the room where it landed behind the couch. I still have that Bible, but I never open it, too many unhappy memories.

I was still not allowed to go out with groups of friends and I became more isolated at weekends and during the holidays. I was too big now for the mothers of friends to invite me over, and I would never get permission to go out and walk around the town centre for example, as most of the other kids did.

I did solve the problem of the hated ballet lessons. They were worse now as I had private lessons and there was no skulking in the back row trying to stay out of sight. I simply stopped going. I wanted some control over my life. My mother would drop me off outside the ballet studio, but as soon as she was out of sight I would scoot off in the opposite direction. Or, I would leave home on my bicycle and go down and play on the swings and slides at the local playground. This was an area specifically out of bounds since a paedophile had haunted the area several years earlier. But the joy of going down the slides and swinging back and forth soaring higher and higher into the sky, seemed reward enough.

It was during one of these escapes that I met my first boyfriend. David was a quiet, gentle soul and I fell deeply in love with him. He was the first person to tell me I was nice, I was fun to be with and that he loved me. He said I was good and he cared for me. I sat in class and wrote him endless love letters and poems. From seeing each other once a week during my absentee ballet lessons, we managed to meet up each weekday after school, and we would walk home wheeling my bicycle as slowly as we dared.

I don't honestly know how I could have been so stupid as to think my mother wouldn't find out eventually, and I suspect it was only a couple of weeks until the axe fell. Although my ballet teacher probably disliked giving me lessons as much as I disliked going to them, her sense of fair play got the better of her and she reported my repeated absences. My mother went ballistic, and I was now timed going to and from school, and on Thursdays, I had to go straight to my mother's sewing class and sit and wait there until she had finished. I was not to be trusted and needed to be watched all the time. Yet it was all so innocent.

While my mother could watch me like a hawk all day, she could not watch me all night. In the early hours of the morning, I opened the bedroom window, thanked God that we lived in a bungalow, and slipped out to meet the most wonderful boy in the world. We walked through the streets in the moonlight and swore undying love. I was particularly touched when David presented me with half a sawn off sixpence, after the musical running in the West End.

We managed three secret trysts before I was found out. Hell hath no fury like my mother scorned and I was subjected to the slipper for an exceptionally long time and the silent treatment for one of the longest periods ever.

I think the friendship with David had convinced my mother that she was losing control. She was constantly on the phone to her parents in London, cataloguing my disgusting behaviour. I was informed that I was the cause of my grandparents' illness and responsible for all heart attacks and other ailments they were suffering. My grandfather burst into tears and told me that all his torture in the prisoner of war camp could not compare with the trouble in the family. That was a particularly low point in my life and I cried for hours after he said that. Goodness knows why I couldn't verbalize that all I wanted was love, a kiss and a cuddle, to be told that I wasn't a totally worthless person. Why was my mother so different from all the other mothers I met? Inside I didn't think I was all that bad, I really tried to be good, but somehow I failed again and again.

Every trip to visit my grandparents resulted in huge rows and bitter words between my mother and her parents. On one occasion my grandfather stood up one night to go to bed and switched off the television while my mother was still watching. That started a row that lasted several days, but however they started, they all ended the same way, it was all down to me, the stress I put my mother through and how difficult I was. From then on it was three against one while I sobbed and said over and over, I would never misbehave ever again, I would be the perfect daughter.

I am my own worst critic. I have tendencies towards neatness and tidiness and think I have a kind and loving nature and would never deliberately harm anyone. I wasn't any different in those days, but didn't understand I was being brought up by the mother from hell. Certainly the phrase 'control freak' was not in common use then, and she was out to control every aspect of my behaviour. Since I had no father and no brothers and sisters, it became a one on one battle with mother as the referee, judge and jury. I was found guilty on every occasion.

I began to play truant from school and my marks went down. I frequented the local café, and made friends with people, all of whom my mother would have considered unsuitable. But for an hour or so each day, I relaxed and laughed with my new allies. Life at home was still unbearable, but there seemed no other option but to return at the end of each day.

In desperation, I swallowed about forty aspirin one day, and then in fright admitted to my mother what I had done. She laughed and told me not to be so dramatic. I ran out crying, but a few minutes later heard her on the phone talking to the doctor. I heard "drink plenty of salt water, eat dry bread and try and make her throw up."

I sat for a while tossing up what to do. In the end, survival won out, and I swallowed glass after glass of salt water with my head hung over the sink as I was violently sick. I was still unsure whether I had done the right thing or not, as it never occurred to me that one day I might leave home and live my own life. I was the only child, my mother was a widow and I had been brought up to believe that I must look after her until she died. I never even considered a future with a husband and children of my own.

My mother next turned to the Social Services for help, and took me to the Child Guidance Clinic. We traveled down to Cheltenham and for the trip she made me wear my oldest clothes, a pair of round toed shoes and my school mackintosh to show the world how awful I was. I slunk into the car, praying that none of my school friends would see me.

Having given a less than glowing reference about me to the counsellor, I was invited in for a talk. I was petrified. Since the age of three and that first aborted escape, I had heard tales of the reform schools where they sent willful girls. The descriptions made the work houses sound like Butlins holiday camps. You were made to wear a thick grey pinafore of sacking material and big clumpy shoes which pinched your feet. Every waking hour was spend on hands and knees scrubbing stone floors with cold water and if you didn't scrub fast enough you were beaten, not with a slipper, but with big sticks. Christmases and birthdays became a distant memory and you were forced to eat scraps and lie on a hard, stone floor at night. Years later as an adult, when I saw the film 'The Magdalene Sisters', shivers ran down my spine and I burst into tears.

When the counsellor started talking I knew exactly what she was looking for, another candidate for the reform school. I told her anything that I thought would plead my case. That my mother was loving and kind and that I was very naughty but I would never do anything wrong again as long as I lived. My mother seemed pleased with the outcome, she had found yet another adult who agreed totally with her that I was a child of the devil and did not deserve to live.

I possibly committed another misdemeanor a couple of weeks later, I can't remember what, but it was enough for the family to decide that I must be sent away. This was the next milestone, and it was one of the best times in my life.

Years later, when Christine was sorting out her late mother's effects, she came across a letter written by her mother May to my grandfather, in which she described how I was being mentally abused. This possibly came about because I had almost lost my temper one night and went for a walk to cool down. I was honestly afraid that I would hit my mother or hurt her in some way. When it began to rain I returned to find the door locked. I had taken a key, but Mother had put the latch on and I couldn't get in. Already half drowned, I went over to see May, who took me in and let me pour out all my misery. I think this may have been the catalyst that involved the Social Services.

3 WALES AND BACK

I was to go to Cardiff and live with my cousins. We drove down in the car and my mother stayed for a couple of days while I was registered at a new school. I settled in quickly and began to enjoy life. I was behind academically, and Welsh lessons were a bit of a nightmare, but I was happy. I was praised for all the housekeeping I did, and my cousins although only a decade older than me, became the parents I had always wanted. I still remember being told

"You'll make someone a very good wife one day." I kept repeating that one sentence over and over again. It was one of the few bits of praise that I had ever received.

For the first time, I was allowed out with friends, I proved myself a reliable babysitter and I began to do all the things that average teenagers were allowed to do, even wear make up!

But it was not to last. After only one term and just when I thought that life was indeed worth living, my mother returned to take me home. Had she missed me? Well, there was no one to clean the house, take her breakfast in bed every morning, feed and walk Boko, prepare all the meals and do the washing and ironing. It was back to cooking raw tripe for the dog, a task that made me heave every time, the smell was so awful, and even now, my stomach flops over when I even think about it. The grass had not been cut either and it took a lot of effort to mow the lawn and get it back into shape and it took me two full weeks to cut the overgrown hedge.

I may have been brought home, but I was to go to a new school. Perhaps the Catholic Church could clip wings? I was packed off to a nearby town where the high school was run by a French order of nuns. By now, I was sixteen years old and in the fifth form and I settled in quite well and was happy at school. The nuns were full of praise and they were always ready to give you a hug and a cuddle. One word of praise would send me to heaven for a week or more. I became a lot quieter and studied the Catholic doctrine. Secretly I contemplated taking the veil and attended mass as often as I could. I spent hours on my knees praying and I bought a rosary, which I carried around with me all the time.

Attending school seventeen miles away meant getting up very early each morning. After a quick bath, there was just time to make breakfast, take it to my mother in bed, clean up the kitchen and cycle the three miles into town to the bus stop. The bus left promptly at 7.45 and waited for no one.

The GCE O' levels came and went, and although I worked quite hard, I had a lot of catching up to do. I did not disgrace myself too much and did well enough to stay on for A' levels. The last two years at school passed uneventfully. School time was fun and I swam and played tennis for the school team and played hockey in the second eleven. I attended a few parties, since Mother seemed to approve a bit more of my friends, possibly because they also attended a school that was for many of us fee paying, and apart from dreading weekends and holidays, I don't think there were any major upheavals.

While most of the world looks forward to the weekends, and dreads Mondays, for me it was the other way around. I adored the start of a new week, it took me out of the house, but as the weekend approached, I would feel more and more nervous.

One event that stands out in my mind was the summer holiday between the sixth forms. We were in London to stay with the grandparents and the subject of my future was raised. Had I considered what to do after school? University was of course essential, but what subjects did I have in mind?

"I want to be a writer, like my grandfather, a journalist," I replied. I honestly think that if I had said I'd planned to purchase a case of red light bulbs, move to Amsterdam, and sit behind a plate glass window, they would have been less shocked.

"Don't be stupid, we mean a proper job."

"Being a journalist means being able to drink others under the table and getting the dirt on them. It's no longer an honourable profession," my grandfather was quite firm about that.

"How about I write books instead?"

"You've no experience of any kind, how can you write books? You'd never be able to do anything like that, do be sensible Lucinda, you need to start working, help repay your mother for everything she has spent on you," my grandfather again.

There it was, the ungrateful, selfish, child only thinking of what she wanted to do, not what she should do. So why ask me in the first place? Would I never learn to keep my mouth shut? If I'd said I wanted to be a nuclear physicist, they would have thought that equally stupid. The trick was to second-guess what they had in mind and react accordingly, but I didn't seem to be any good at that. For the moment the subject was dropped, but by Christmas, the subject was in full swing again. The family gave me my final options in the holidays. I was allowed to choose between being a secretary, a nurse or a teacher, in the extremely unlikely event that I was not accepted at a suitable university. If I was accepted, we could discuss subjects later, although my highest marks were always in English.

It was not a difficult decision to make. I had a firm picture in my head that being a secretary was tantamount to becoming a lackey to some male, of which species I had very limited experience. I fainted at the sight of blood, so nursing did not seem a wise choice, so that left teaching. It was definitely the best of a bad bunch, and, as I was quite determined to have a career, I considered it the easiest to cope with, in the very unlikely event, I was ever to rear a family.

I dutifully sent off the appropriate forms. From home, I applied to colleges close by, as my mother informed me I could commute daily. From school, I filled in a different set of forms, to colleges farther away, to read the subjects that held a real interest for me, History and Sociology.

This was one of the few times Mother seemed a bit nervous and I was soon to discover why. One of the prerequisites for being accepted to teacher training college was a full medical. Before taking me to the doctor, Mother told me to tell them that as a child, I had had water on the knee, but I was only to tell them this if they asked me about previous illnesses. This was the story I had grown up with, so why the reminder? But what if I hadn't had water on the knee, what if it was something else? Before I could ask, my mother pushed me out of the car.

Many years later, and quite by chance, I found out the truth, when an old friend of my mother whom she had not seen in years pitched up on the doorstep. She told me that when my mother was in the army, she had asked for compassionate leave to visit her fiancé who was to be posted overseas. They turned her down. She swallowed a bottle of HP sauce, guaranteed to send a temperature sky high, and queued up outside the MO's tent but he was called away, and by the time he returned, her temperature was back to normal.

Plan B was to bathe in cold water, put on wet pyjamas and go to bed with the window wide open, in Wales in winter. This time my mother succeeded in making herself really ill. She contracted pleurisy, which later developed into tuberculosis. In time, she recovered, but it flared up again while she was carrying me and I was looked after by my paternal grandparents for several weeks shortly after my birth, while my mother was recovering in a sanatorium.

I passed my medical with flying colours, all 'no abnormalities detected' in my X-rays and I got the all clear, but I hadn't forgotten mother's nervous behaviour and I asked her about it again. She simply denied that anything was wrong, in fact there was no need to mention to anyone that I had ever been ill and in hospital with TB. It's a shameful disease she told me, only attacking those who lived in squalid conditions. But, she added, if I ever had the Heaf test, then it would show positive and I could be in big trouble.

That brought back memories of Mother keeping me at home one day from school when the school doctors and nurses made a visit to administer the BCG for tuberculosis. Perhaps if no medical had been necessary for college, I might not know to this day that I'd had tuberculosis.

My paternal grandfather had recently passed away and left me a small inheritance. I was not told this, but it coincided with an amazing gesture from Mother telling me she would give me her car. This would make commuting even easier. While she was determined I should remain at home, I was just as determined to get a place in a college as far away as possible.

We had flown over to Dublin for the funeral, and I had a great time with my cousins. My mother was extremely upset because I didn't go and visit my father's grave. Quite frankly, it never entered my head! I had no idea which cemetery he was in, and I had been too busy visiting the attractions of Dublin to think about my father who had died when I was two years old. But she refused to talk to me on the return trip and for a further three weeks after we got home. What was so unfair, was that she didn't visit his grave either!

I don't think my application impressed them very much at our nearest college of education, as they never even called me for an interview. I was invited to one near Birmingham, this allowed possibly for a weekly commute. However, they offered me a place on the Divinity course, and since my thoughts of becoming a nun had receded more than a little, I deliberately made a hash of the interview, in the hope they would withdraw the offer. They did.

Then I was summoned to Liverpool. Catching the train at Cheltenham and traveling north was a big adventure. The college of education itself was nothing much to write home about. It occupied several acres of previously abandoned Nissan huts once used by Her Majesty's Forces, and had not been occupied since the end of World War II. The air was dirty, the college was next to a busy railway line and I found it difficult to understand a brand new version of the English Language. But they offered me History and Sociology and I was accepted.

On my return, my mother was in a quandary, but I think she may have consoled herself with the thought that Bristol University was not too far away and it was only a matter of time. It wasn't to be.

4 LIVERPOOL, COLLEGE DAYS

To everyone's horror, I failed all three of my A levels, and it was Liverpool or nowhere. It would be just too much to have a daughter without tertiary education and, after much debate, I was allowed to accept the place offered. But the months before the start of the new term in October gave everyone plenty of time to remind me what a failure I was. That was mean, because no one in my family had ever attended a university, and even the tertiary education was doubtful. But of course, my mother was a widow, she had struggled to bring me up alone, and the majority of my education had been at private schools.

The car was no longer on offer of course, so my mother drove me up to Southport in the first week of October in 1967 to the residence. This was the time when teacher training courses were crammed full, which is probably why they utilized the old army barracks, it certainly doesn't train teachers today.

I breathed a sigh of relief as my mother's car disappeared out of sight on its way back to the Cotswolds. At last I was free. I had escaped! I did a little dance on the pavement before I went in to meet the other students.

Our principle was a dragon of note and at our welcoming address she informed us that if we were to fail a single exam, we were out, if we failed a teaching practice, got married, or fell pregnant, we were also out.

Our second address was the local bank manager, who pleaded with us to open an account into which we could deposit our grants. Since I was on a full grant, I received the princely sum of £52 per term, but my mother had opened a bank account for me at home, so I didn't listen too closely. I did however listen in total amazement to the next speaker, the college doctor. He explained that as we had come this far, it would be extremely silly to get pregnant, remember, we would be chucked out immediately. If we required the birth control pill, all we had to do was knock on his door.

At first, I tried to buck the system by refusing to join the Student's Union. I had a horror of union activities, that had been drummed into me at home and I decided to steer well clear of them. However, since the entrance to the canteen was through the Student's Union common room, and since non-members were not allowed to enter unless they had paid their membership fees, I was faced with the decision to either join, or starve to death. I paid my annual subs. This was another thing I would have to lie about when I was home for the holidays. I could never admit to being a union member, my mother would go ballistic!

I must admit to going wild in that first year at college. I was like an animal let out of a cage. I played the social game to the fullest extent and was out every night. We were lucky in that first year, as the strict rules for living on campus, didn't yet apply to us. There was not enough space for first years to live on the college grounds, so, at enormous expense to the taxpayer, we were put up in hotels in Southport and bussed into college each day.

I found the work at college fun, and I got the clearest grasp of Maths so far in my life, as since the 11 plus, numbers have always put the fear of God into me. I was going to need those numerical skills later in life. There were seven of us in our group and we all had a ball. I shall always remember my college years with great fondness.

However, I could not get completely away from home. I had to phone Mother every Sunday, an expensive drain on my grant. The call was to be precisely at two o'clock and this often meant planning my day to be sure I was next to a public phone at the exact time. Not that the phone calls were enjoyable, I was, in fact spending precious money to listen to verbal abuse. Nervously I would pick up the receiver and punch in the numbers.

"Hello Mummy."

"What do you want?"

"You know I always phone you on a Sunday, you asked me to."

"Huh! Since when did you do anything I asked you to?"

"How are you?"

"What do you want to know for? You're not really interested in how I am, you're too busy having a wonderful time with your little college friends. Don't pretend you care about me."

"If I didn't want to know, I wouldn't have asked."

"You just want to tell me about all the wonderful things you're doing, not that I believe a word of it."

"Well I did get top marks in our Sociology survey."

"Is that supposed to impress me? After all that private school education I had to pay for. Waste of time all that Sociology nonsense, obviously the standard wasn't very high. All it does is make excuses for people like you and their bad behaviour."

"Mummy, please stop it, I've not done anything wrong."

"Oh, trying to whitewash your bad behaviour again? That's how you've always seen it. I see it quite differently, you've been impossible from the day you were born. Don't expect me to be impressed by anything you do."

It didn't matter what I said, she always had a derogatory answer.

And it was not only the words themselves, but the sneering, belittling tone she used every time she spoke to me.

I tried to hide all this from my college friends, but it was not easy. From Monday to Saturday, I could relax, work hard, play hard and enjoy life, but Sunday always loomed on the horizon. Then there were the holidays of course.

It's impossible to explain to anyone who has not been indoctrinated from birth in 'what to believe and how to behave', how difficult it is to break away and reject your earliest teachings. For as long as I could remember, it had been drummed into me that I owed everything to my mother, who had struggled to bring me up on her own. I was expected to be the perfect, worshipping child who would always be there for her as and when she demanded. I didn't have the courage, the confidence, or the money to walk away. At the same time, I was also conscious of the fact that if I was ever to stand on my own two feet, I needed a good education with qualifications if I was ever to break free.

From day one, my mother decided to charge me rent to stay at home when I was not in Liverpool. So I needed a job each vacation. I was a chambermaid at several hotels, a waitress at a local coffee shop and a washer up in kitchens. I worked at the local food factory in town, and when they went out on strike, it left seven of us temporary students to run the whole place. As a member of the *Student's Union* and not the *Bakery and Allied Workers Union*, we were not sanctioned to stop work.

Not all holiday jobs were frustrating. For two seasons, I worked on the archeological digs on the edge of town. Most of our town was built on Roman remains, and prior to any new development, a full archeological study must be carried out.

My social life was somewhat limited. I had a few boyfriends at home, nothing too serious at first, but then it was difficult to be scintillating company when you left the house with "Are you really going out and leaving me on my own?" ringing in your ears, and hours of frosty silence awaiting your return. I have always envied (I did a lot of that in those days), those people who can compartmentalize their lives, put things at the back of their minds and switch off. I have always worried a lot and find it difficult to forget clouds which loom on the horizon.

Liverpool in itself was an experience. It was so very different from the cute Cotswold villages I was used to. The streets buzzed with traffic, the docklands area was fascinating yet forbidding, and the shops were so much larger. Each year we were required to do a teaching practice for several weeks in the nearby schools. Few of us knew what was in store for us. Most kids just lie in wait for the student teacher and plan well in advance, how they can make their lives a complete misery.

My first venture out into the community opened my eyes. There were children who couldn't come to school because they did not have enough clothes. Some told me about the various 'uncles' who lived with them on different nights, while others came to school covered in burns from falling pots of hot food while feeding the younger ones. Many were covered in bruises and some were absent because they were appearing in court, or disappeared altogether when they were taken away into care.

Our area was recognized as the largest council estate in the United Kingdom, with the highest crime rate and the lowest illegitimacy rate, since it was home to a large number of Roman Catholics of Irish descent. Most of the inhabitants had been relocated from the slum areas around Scotland Road, and the estate consisted of acres and acres of identical council houses. It was very easy to get lost, especially where street signs had been vandalized. Although the housing was in place, the social facilities were very limited and strong family and cultural bonds had been broken in the move.

By the third year, I felt I had a good grasp of this teaching thing and approached my third school with a lot more confidence. It was in Liverpool 8, near the docks, an area where you removed the rotor arm from your car if you wanted it to be there at the end of the day.

In many ways, I'd had a very sheltered upbringing and all this was a complete culture shock, meeting so many families whose lifestyles were to me, chaotic and totally incomprehensible. For years, I had suffered physical and mental abuse, but because I had never been covered in bruises where they showed, nor suffered physical deprivation, I did not equate it with my own experience at all.

I was heartbroken over very bright children who were leaving school early to work in the local biscuit factory, not realizing that often advanced education meant alienation from their family background. It shows how strongly we are all bound to family and I did not equate it either with the times I cycled through the council estate to and from school suffering the jeers at my boater, white gloves and lace up shoes.

On the lighter side I learned another lesson during one of our sociological surveys, a census on leisure time pursuits. Armed with my checklist I hesitantly knocked on the first front door. It was opened by a slatternly looking woman, with a cigarette hanging out of her mouth, a baby clamped firmly to one breast, and a toddler swinging on her torn skirt. After introducing myself, I manfully ploughed my way down the list of questions. When I reached "do you play a musical instrument?" my courage failed me and I just ticked the 'no' box. She may have been the lead violinist in the Liverpool Symphony Orchestra for all I knew, but somehow I didn't think so.

A fellow student did have the courage to ask the same question, and couldn't understand why the man laughed so much when he said he frequently played on his organ. I guess we were so very naive in those days.

I had three narrow escapes during my teaching practices. I sent Billy out of the room when he was totally disruptive and he walked home through heavy Liverpool traffic. I was accosted by Pamela's father after school, blind drunk with his snarling Alsatian dog, because she had been sent home in fresh clothes after having an accident; and thirdly, when the assessors walked in on my finals, it was to find the classroom in an uproar as the darling tadpoles had turned into frogs overnight and escaped from the tank. All of these incidents left me fearful that I would fail at college as well. Phoning home for some comfort and encouragement was quite out of the question.

In year two, we moved into residence on the campus and the college rules were strict, even for those days! We had to sign in by 10.30 pm every night and weekend passes to be away overnight from college, had to be approved. There were no entertainment facilities in the area, the nearest cinemas were in Liverpool and even if you had a car, it was impossible to get back before the perimeter gates were locked. If you went shopping and used public transport, you had to leave the city before 5 pm to make sure you got back in time. We all cheated and the few people left in the Nissan huts, were responsible for signing in at least thirty absent people, the price was usually a packet of cigarettes.

The first year at college was a complete break from my mother, except for the weekly phone calls and vacation breaks. First years were not allowed to go away at weekends, so I had a cast iron excuse. But all that changed in year two, and my mother decided that I must now have the car, whether I wanted it or not, so that I could travel home for weekends at least twice a month. If I thought that having a car spelt freedom, I was mistaken. It's several hundred miles from Liverpool to the Cotswolds and I found the journey both tiring and expensive. There was no offer of petrol to go with the car, and the £52 grant per term did not stretch very far. I made a bit by charging other students who were travelling in the same direction, but no one else lived further south than Birmingham and it was a lonely, sometimes frightening journey in the dark. I also didn't look forward to the reception when I reached home.

This was the time of the student riots in Paris and my mother had plenty to say about that. We were all a waste of space, we felt the world owed us a living and we were being indoctrinated with communism. We were selfish parasites, especially those who studied Sociology, we were taught that all behaviour was acceptable and had some fool reason for doing what the hell we liked.

In fact, that last part was true. As I studied both Sociology and child development, I learned that some of my peculiar practices were not as strange and 'devilish' as I had been told. I'd had a spate of stealing tins of fruit from the larder and eating them in my room at night - they told us about compensatory eating. There was a lecture on why children told lies - it was a learned response to the over-reaction they would get if they told the truth. That explained a lot as well. I was foolish enough to quote these examples to my mother, which of course only added fuel to the fire.

As the term drew towards a close I began to really dread going home. The weekly phone calls had been more vitriolic than ever before, and it got to such a pitch that I bravely decided not to go home. I would stay in Liverpool over the Easter period. However, I had nowhere to live, so the answer was to get a job that provided accommodation.

I became a live-in chambermaid at a large hotel in Southport. I had plenty of previous experience from other vacation jobs and I quite enjoyed it. The hours were long and the pay very poor, but I was getting by, it kept me busy and I had a respectable roof over my head. I remember not telling my mother where I was, but to put her mind at rest I did write to her best friend May, explaining that I was not coming home and that I was working in a hotel and was quite safe.

I had only been at the hotel for a couple of weeks before I was summoned to the telephone. It was my mother, and she sounded so sweet and kind and said how much she missed me and please would I come home?

I fell for it, gave immediate notice, jumped in the car and drove south. What a mistake! The moment the door opened the sweet, loving mother disappeared and everything was back to normal, only worse if that was at all possible. My bid for independence and freedom had failed, and once again, I had been brought to heel. My mother had me exactly where she wanted me. I spent a miserable couple of weeks at home, I don't think we left the house once, before I escaped back to college. Except for one errand I was sent on.

My old dog was by now well past it, and Mother asked me to take him to the vet. He told me that Boko was in a lot of pain and it would be kinder to put him out of his misery. I phoned Mother from the surgery and told her the news. She told me to make up my own mind, so with many tears I held my old friend while the needle was inserted. For the next forty years, whenever animals were mentioned, I was pronounced as unfit to own any, if I took them to the vet it was only to have them put down.

The car I had inherited was the sixty-fifth mini to roll off the production line, and we were the first in the area to own one. For several weeks we had to push our way through the crowds as we approached the car, it was almost our 'fifteen minutes of fame'. I think the main attraction, apart from its small size was the side-on engine, and I could see that several of the men would have loved to ask my mother if she would open the bonnet, so they could have a look, but they were much too polite.

From being brand new in 1960, nine years later, she was not quite as smart, but although I knew I couldn't really afford her, I was very proud of my car. The Morris Minis in those days were very basic, with only a speedometer and petrol gauge on the hollowed out dashboard, and a wire string to open the door suspended above the exposed inside door storage area. Since her number plate was 104 AD, I named her Domino. She was white and I have no idea how many miles she'd done when I got her, but with their high revving 850cc engines, minis were not designed to last forever. When you're young, you never expect cars to break down.

By the end of my second year, the money did not stretch far enough to allow me to run a car, there was something major wrong with her, and I couldn't afford the repairs. I decided to leave her behind when I returned to college the next term. My mother flatly refused to let me do that. We only had a single garage attached to the bungalow, and if there were two cars, Domino would have to be put in the garage, or, my mother would have to move her every time she wanted to drive her own car. I pleaded poverty, but to no avail.

By chance, my problem was solved by a friend, whose parents had a second house and an empty garage. I made arrangements to house Domino there, had her raised on blocks to protect the tyres and disconnected the battery.

My mother was absolutely furious and approached me with the infamous slipper. But enough was enough. I was almost twenty-one, and getting a hiding at that age was getting to be ridiculous. I don't know where I got the courage, but I shouted at her and took her quite by surprise.

I also had an ally in the dog, the second generation of Cairn Terriers, who usually barked his head off when my mother dragged me kicking and screaming into the bedroom to administer punishment. He saw the delay as his opportunity, and attacked my mother, biting her on the leg. I still got the silent treatment alternating with the verbal abuse, but I think that was the last time she ever picked up the slipper.

In the second year exams, much to my amazement, I came top of the year. Being away from home for several days at a time helped me to concentrate and I enjoyed all my subjects. It was suggested that at the end of my third year, I transfer to Liverpool University to do a final year course that would give me the newly introduced B.ed degree.

With great excitement, I applied to Gloucestershire County Council but sadly, they turned down my application for a grant. That year they had computerized part of their system and had made some sort of financial loss, and their argument was that I was quite capable of teaching with my three year diploma, so they were off the hook.

I spoke to Mother about it, as I thought maybe she might be able to make a plan. I was left in no doubt about that. If I had fanaticized about her co-operation her first sentence soon put that to rest.

"And just where am I supposed to get that kind of money?" she shrieked.

"You had your chance and you failed. Now you want to fail again and make me poorer as well? It's about time you stopped all this studying and came back and started work and paying tax like the rest of us." As I was recounting my tale of woe to my favourite lecturer, she gave me the following words of wisdom that I have never forgotten.

"You young people don't realize that your education doesn't stop the moment you walk out of college. You'll go on learning all your life and there is no time limit to getting a degree, you have the rest of your life to get one."

I am now in my mid sixties and I still don't have a degree, if you discount the *University of Life*, but I have not given up hope that one day I will complete that extra year. On the other hand I have certainly learned a lot, especially in the last few months.

My twenty first birthday party was an occasion I prefer to forget and I still cringe whenever I think about it. Mother hired a room in a local pub, constantly reminding me it was all at great expense, and my college friends were all invited. Several of them slept on the floor in the bungalow, although my mother did not approve.

The actual party was a disaster. None of my new friends had met my mother before and they were not sure what to make of the sour-faced lady who stood at the edge of the room, arms folded across her chest glaring at everyone. This time she was making no effort to be nice to anyone. She was so obviously there to see that we didn't misbehave or enjoy ourselves. We were light years away from the world of the chaperone. This was the end of the sixties. Mary Quant designed new, young fashions, Carnaby Street was in full swing and those dirty, unwashed louts singing in collarless suits knocked the older generation sideways. It was the time for the young, the newly liberated generation with the pill, the spending power, and a voice to express new ideas openly.

All this was worse than a red rag to a bull. My mother was totally out of step with the modern world, growing older and more bitter by the day, with few friends and no family relationships at all. Up until that time, I never remember her going out on a date, nor having any admirers, and I can understand much better now, that she felt that life was passing her by, as indeed it was.

Worse was to come. We all piled into the cars to go home after the party and someone threw up outside the house, I guess from drinking too much. After that, I never heard the end of how awful my friends were.

Returning to college the following term without the car, I had a cast iron excuse not to go home as often, but the pressure mounted, so I took to hitching down the M6 motorway most Friday nights. I had lots of interesting conversations as I chatted to the truck drivers, and being raped or molested was the last thing on my mind, or on theirs either. Perhaps I was just lucky, or too ugly, but in my experience, they were the 'true gentlemen of the road'. I enjoyed many a greasy meal in the motorway truck stops, and was passed like a long distance parcel from one lorry to another.

"Hey there, got a young lady for the Cotswolds here, anyone taking the Bristol route?" I would be offloaded from the steel carrier onto the egg truck and again transferred to the distillery wagon.

My mother never enquired how I got to and from Liverpool. She must have guessed that I was hitchhiking. Was it safer in those days? Getting me back for a couple of days so that she could castigate me, was more important than my safety.

At no point in my life have I ever been considered beautiful, nor even vaguely pretty. I never had a chance to be vain, my mother saw to that, so, along with my very low self-esteem, and partly due to the compensatory eating, I grew quite fat. Well to be honest, I grew very fat. At my maximum, I was well over 11 stone, and the cry was "Lucinda, you are a fat girl and you will always be a fat girl."

In line with my mother's efforts to turn me into a lady, she had always dressed me beautifully, if light years out of date for a 60's teenager. It was all part of the external showcase to the world that everything was fine. But my mother had been blessed with a talent for dressmaking, and she added tailoring to this when she attended sewing classes while I was still at school. At my largest weight, I had a series of interesting tent-like dresses, and she even managed to make me reasonably respectable for the May Ball.

At school in Cheltenham, I had made friends with the daughter of one of the local publicans. Mother didn't really approve. She forbade me to enter the bar and lounge of their public house. However, Sarah had contacts, with the local agricultural college students, sons of wealthy farmers and minor royalty. I'm not sure how much they ever learned about growing crops, but our town seemed a good place for them to sow their wild oats and test out the local livestock.

Again, my mother was faced with another dilemma. She wanted to boast how well I was doing, and perhaps she hoped for a glittering match, after all, she was the daughter born of great wealth, servants and acres of property. At the same time, she wanted to keep me tied to her apron strings until the day she died. I begged and begged to be allowed to go to the May Ball, I had been invited as part of Sarah's party. After weeks and weeks of pleading, my mother relented, and I stepped out in a dark red, shimmering taffeta evening dress, my first pair of very low heels and a pair of stockings, at last!

It was a night to remember. There were tables groaning with food, two bands in the marquees and everyone who was anyone was there. I paired off with Jack, who although a student at the college, was the son of an Oxfordshire widow who was in dire straits. For weeks and weeks, I kept up the pretence of a large estate and great connections in the hope that my mother wouldn't make too much fuss about our dating. But Jack had a very special way with my mother. When he brought me back after an evening out, I was under strict instructions to bring him in, whether he wanted to or not! This was pretty terrifying, as I was never sure what she would say, and if he heard of my earlier misdeeds, would I ever see Jack again?

"So where have you been? Drinking in a pub I suppose?" said with a sneer. I mean where did she think we went? There was absolutely nothing else to do in our area once you'd seen the weekly film at the local flea pit.

"Oh no," Jack would reply, "we just drove into a field and made mad passionate love all evening." This was a response my mother did not expect, and it took the wind right out of her sails. Sadly when I tried it, it didn't work at all!

"Can I get you anything before I go?"

"Off out again are you?"

"Mum I've not been out for two weeks."

"Lucky you, I've not been out for years, not that that bothers you of course. No, don't bother to get anything for me, I will just have to cope by myself, like I've always done."

"I'm only going to the cinema. Would you like to come as well?"

"With you? I certainly don't want to spend time with the low life you like to mix with."

"But it's Patrick, he's in the church choir. You know him, he's training to be a pharmacist."

"Well I'm sure his mother doesn't know he's mixing with you, I'm sure she'd put a stop to it and I've a good mind to tell her all about you."

"Tell her what?" I was aghast, would my mother talk to Patrick's mother?

"I think it's only fair that she knows about the lies you tell. No one can believe a word you say. And what about the money you took from my purse? She won't want her son mixing with a common thief and a liar. It's my duty to warn her who her son's got mixed up with."

"Mum please don't say anything, please don't."

"I think she should know. You're hardly good company anyway, so what are you offering? Sex? Is that how you keep these young men? I can't see why else they should want to spend any time with you. Go on, go on out and leave me here all alone. You obviously don't want to spend time with your own mother, after all I've done for you, but then you always were selfish, only thinking of yourself. Don't worry about me, I'll be fine here on my own, you won't give me a second thought the minute you're out that door. I don't know what he sees in you, a big fat lump who doesn't know how to behave. Go on, clear off."

And so I would embark on a date with those words ringing in my ears, knowing that they would start again the moment I walked back into the house.

Despite my size, I did have several boyfriends. There was Jeff of course, I met him in my first year in Southport. I had hitched south to stay with him a couple of times and it was on his narrow, two foot six bed that I lost my virginity, at the tender age of nineteen. I raced back to college in a panic. What if I was pregnant? That would only prove to the world that everyone was right and I was wrong. I would run away permanently rather than face my mother.

Fearfully I made my way to the college doctor's surgery. He examined me from three feet away, and asked me if I was in a permanent relationship, or if I intending to go on the game?

I was mortified – a prostitute!

I assured him that I was engaged, and he gave me the prescription and I raced round to the chemist. I felt like a marked woman as the pharmacist looked sternly at me, then glanced down to look at the third finger of my left hand. I'd never even thought to wear at least a curtain ring. Worse was to come.

She made up the order and demanded ten shillings. I didn't have a cent on me, I was absolutely broke. I flew out of there, certain that if I didn't start the course of pills immediately, all those little visitors would be swimming away intent on making me pregnant.

I asked Hazel, one of the students from Ethiopia if I could borrow ten shillings. She was already a mother, and so very understanding. I'd naturally assumed that she was married, but she just laughed and replied "Certainly not."

Apart from her understanding, she was also extremely rich. She drove a BMW, and always had masses of money to spend. When she wrapped her first car round a bollard, her father replaced it within a week. I understand she was related to King Haile Selassie, and her parents ran a civet cat farm outside Addis Ababa.

Although I didn't want to tell Hazel why I needed the money so urgently, she teased me until I confessed. I was feeling so ashamed, but her reaction was to give me a big hug with the proviso that the money was a gift and not a loan.

I raced back to the chemist and retrieved my small brown paper bag. As I took the first pill that night, my hands were shaking so badly that the first one sailed right out of my hand and disappeared out of sight down the plughole. Now I knew that I was definitely going to get pregnant.

I think Jeff was really fond of me, because he became involved in a very nasty incident when my mother found out that I was staying at his flat. She passed on the terrible news to my grandfather, who phoned and threatened Jeff with abduction if I didn't leave there immediately. I fled back to college extremely upset and embarrassed. I was getting on for twenty-one, so I'm sure the threat was not really valid, but I believed it at the time and knew that yet again, my mother had almost succeeded in breaking up yet another relationship as she had done so often in the past. How my mother found out I shall never know, had I made a diary entry and left it at home?

But Jeff stuck by me, and since I did not dare go to see him at his place, he traveled up every weekend to visit me at college. We were lucky that he could stay with his parents, as many of the visiting boyfriends didn't have family in the area, so they stayed in the residence. One night there was a raid, with the staff lined up outside the Nissan huts to catch anyone who tried to escape. There were bodies flying out of windows, doors and the fire escapes. A few men flung themselves half-naked over the perimeter fence, and one bright young man got away with it by taking a shower while singing in a falsetto voice.

Things calmed down for a while after that, but before long, there were almost as many young men sleeping in the res at weekends, as there were women in our girls' only college.

Jeff and I subsequently became engaged, and I might have married him if it were not for one thing. We were sitting in the car late one night when he said:

"Will you leave college at the end of this term?"

"What do you mean leave college, why can't we wait until I have finished?"

"What's the point?"

"What do you mean? I can't teach if I don't finish college and qualify." The thought of leaving college early had never occurred to me.

"You don't need to qualify. I'm not going to let my wife go out to work. I'll look after you. It's my job to earn the money."

I sat there for a while and silently handed back the ring. I'm not sure where I got the firm intention that I would be a career woman, but I knew that I needed to have a measure of independence.

There are days when I wish I had given up college and become the little woman at home. Would my life have been easier? Yes, but would it have been as interesting? Certainly not!

I had shuddered to think how I was going to introduce Jeff to my mother after the 'abduction' episode, but Mother never got to meet him after all.

After Jeff there were a few other boyfriends, I seemed to go for long-term relationships and altogether I was engaged four times. It was a bit of an enigma to several of my friends that I got and held any boyfriend, for as I say, I was not a fashion plate, and neither was I scintillating nor promiscuous. I think the thing that attracted them was my submissive behaviour. I was always grateful for the smallest attention, always fell in with their plans and never complained. I did my best to please and made them feel big and important.

The last great college romance was a handsome Swede by the name of Hans. Now he saw me coming and took full advantage. Hans borrowed my car and crashed it into a Liverpool bus. He caused more damage to the bus than the car, and it was the first and only time I have ever lied to the police, when I told them later that my car had been borrowed without my permission, and I had no idea who'd taken it for a joy ride.

Hans also borrowed cash, which he never repaid, and it was with tears running down my face that I gave him a lift to the passenger boat at Liverpool and waved him goodbye. He had invited me to Gothenburg for Christmas, and no matter what my mother said, I was going.

There was one small problem, I didn't have a passport. In the Lower Sixth, I'd been to France on a student exchange and I was forced to travel on a temporary permit since they refused to issue me with a British passport. I had of course been born in Dublin, and as such, didn't qualify for one. This seemed particularly hard, as I'd lived in England since I was ten and completed most of my schooling there.

I applied to the passport office in Liverpool and was told I would have to swear allegiance to the Queen and take an oath. I was quite happy to do this, but it was expensive, and by now I was completely broke having given all my cash to Hans. I returned to college, plotting how I would get the money. I dared not sell the car and anyway it was still not officially in my name, and the logbook was safely locked away at home.

The only option was to get a job, so I applied to work at Littlewoods on Saturdays. I was given one hour's basic training and let loose on the food market tills. I was hopeless. In those days, the tills were more basic and didn't tell you how much change to give. Although my Maths had improved, I still couldn't work out sums very fast, so I'm sure that most times the change was not correct. I also had problems with charging so much money to some of the poor, elderly people. As I watched them scrape for their last few coins, I would move them along, and forget to ring up a couple of items. I just hope the statute of limitations is now up on the crimes I committed, but it was never out of malice, and I never took a penny for myself.

I need not have worked so hard. A couple of weeks later I had a letter from Sweden in which Hans told me that he would not be in Gothenburg for Christmas as he was going to Canada to visit his fiancé. I was distraught. I lost my appetite and refused to eat. After a few days, I didn't want to eat, and after some persuading when I tried, I just felt sick. Maybe I had anorexia, it was long before the disease hit the headlines, but I had all the symptoms. I got thinner and thinner, until I was feeling too weak to get out of bed. My weight went down from over eleven stone to just over seven stone in less than two months.

The college matron was fantastic and because the sanatorium was full with an outbreak of chicken pox, she arranged meals that were nourishing slops and slowly I grew stronger. As part of my new image, I was persuaded by my friends to change from brunette to blonde and they applied a home colour. It went horribly wrong and my hair turned green. When I arrived home at the end of the term my mother didn't recognize me when she opened the door and slammed it in my face.

The following January, I decided that I was through with the male species and concentrated, for the first time, on my studies.

As the Easter holidays approached, I again became more and more nervous about going home. I guess it was a grown up version of running away from home, but I just couldn't face the prospect of sitting in the house day after day, walking over eggshells with every word I uttered, waiting for the axe to fall. I was happy and relaxed at college, so I decided again, not to travel south. There was little chance of getting back my temporary job as a chambermaid at the hotel in Southport, I'd left them in the lurch last time.

My salvation appeared in the guise of the Liverpool Settlement. I don't remember if the settlement was run by the church or the government or was a private affair, but I do know they were wonderful. Situated in a very grimy backstreet of Liverpool, close to both cathedrals, it was run as a kind of hostel for those in need and also as a youth club. I had helped out at the youth club as part of my Sociology course, and continued after the few compulsory visits.

I think any help I could give them was limited, as the children who frequented the club had a distinct sub culture of their own, and when they talked they took the last sound of each word and put it at the front, thus the word 'table' became 'bleta,' 'cinema' became 'maecine' and so on. The kids were so adept at this, that they would chatter away for hours and no one could understand them but themselves.

I moved into a small dormitory which, since it was holiday time I had all to myself, and took time out to lick my wounds. I was scared to go home and I was scared about not going home.

One of the friendly counsellors would sit and chat and I didn't realize it at the time, but it was my first introduction to counseling and it helped. He reminded me that I was not a complete failure, after all, I would qualify soon and the government at least, was prepared to let me loose on classrooms filled with innocent, enquiring minds. I could start to believe that I had a lot going for me. He also pointed out the frustrations and pent up anger that my mother must have harboured for years. She had not made a life for herself, but tried to re-create a life through me. I'd never thought of such things before. It was true that my mother did little to help herself, no efforts to create a normal social life, make friends or be independent.

This time I remained at the Settlement for the whole holiday and returned to college for the last term, uplifted and refreshed.

We had all applied for posts, and I was accepted by Warwickshire, and Inner London. However, there was a lot of discussion among us as to what we would really like to do the following year. We had all been at school since the age of five, then straight into college and now, we were poised to return to school again. Hardly a rounded education, most of us had little idea of the real, big, bad, outside world.

A few of our lecturers encouraged us to think about taking a year out, and some of our group decided we would do just that. We could put our posts on the back burner for twelve months and swan round the Continent, waiting on tables, picking potatoes, washing up in hotels. It didn't matter what we did, it was just for the experience. The dawning of the 'gap' year.

When I mentioned my plans to my mother and grandparents, they were furious. The condemnation started again. I was a parasite on society. I had accepted a full grant - never increased in three years - and it was high time that I got off my backside and out into the workplace and started paying tax. There was heavy pressure on me to live at home and teach in a local school, but luckily, there were no posts available and I eventually got a position in Bath. It was only thirty miles away, so I couldn't travel that distance every day, but of course I could go home at weekends, that is, every weekend.

Sadly, I told all my friends that I wouldn't be joining them on our European adventure. My freedom was at an end, I was being reeled back in again like a helpless fish.

5 BATH

I remember my interview at the primary school in July of 1970 quite clearly. If the school was worried about engaging a young woman straight out of college, this was no problem I told them. I didn't have a boyfriend and I had set my sights on being a schools' inspector by the time I was thirty-five. I was totally career minded and marriage was the last thing on my mind.

I got the job.

There were ninety-six children in the class, ranging from reception to going on eight years old, with three teachers all in one room. It was a fine example of the new modern style of teaching. We divided the work up amongst us and I was to be primarily responsible for English and reading.

However, three years of teacher training college had not prepared me for two things, taking the register and handling the dinner money. I had never encountered a register before and it took me quite some time to match thirty odd little faces with the correct names and ensure they were actually there. Next I needed to collect in the money. Some children paid the full rate of one shilling and eight pence per week for their daily school lunch, some only stayed for two or three days each week, and some younger siblings paid a discounted rate as the second child, with the third in a family being free. Another portion of the class qualified through the social services for free dinners and must be marked down as prospective diners.

Multiples of one and eight pence and proportions thereof and working out the correct number of children who were staying at school was a nightmare. There were no calculators to help me either. It took me until the first break on that first Monday morning to make an informed guess as to who was staying and if I had the correct amount of money to hand in. To make matters even worse, it seemed that every child needed change. I was still in a cold sweat at lunchtime as I waited to see if all my class was fed.

It was in that first term that I felt that I was making a difference. I had identified one little boy I thought was deaf. I asked to see his mother, and after school one afternoon, she reluctantly entered the classroom.

"Have you ever noticed that Timothy doesn't understand you?"

"Yeah, well, he's a bit thick an' all," she didn't seem to mind much.

"No, I think it's because he can't hear too well," I explained

"What d'ya mean?" She looked at me aggressively.

"I think there may be a problem with his hearing. Have you ever had him tested?"

"What for, 'elfy enough aint he?"

"Well yes, but I don't think he can hear what people say to him."

"You saying that my boy's got summat wrong with him?" I thought she'd hinted at that herself in the first place.

"No, not at all, except that maybe you should have his ears checked out. Maybe take him to the doctor?"

She shuffled from one foot to the other. "Waste of bloody time that is. He'll only say that my boy's fine, nothing wrong with him, only a bit thick and stupid."

As she left, I felt awful. Somehow, I'd failed to connect with her, and what was more, I had failed to help Timothy.

But I was wrong. Next day he was missing from school and when his mother brought him in the following day, she came to tell me that the doctor had made an appointment with the ENT specialist, or "Ear Man" as she called him. Timothy was found to be eighty-five percent deaf and was fitted with a bright new hearing aid, which he wore to school with pride. He cheerfully ignored the teasing from the other kids, as, for the first time in his life he could fully understand what was going on around him. He did very well in the time I taught him and proved to be a bright, responsive little boy.

I remember wondering how he could have reached the age of five without anyone else, especially his family, ever noticing. I told myself that I was an excellent teacher and I was also being paid for the privilege as well!

My first flat was in a basement at the back of a large house and it was damp and dark. I'd answered an advertisement in the paper from a girl wanting a flat mate and my mother and I traveled down to Bath to interview her and look the place over. I could have died with embarrassment. I was twenty-two years old, I didn't need my mother to conduct interviews on my behalf, but there was no getting away from it.

Luckily, Gwen took little notice of either of us, she had just got engaged, and if Godzilla had applied for the vacant room, I doubt if she would have noticed. She was quite sweet, but the tales about her boyfriend began to get on my nerves. When Gwen wasn't talking about her darling, perfect Willie, she was reading the Bible. I had long got over my brief flirtation with the church.

Much as I loved teaching, I missed the studying at college and the opportunity to stretch my mind, so I walked down to the local college and found they were offering an A' level course in Sociology. I immediately signed up and set aside two evenings a week at night school.

Our first assignment was “Religion is the opiate of the masses,” Karl Marx. I have since learned that this is not the precise quote, but as our lecturer explained, if God did not exist, then man would have had to invent him. While I had lost a lot of faith in the church, I was incensed by this introduction to communism as I termed it. I rushed back to the flat and wrote an impassioned support of God and anything else I could dredge up about the saints and sanctities of the church. I was not particularly surprised to see my low mark, as really it was a terrible piece of writing with nothing to back up any points except pure, raw emotion, and the result of an upbringing where you didn’t question anything taught by those older and wiser.

I was still commuting home every weekend, even though I didn’t want to. And things didn’t get any better, only now, all teachers were communists and all the young thought that the world owed them a living. Without a doubt, I was helping to perpetuate this myth. I didn’t dare tell Mother about the Sociology course.

I changed flat when I returned for the second term in January. Once again, I answered an advertisement in the paper and felt that Sue and I would get on much better than I had with Gwen and anyway, Gwen had swanned off to get married, and rather than find another flat mate for the damp basement I thought it wiser to move. The new flat was also approached by a flight of steps going underground, but the two bedrooms and the kitchen were on the first floor. That only left the lounge and bathroom to get damp.

In a fit of energy, I re-painted the whole flat, and I would like to apologize to the landlord, for my simply awful choice of bright, primary colours. I found it more fun to paint, than clean, so everything got painted, the dust, the dirt, the spiders and the cobwebs.

Money was often a problem though. From £52 grant per term at college, I now got £54 per month teaching salary after deductions, but it never seemed to stretch from one month’s end to the next, and I often felt despondent after three years hard work. Now I was struggling financially even more than when I was a student. The money had to cover rent, food and electricity and of course, petrol for the weekly trip home. Towards the end of every month, I would stand in the bank queue clutching my personal cheque made out for a few pounds, praying that they wouldn’t find out that I didn’t have any money in my account. I went into overdraft every month and never seemed to make ends meet.

The year of 1971 continued and I decided that I would have as much of a social life as I could during the week, even if the weekends were out. I joined the Young Conservatives and became actively involved, with another Young Conservative. Leonard was tall, suave and very well dressed. He took me home to meet his parents and they too were charming. I fell into the habit of having dinner there once a week and I almost became part of the family. Leonard was also understanding about me disappearing every weekend and not inviting him back to my home. Mother had broken up too many friendships in the past to make me want to risk it.

That Easter we all went down to the Young Conservative Party Conference in Brighton and I shook Edward Heath's hand. My one millisecond of fame! It was all very exciting, but it was over all too soon.

Before having the weekend off I had to phone my mother and break the news that I would not be driving up on Friday as usual. To give me extra courage, I took a friend with me. As expected, Mother went ballistic. As we left the phone box my friend was shaking even more than I was.

She said, "I never really believed what you said about your mother, but now I do, every word of it!"

Although I got on with Sue, my new flat mate, she was certainly strange. Looking back now, I have a nasty suspicion that she was on the game. Since this was the early part of the seventies, we prided ourselves on being very broadminded about life, so I was not unduly surprised or worried when I met Sue's boyfriend exiting her bedroom early one morning. I was a little surprised to see yet another boyfriend exiting at approximately the same time the following morning. I never saw either of them again, but I was envious as Sue seemed to have several very nice looking, well dressed boyfriends, who didn't seem short of a bob or two. And so it continued, with a different guy almost every day. When I asked Sue about them she was deliberately vague and pulled me into her room to show me yet another pair of new shoes that she'd bought.

That was the trouble with Sue, she spent money like it was going out of fashion, and she didn't always have the rent money at the end of each month. I was beginning to get a bit frantic. From my £54 a month salary, the rent cost £18 each and if I had to subsidize my flat mate, that left me with very little to live on. As it was, Domino desperately needed a new battery, and I had to park her at the top of a hill if I wanted to use her. Luckily, Bath is full of hills, but sometimes it meant driving round and round to find a suitable parking place on the street, and I had to walk two blocks to and from school as the staff car park was on level ground.

Sue suggested that we look for a cheaper flat. She told me she was taking delivery of her new car, and she needed a place with a garage. Trying to find out how she could afford a new car when she didn't have money for the rent elicited a different reply each time. I began to have serious doubts about Sue, but I didn't have enough courage to get to the bottom of it. We began to flat hunt.

I continued to go out with Leonard, but became a little uneasy. I liked him a lot, but didn't want to marry him. I had noticed when I visited Leonard's house, that ring catalogues were casually left open on the coffee table and once, I found swatches of white wedding dress material together with a pile of dressmaking patterns.

In June, Leonard traveled to Europe for two weeks with his parents. The Bath Festival was on, so I attended a concert to hear Yehudi Menuhin play, and went swimming in the Roman Baths, but I met no one new and time was running out.

I sat the exam for my Sociology A' level and afterwards a friend and I went back to my place for a drink to celebrate. Sue was in and insisted she take us both out to a fabulous new club, she had friends there, so we could get in free. I was quite nervous about this suggestion, as apart from going out with a group of college friends, and groups of the Young Conservatives, I had never been to a nightclub unescorted. However, it was my window of opportunity, Leonard was due back in three days and we were sure to pick up where we'd left off. I wondered if drifting into marriage was the right way to go. On weekends I was getting a lot of snide remarks from my mother, I was approaching 23 and still not married. But she always added,

"Who would want me anyway?"

Sue made a grand entrance into the club and soon we were all sitting at the bar while Sue ordered the drinks. She then disappeared onto the dance floor, leaving me to pay for them. My night school friend was asked to dance, and I was left sitting on a bar stool all by myself which made me feel very vulnerable. I picked up my drink and slid over to a small table deep in the shadows hoping no one would notice me.

"Will you dance with me please?"

I looked up to see a slim young man of medium height, with very short blonde hair and bright blue eyes bending over me.

"No thanks."

"Why not?" I froze. This was a situation I could not handle. "I, uh… don't feel like it just now."

"Come on, one dance won't hurt." His persistence began to make me angry.

"I said no. I don't know you and…"

"My name is Jeremy."

"I still don't know you, we've not been properly introduced by a mutual friend. I'm not here to be picked up by a total stranger." Jeremy walked away.

I felt very uncomfortable and would have got up and left, except that we had all come in Domino and I couldn't just leave the others to find their own way home. From the glimpses I caught of Sue, she was having a great time. Someone I knew walked into the club and I rushed over.

"Thank goodness you're here," I gasped grabbing his arm. "I don't know what came over me, I was going to have a drink at home to celebrate the end of the exams and somehow I found myself here and I don't know anyone and I don't usually behave like this as you know and now this strange guy is trying to pick me up and of course I said no, because I don't know him and..."

"Hi, hello Leslie, how are you?"

"Doing well Jeremy, not seen you in a long time."

"No, I've been overseas. But...I see you two know each other, so now will you introduce me, formally?"

I couldn't believe it, this creep actually knew one of my friends!

Leslie smiled and said, "Lucinda, this is Jeremy Landon, Jeremy, meet Lucinda Donagan."

"Now, you can't possibly refuse me a dance, can you?" Jeremy smiled and reluctantly I walked with him onto the dance floor.

"Do you live in Bath?"

"Yes."

"And what do you do?"

"Guess."

Jeremy took a step back and looked at me. "I guess that you're a secretary, am I right?"

Idiot!! I thought, couldn't he see the length of my nails? They were far too long for typists' nails.

"No, nowhere close," I replied.

"Tell me then."

"I'm a teacher."

"Wow!"

I was not sufficiently interested to ask him what he did and almost managed to escape at the end of the music, but I was not quick enough. Didn't they pause longer than two seconds between records in this place? Reluctantly I danced one more dance, but I was leaving immediately it had finished. I'd seen Sue disappearing out the door with some guy, and I'd not seen my other friend for a couple of hours.

"Would you like to come out tomorrow evening?"

"No thank you."

"What about Saturday then?"

"Sorry, but I am going away for the weekend," home of course.

"Well lunch on Thursday?"

This time I paused. School dinners were pretty awful at the best of times, and as staff I could hardly leave most of it and set a bad example. There was also the thought that I should be safe enough in daylight and it's difficult to turn down a free lunch.

"Well all right then, but I only have an hour."

"No problem. I'll get you back in time. Where shall I pick you up?"

I told him and as soon as the music stopped, I darted away, grabbed my bag and drove home alone. Sue never made it home at all that night, and I never bothered to ask her where she'd been.

Thursday came and I was so sure that Jeremy wouldn't pitch up, I didn't even go to look for him. Then they told me that there was a taxi waiting for me outside. Reluctantly I walked to the front gate and sure enough, there he was, not sitting in the back, but in the driving seat.

"Oh great," I thought. "A taxi driver, Mummy will be pleased." Something about Jeremy brought out the very worst in me. Every hair was standing up on the back of my neck, and I hesitated before getting into the cab.

He was very smartly dressed and he drove fast with confidence. I was expecting to go to the nearest 'greasy spoon', but we drove to one of the smartest hotels outside Bath and Jeremy ordered smoked salmon with all the trimmings. I didn't even get a chance to look at the menu, but I guessed that it wasn't going to be cheap.

He'd recently returned from overseas where he'd been in the Army, he was now in civvy street and looking for opportunities for employment. Driving a taxi was just to provide some pocket money while he looked around. The job was also flexible and allowed him to attend the odd interview. He was an engineer by profession. Well, that didn't sound so bad, but I still decided that I wouldn't see him again.

At the end of the meal, the waiter brought the bill. Jeremy glanced at it briefly and put his hand in his pocket. He put his hand in another pocket, looked inside his jacket and each time it came out empty.

"Oh lord, I've left my wallet at home. Hell, I don't have any money on me at all!"

I was horrified. I could see the headlines already.

Teacher arrested for not paying for meal in up-market Bath hotel.

"Do you have any money on you?"

Numbly I nodded. I'd actually drawn money for a taxi in case I needed to get back to school. "I'd really appreciate it if you could settle up. If I have to go home and collect my wallet, then it will make you late back at school, and I doubt they'll let both of us leave without paying."

I looked at the bill and my heart flipped over. It amounted to what I earned in a week! As I counted out the money, I wished I'd eaten a great deal more, as today's lunch would have to make do for supper.

We were five minutes late back at the school gates.

"Give me your address and I'll bring the money round to you on Friday."

I was reluctant to let him know where I lived, but I was even more worried about being late and I desperately needed the money, so I told him and hurried on into the classroom.

By late Friday night I was sick with worry. I just couldn't ask my mother for a loan, what was I going to do? At one minute to midnight the door bell rang. I was so relieved that I invited Jeremy in for a cup of coffee. We talked until dawn.

I mentioned that Domino needed work on her urgently, she was very difficult to start, and I was nervous about her breaking down and leaving me stranded.

"No problem. I told you I was an engineer, and I can give her a complete overhaul for you. No charge, it'll be my pleasure."

Once again, I was caught on the wrong foot. Would my greed get the better of me? Yes. We arranged that Jeremy would drive home with me later that day, which was the start of the school holidays, leave me at home and then return to Bath to fix up the car.

Looking back, it was a really stupid idea, just handing over my car to a complete stranger, but I was also sick to death of having to park her at the top of hills and walk miles to my destination. On the odd occasion when I had to leave her on level ground, I was also sick of asking people to help push her for me.

It was only years later that I discovered that Jeremy should have been working that Friday night, ferrying *fare paying* clients from one point to another. That he could completely ignore his responsibilities and not give them a second thought would never have occurred to me.

Was I really stupid then or is it simply the wisdom of age? Why didn't I question why he drove me to lunch in a taxi when he should have been working? Why didn't I wonder why he didn't have the money to pay for lunch if he'd been collecting fares all morning? I simply never thought to ask, yet it seems so obvious to me today.

I arrived home late that Saturday evening as we'd stopped for a drink and then sat in Domino and talked and talked and talked. I made some excuse to my mother, something about a cracked distributor cap, yet another lie, and although she was angry, she decided not to make too much of a fuss. I think she weighed up the options of Domino being out of commission and thus not able to transport me home, to the dangers of letting a 'long time' friend, give her a complete and thorough service which under ordinary circumstances I couldn't afford.

The holidays spent at home stretched ahead and my mother and I did our usual sitting in the house and going down to Cheltenham, Gloucester or Swindon to look in the shops. By now, I had a more modern wardrobe but nothing too extreme.

"What's that you've got on?"

"This?" I looked down at the red and white mini dress. "I bought it a few months ago."

"Pretty disgusting, I wouldn't be seen dead in anything as short as that."

"It's not that short, only a little above my knee. Most fashions these days are a lot shorter."

"Oh yes, it's all about the young now isn't it? Everything's for them, nothing for normal people. That's what you're all taught these days, how the world owes you a living, how everything's your right. It wasn't like that in my day, we knew how to behave. We had honour and respect for our elders, we would never go around like you young people today. We behaved properly. What happens now? Protests about this and that, sit-ins at universities, education is a privilege not a right."

"Yes Mother. Things are different I guess, but it's not my fault I was born when I was."

"How I wish you'd never been born, you've caused us all so much grief and pain. If I'd known how you were going to turn out, I'd never have had you. You are such a disappointment to me, I'm ashamed of you."

"But why, what have I done…?"

"What have you done? You go along with all this modern stuff, you believe all that rubbish they taught you in that college, and you think you can behave just as you like. You mark my words Lucinda, you'll come to a sticky end one day, don't say I didn't warn you."

So it went on, day after day, all day, every time my mother opened her mouth, not one kind, or even neutral word.

I had a frantic phone call from one of my friends in Bath, she had seen my car, at least she thought it was my car. Had it been stolen? I reassured her that I knew all about it and that Domino was in very safe hands. She didn't agree, she'd seen it parked by the roadside and it only had one front seat, and no back seat at all. Furthermore, the bonnet and boot were now painted matt black! Did I know about that?

Uh, no, I didn't.

And then some guy came along, got into Domino and drove her away faster that she had ever seen any mini move!

My first thought was good, Jeremy must have fixed the battery, my second was, matt black?

I decided that I needed to get down to Bath urgently and repossess my car while there was something left of her to repossess! I walked to the outskirts of town and stuck my thumb out and a few hours later, I knocked on the door of the address Jeremy had given me. The door was opened by a middle-aged lady who asked what I wanted.

I replied that I was looking for Jeremy. She hadn't seen him for several days, but when I did see him, I was to tell him that she wanted to talk to him urgently. But he did live here?

Yes, but not for long!

I was now more than anxious to get Domino back. I asked if I could wait for him until he returned.

No, because she had no idea where he was, if he would ever return and she didn't know me from a bar of soap.

I had the feeling that she wasn't too impressed with me – was it because I was a friend of Jeremy's?

I didn't know what to do, but just as I was leaving, I heard a loud roar and Domino swung into view from around the corner. She certainly looked different.

Jeremy offered to show me what he'd done, but there was nowhere for me to sit. He had indeed removed both the back seat and the front passenger seat.

We sneaked up to his room, at the time, I was so furious that I didn't notice the sneaking part. Jeremy opened the outside door very quietly and raced up the stairs as quickly and quietly as he could. I followed close behind him, I only had eyes for the car keys in his hands.

"Is that you Mr. Landon?" called a voice from the bottom of the stairs.

"Shush," Jeremy said.

I was in no mood to shush, but well trained, I lowered my voice. Jeremy persuaded me that what he'd done was in fact a good thing. It was easy to pop the seats back in, that wouldn't take a moment.

It's almost impossible to convey on paper just how persuasive Jeremy's skills were. He could, as the saying goes, sell fridges to Eskimos and heaters to Africans. How many times would I be persuaded to do exactly what I didn't want to do? Countless, more than I can even begin to remember.

At the end of the day, it had been decided that we would get a flat together and … that was the start of a whole new life.

Much to my own amazement, I phoned my mother and told her that I would be staying in Bath for the rest of the school holidays. I can't remember now what excuse I made, or what lies I might have told, but the die was cast.

The truth was that I was totally infatuated with this charismatic man. Everything I had wished to do, he'd already done. He'd traveled, had adventures, he was a free spirit. I worshipped the ground he walked on.

He told me tales of warm climates where you could swim in the sea after dark, he spoke of camels and Arab chiefs and the beauty of Cyprus where you could snow ski in the morning and go water skiing in the afternoon. He painted beautiful pictures of Australia, and vast deserts and Greek donkeys with flowers in their ears. There were adventures from his days firstly in the Army, and later in the SAS, but he'd had to leave the special forces when he broke a finger during a motor rally in Malta, driving for Ford.

And I sat and listened, and believed and imagined and wanted to see all these things too, and above all, be warm. How I hated the grey skies, the frequent rain and the fact that I was unnaturally cold most of the time.

However, my senses hadn't left me entirely, a few doubts did creep in every now and again. But it wasn't going to be easy getting out of the net.

The following day I was taken to meet Jeremy's parents. A really charming couple they both made me very welcome. I was a bit puzzled as to why Jeremy had his own flat in Bath, but he told me that he liked the odd pint, and knew that his mother didn't approve. Also, his parents went to bed every night at ten, and he didn't like to risk waking them, as they were both light sleepers and got up very early in the morning.

Many of my very small disbeliefs about Jeremy were smothered as I glanced round his parents' front room. There, in a glass case in the corner, was a curved sword that certainly looked Arabic and reclining on the settee was an embroidered cushion from Dubai. There were a large number of post cards from foreign places stuck on the fridge door.

I was re-assured, all the tales were true. I had in fact met someone very special, very different, someone who was as dashing and traveled and romantic as all those heroes in my make believe world all those years ago. He was such a strong personality that he gave me the courage to break away from home. He was someone I could lean on.

By now, of course Jeremy was no longer a taxi driver. It's just not done to leave your taxi parked outside your girlfriend's flat all night and still expect to be employed. By now he had moved on to drive something much bigger, a cement truck.

Since it was still the summer holidays, I traveled with him each day, viewing the world from our lofty perch, as the cement bin turned slowly behind us. I tried driving it once, but I didn't even have the strength to push the clutch in fully or turn the wheel. I marveled at all the clever things my newfound lover could do and fell even deeper in love.

We spent an idyllic couple of weeks barreling around the beautiful countryside around Bath, and I remember one particularly memorable day. We'd arrived at a farm to deliver cement for new pigsties and in a fit of insanity rescued a kitten from drowning. This left us in a bit of a quandary, as although I had yet to meet my landlord, I was well aware that the rules clearly stated 'no pets'.

When we returned to my flat that night, it was to find a note from

Sue announcing that she had moved out, something about a job in London, the first I heard she was even thinking of leaving Bath.

“No problem,” said Jeremy. “Let’s find a place for the two of us, where they do allow animals.”

We found somewhere, miles out of Bath but it did not solve our problems.

6 WILTSHIRE

The rent on the cottage was astronomical, but Jeremy assured me he brought home good wages and so we could afford it.

I went back to teach at school the next term, and for a few weeks Jeremy dropped me off at the railway station in the morning where I caught the train to Bath. Most evenings he was at the station to pick me up again, but on the rare occasions that he was held up at work, I took a taxi.

Today, it's widely accepted that people live together before they're married, but this was the early seventies and I felt a mixture of wild adventure, brazen wantonness and fear. I'd not forgotten my grandfather threatening Jeff for allowing me to stay with him. I was not in contact with my mother, but I was terrified that she would find out and make trouble. For the sake of appearances, I bought a curtain ring in Woolworths and put it on as I left school and took it off as I walked back through the gates the following morning.

I fretted about the situation, but one magical evening Jeremy asked me to marry him. Well that's not quite accurate. On that first trip home at the beginning of the holidays, Jeremy had announced that he was going to marry me. I laughed loud and long and simply thought, "Oh yeah, sure." This time he didn't actually ask me either, he simply said that we should now set a date.

It was the answer to all my problems and fears. I contacted my mother to tell her, but her only comment was a threat to inform the school I was living in sin, and therefore not fit to teach impressionable children.

I asked her to meet me in a coffee shop in town, hoping that might be a safer venue, but things were now so bad between us that I gave up and fled back to Bath. She had started screaming and crying in public and I was so embarrassed I fled. Her last words rang in my ears.

"Go ahead and marry him, but you'll regret it. And don't come running back to me."

Jeremy's parents knew we were living together but they did not condemn us. Now everything was going to be all right, as we were getting married. It would all be legal and above board.

It was left to me to arrange the venue and this was a problem, as we lived on the border of Wiltshire and Somerset and no one seemed to know which parish we were in. We didn't get married in church, the thought of walking down the aisle in silence, no organist, no choir, no flowers and not even a proper wedding dress, was just too dismal. I had one long dress I'd bought for dances and that would have to do. After paying the rent and finding money for food and petrol, we had very few pennies left over. In the end, the staff at school was wonderful and between them, they put together all the food and even a wedding cake.

We both took a day off work and a few friends and Jeremy's parents turned up at Frome Registry Office. I discovered later that Jeremy had borrowed money from his father to pay for the ring and a pair of shoes, as he only possessed gym shoes, and trainers were hardly suitable for a wedding.

Living together it was impossible not to see my husband-to-be the morning of the wedding, but I didn't want us to drive to the venue together so I ordered a taxi. I was mortified to see that the taxi driver was the one who occasionally collected me from the station, the same taxi driver I'd chatted to about my husband. It was impossible to look as if I was going any place other than to my own wedding. Unwillingly I climbed in, trying to hide the bouquet of flowers and the absence of the curtain ring on my finger.

I don't remember the wedding too clearly, except that it seemed clinical and that I cried all the way through, I've never been able to work out why.

The party went on well into the night and as the last guests left, we were ready for bed.

"The car is still outside the garage," I said to Jeremy.

"Then go and put it away," he replied.

"But I'm still in my wedding dress, and it's dark out there and isn't that a man thing?"

"Not necessarily, I'm too tired, you put it away."

"And what if I won't?"

"Then don't expect to share a bed with me ever again."

I was shocked, but I'd been so well trained. While I baulked at walking up the dark back path and maneuvering the car into the garage, I was afraid to test Jeremy's declaration. I meekly went outside and did as I was told. This set the pattern for our whole marriage, but it did not occur to me to do anything else but fall in line with his wishes. Yes, I guess I was spineless, but years of pandering to a domineering mother had taught me to obey, and obey I did.

It was different the following morning as Jeremy was kind, loving and cheerful, and I instantly forgave him his orders from the night before. But as I made the bed the following morning, I asked myself just what had I done? It was too late to go back, as far as I understood life, you made your bed and you lay on it.

The honeymoon lasted two days. Saturday was a trip to the coast and on Sunday his parents came around for tea. Monday saw me back at school and Jeremy back in the tar lorry. At some point between July and October, he had not only lost the job as a taxi driver, but that of driving the cement mixer as well. I hadn't complained too much at the time, as I was exhausted washing his dust laden overalls by hand. I hadn't reckoned on the tar being a whole lot worse than the cement. In total, I had met and married Jeremy in eleven weeks and three days, not long, when you think about it.

Driving the tar truck also included weekends, as road works were often planned out of hours to cause minimal disruption to traffic, so I would go along too, I had a horror of being left alone. The spectre of my mother was lurking in the shadows all the time. I was scared that somehow she would appear and take all my new found happiness away. I had not even invited her to the wedding and I was even too scared to tell her I was married.

One weekend it was raining heavily and the road workers refused to take delivery of the hot tar. When Jeremy phoned the depot they told him to get rid of the load, not an easy thing to do in the Wiltshire countryside. We slowed down alongside a couple of gateways, but it didn't seem right to deposit tar in anyone's access road. This was dumping on a grand scale!

Jeremy had a brainwave. "We'll take it back to the cottage and lay a tar driveway from the road to the garage. The landlord will be pleased and he might even reduce the rent for a couple of months."

It appeared to be a good plan, so we drove home as quickly as we could and Jeremy backed the truck up to the garage doors and lifted the bin. It rose higher and higher, but the tar was going nowhere. Even almost vertical, the tar moulded itself to the bin and refused to budge. Jeremy tried driving forward a little and braking suddenly, in the hope it would jerk the tar free. This had only limited success. One huge lump was catapulted off the back and landed in front of the garage doors.

By now, Jeremy was in a furious temper. He could see his plans failing and that did not sit well with him. He drove farther down the drive, stopping and jerking several times until we had a series of small mountains all along the path. But that still left most of the tar firmly settled in the bin.

Jeremy jumped out, handed me a spade and told me to get the rest of it out. It was still pouring with rain, I was soaking wet and I began howling my eyes out as I climbed up into the bin. I did the best I could, but by now, the tar was nearly solid and I could only get a few small spadefuls off the top.

Jeremy reappeared with a pickaxe but it was hard enough lifting the axe without wielding it, and I proved even more useless with that than I had with the spade. My new husband climbed back into the tar lorry, and giving me just enough time to fling myself off the back, he roared off to take it back to the depot.

I was left to flatten out the remaining tar which had dropped out, but by now, we had a series of large black, solid, gigantic molehills from the garage to the road, including an extra large one at least three foot high, right outside the garage. What made this even worse was the car was still in the garage and the chances of ever getting it out again were slim. On the bright side, the imprisoned car was not Domino, but a large, black Rover 8 that Jeremy had bought in barely running order. Now, it looked as if we were back down to one car again, and I dearly wished that Jeremy didn't drive Domino as if he was competing in the Formula One. I didn't have the courage to ask him to slow down.

When Jeremy eventually returned much, much, later that night, it was with the news that he'd been fired. He'd now had three jobs in less than six months.

This was to be the story of our lives as Jeremy hopped from one job to the other. Yet, at the time it didn't seem important. Why? Because living with Jeremy was like being on a roller coaster. He would be down and depressed for about five minutes but after that, he would leap up like a spring lamb and begin planning the next phase of our lives. He was a fountain of energy and each new day was destined to bring yet another exciting experience.

If I was worried or anxious, he would hug me and reassure me and chase all the devils away. He was my rock and my refuge and I worshipped the ground he walked on. Where I was shy, quiet and terrified of authority, Jeremy was outgoing, brave and optimistic. If anyone could ever take the world by storm, it was my fantastic, wonderful husband. I knew that one day he would make it really big and I hoped that I would be there by his side.

I spent many happy hours dreaming how I was going to spend my millions. Each day was a new adventure and while I had moments of despair, Jeremy was always there to cheer me up. It got that I needed to be by his side most of the time I was not at work and emotionally, I became very dependent on him, although I was not consciously aware of this at the time. I just knew I felt frightened and lost unless we were together.

I decided that it was time to face my mother, I would just have to be brave, and one weekend we drove back to the bungalow. As soon as she opened the door my mother guessed we were married. She began crying, weeping and wailing. At one point she even crawled across the floor beating her fists on the carpet.

Jeremy was good with her, talking to her in a calm voice until he eventually persuaded her that we should take her out for a drink. To my surprise she agreed, but half way through the evening Jeremy said the fatal words, “There, I told you, you should come out, you’re enjoying yourself after all.” Immediately her face went rigid, and she demanded that we take her straight home. The evening did not end well.

A couple of days later Jeremy bounced into the lounge and announced that he had an interview. It never failed to amaze me how quickly he found work.

“I’m attending the presentation first,” he told me. “This is the real answer to our future. This is going to be the perfect job for me, we are going to make a million in no time at all. Do you want to come along?”

7 LONDON

Five minutes into the presentation I knew it was a waste of time, but Jeremy was totally enthralled. I made a few cautious remarks but it was like trying to stop a herd of charging elephants with a fly swat. The result was that Jeremy moved up to London to stay with a friend, we gave up the cottage with the tar molehills, left the cat temporarily with another friend and I moved in with an aide at school.

I heard nothing for several weeks and after payday took a train to London, to find that Jeremy had not been coming in before 3am each morning. He was selling encyclopedias door to door in Coventry of all places, driving up and back every day after training in the morning. When I finally got to see him there was no persuading him he should give it up. He had been promoted and was now area manager, but to date had not been paid a cent.

I returned to Bath and took an evening job on a hot dog stand, fearful that I would be seen by the head, the staff or one of the parents. I was lost, lonely and fearful and I was the self-fulfilling prophesy of everything my mother had said.

Then Jeremy came back. Why? Because he could not bear to think of me working in such dangerous conditions at night, I could be mugged or raped. He marched me down to the hot dog garage and handed in my notice.

To make matters worse, I had already given in my notice at school, which, I like to think they accepted reluctantly. As soon as I arrived the next morning, I asked the Head if I could cancel it and continue working.

"Sorry, your job has already been advertised."

"Then can I apply for it?"

"No, that would take a lot of explaining, the date for applications has expired and in fact we're interviewing this afternoon. It wouldn't be ethical to add you to the list at this late stage."

It wouldn't? Perhaps they had accepted my resignation with alacrity! But I did have to work out my notice, and it was not long before Jeremy found another job, I think it was another driving job. We moved into a rented room on the ground floor in the centre of Bath and we went to reclaim Premix the cat.

It's really amazing what you can do with one room. I portioned off one area as a bedroom and another as the dining area and pushed the couches over by the windows, which I sealed with sticky tape to keep out the worst of the draughts. We had one small table top stove in which Jeremy managed to melt our one and only plastic plate, and the week we had enough spare money to buy a bottle of fruit squash, we celebrated by dancing madly round the room.

For leisure, we played tennis against the back wall, until one night we heard a rumbling as the plaster behind the wallpaper disintegrated and bulged out like a vertical moonscape. We stopped playing tennis. The room came partly furnished, with two single beds of different heights. This problem we solved by propping up the lower one on four empty paint cans. On occasion, these would slide apart in the middle of the night and deposit one of us on the floor. The thing I hated most was the bathroom on the first floor above us, which we had to share with two other families.

During his time in the army, Jeremy had become quite proficient at karate, and often performed party tricks for our friends. This was highly amusing and made me so proud of him until the night he sliced though one of the dining room chairs with the side of his hand, and then chopped the doorknob, which promptly fell off the door and landed on the floor. After that, we had to use the remaining doorknob on both sides of the door, so everywhere we went I carried it in my handbag.

The rest of our leisure time was spent moving Domino from one parking spot in the street to another. We didn't have a garage and the street-parking limit was only two hours. If we overslept at a weekend, we knew we would get a ticket. Life never seemed to let us relax.

The school term ended and I was now unemployed. I had applied for every teaching post within commuting distance, but there weren't many posts available only one term into the year, and it was with a sense of desperation that I took a much lower paying job with the South Western Gas Board as a clerk, or rather, clerk's assistant.

This was even less fun that serving on the hot dog stand. I was given figures to check and forms to fill in, and by half ten each morning I had finished the day's work. I took my knitting in, but this was frowned on. I substituted wool and needles for a book and was told that was not allowed either, I was not getting paid to sit and read. I asked for more work to do and after proving I was proficient in the alphabet, they allowed me to file. I filed everything in sight and was still finished well before lunch.

Friends and long lost relatives were amazed to hear from me as I wrote long, boring letters to everyone I could think of every afternoon. I wandered down into the control room and asked endless questions about how everything worked, and even filled in for the manager's secretary when she went on leave. It never occurred to me to walk away from the job, no matter how mind numbing it was. I still applied for every vacant teaching post, applying farther and farther afield.

As Christmas was approaching, I thought I should make peace with my mother. The telephone conversation went reasonably well and ended with an invitation for us to spend Christmas together. I accepted. We counted out our pennies and thought, if we did without a gift for each other, that would leave just enough for petrol and a small present for my mother.

I phoned again early on Christmas Eve, only to be told that it was no longer convenient and the invite was withdrawn. I think I went into a mild state of shock, because for the first time, I felt I had a right to shout at my mother. And I did. I told her how awful she was before hanging up on her.

When I told Jeremy, he responded quite cheerfully, and we went out and bought a very, very old black and white second-hand television as our Christmas present to each other. We did not possess a TV license. We trawled a nearby supermarket at around 4.30 pm and picked up a steak for Christmas dinner the following day, a real treat.

Christmas day 1971 was one I'll always remember, not for the wealth of presents, but the first I had spent away from home, now happily married, watching TV and munching on a steak, I thought that life wasn't so bad after all.

January brought a surprise visit from my mother, had she been feeling a bit guilty over the cancellation at Christmas? What was really amazing though is she brought someone with her. My mother, for the first time in twenty-three years had a boyfriend! His name was Paul and he was a really nice person, I took to him straight away.

My mother's first words on entering our small kingdom, with a garden and without a bathroom were;

"What a dump."

"We can't afford anything else right now Mum."

"I'd be ashamed if my mother ever saw me living in a hovel like this. Of course I've never sunk that low in my life."

"Mum, it's clean and we pay for it and…"

My mother ignored my words as she looked around. "Where's the bathroom, and the kitchen?"

I pointed as I said. "The 'kitchen', is over there by the back door."

"And the bathroom?"

"It's on the first landing."

"You don't mean to say you share with other people do you! How awful! To think, after all I've done for you, all that private education that you should end up like this!"

"Well we do have access to a garden, it gives us extra space."

Paul tried to pour oil on troubled waters. "Now Margaret, they're young and just starting out."

"I'm sorry Paul but when I started out I never sank this low. But then of course I didn't associate with the kinds of people Lucinda likes to mix with, but then no decent person would be seen dead with her."

This was so charming, Jeremy was right there and listening to every word. I was so scared that he would say something that would escalate things into a full scale row.

"Now Margaret, that's not fair, give them some time to get on their feet. That's enough. I think you've done wonders with one room, both of you."

"Thank you Paul, would you like tea or coffee?" I asked.

"A cup of tea would be lovely, and I'm sure your mother would like some as well, wouldn't you Margaret?"

"I might as well have some tea after driving all the way down here."

Paul was much kinder and complimented me on how nicely I had done everything up. He made a friend for life. They didn't stay very long but I had a small glimmer of hope of a new relationship with my mother at long last. She seemed to defer to Paul a little, he was certainly sympathetic to our situation, and he didn't condemn.

But as 1972 progressed, in fact only a week or two later, Jeremy's latest job went wrong, as so many were to do in the future. Overnight, I found I was now married to an antique dealer.

I guess Jeremy must have got talking to someone, maybe in a bar, but suddenly we were immersed in a domestic version of "Antiques Roadshow." The flat, a rather posh name for our one room without bath, was crammed with library books displaying and describing any artifact over a hundred years old.

Jeremy studied each night, all night and during the day, he worked as a sales assistant in an antique shop. He had, he pronounced, found the real career he was born for, all other jobs had been a fill in until he found what he really wanted to do. Unfortunately, his new boss seemed loathe to part with any money for the time and effort that Jeremy put in, but instead paid him in kind, all kinds of things. Slowly our flat filled up with gross, overbearing Victorian wardrobes, Edwardian chests of drawers, Georgian tables and Victorian snuffboxes, until it became so bad we could hardly move.

If I'd had the courage to be brutally honest with Jeremy, I would have voiced my opinion and told him that everything he brought home was either falling apart, a fake, or wood infested. From a total of two living in our ground floor 'flat' with garden and no bath, the population rose by several thousand as we shared our slice of paradise with a myriad of small wood eating insects and one cat.

We were desperately short of money and food became a problem, and there were other bills to pay. I doubted if Bath Electricity would accept payment of one 19th century insect infested sideboard in return for the quarterly account. They didn't, and consequently we lost our electricity. I could never persuade Jeremy to plan ahead, he lived for the moment.

So, we had £5 to spare? Great let's go for a drink and a burger. But the electricity bill / rent / car tax is due! Has the bill arrived yet? No but.... Then it's ours to spend tonight.

Like a lamb, I put on my coat, tucked the doorknob into my bag and followed him into the street.

After a few months the antiques world lost its glamour. Jeremy's new boss was now living at Her Majesty's pleasure so there was no chance of earning anything.

Jeremy decided to go back into engineering and he started work as a garage mechanic. For the first couple of weeks he used Domino to get to and from the garage, several miles out into the countryside, but one night he arrived home in a white jaguar. I was a bit stunned, but he assured me that it was in part payment for labour and he would be paying the rest off weekly.

I felt like a queen as I hopped in for a demonstration drive. I pushed any misgivings I had firmly to the back of my mind, especially the voice that wanted to scream,

"Don't these guzzle petrol like Boeing aircraft?"

I needn't have worried, it was not destined to take in much more fuel. Two weeks later, it blew up on the M5 on the way to work. Jeremy didn't tell me about the incident right away, pretending that he had parked the car down the back road behind the flats, and he began hitching to and from work.

In the meantime, we had been house hunting. Jeremy assured me that it was quite possible to become a house owner without a penny to your name. He was right! We trailed round hundreds of properties each weekend and soon learned that:-

"Needs a coat of paint," was equal to derelict.

"Ripe for renovation," was equal to derelict.

"Needs a loving owner," was equal to derelict.

"We want a cottage in the country," we told the estate agents only to be sneered at and directed to yet another new housing estate where the views through the middle of the walls were cheerfully described as 'settling in cracks'.

But we persevered and after a long search, we knocked on the door of a house near Melksham. If I had followed my instincts I should have jumped back into the car and driven away.

8 MELKSHAM

Standing in the hallway was a young lady about my age, wearing a t-shirt and leopard skin print trousers. One of those sayings that my mother had so often repeated popped into my head. “Never trust a female in leopard skin, or any other wild animal print clothes.” Yet again, I pushed these thoughts right to the back of my mind as we took a conducted tour of the house. There was a garden at the back, and as an added bonus, a slightly tumbledown garage across the road, together with several feet alongside the River Avon complete with fishing rights.

The only drawback was the closeness to the road, as the traffic went by approximately six inches outside the front windows, but we felt the advantages far outweighed this one fault and fell in love with it. We made Sally and Ben a firm offer that they verbally accepted.

I just knew that this was the house for us, after all, Sally had two Cairn terriers from which she was going to breed and if that wasn’t a sign, I didn’t know what was.

Now all we needed was the £7,950.00 to buy our cottage in the country. For Jeremy such details were not the slightest problem, leave everything to him, he would sort it out. I did and he did. I only learned long after, the full extent of his ‘courage?’ He approached one building society for a loan which they granted, remember Jeremy could sell fridges to Eskimos.

With the loan firmly in the bank masquerading as our hard earned deposit, he next got a mortgage from the bank, showing them his salary slips from an earlier job. What I didn’t know, was that since the Jaguar had exploded and Jeremy had been hitch hiking to work, he’d been late so many times that he was in fact unemployed. I never asked about the rest of the payments for the now defunct car. I just didn’t have the courage, and it would make him so angry.

But in the end he pulled it off and we finally moved into our new home in April.

Jeremy had applied to another Bath company for a position as a mechanic. Heaven only knows what he said at the interview, but he walked out a Project Manager. He’d landed an amazingly good job, with good career prospects. At last he had found his niche he told me, and did I realize how good the pension package was? I was offered a post at a primary school in Trowbridge on the bus route from

Melksham and our new home.

As Jeremy explained, that was not important as he now had a company vehicle, a grey Morris Minor van with the company name blazoned large and bright on the side, but the petrol was free and we used it at every opportunity.

We settled into domestic bliss. We became firm friends with Sally and Ben who'd moved just down the road, and life seemed to have turned out just as I had hoped. Since things were going so well, I thought a visit to see my mother was in order. I wanted to prove to her that we had settled down, we were paying our taxes, that we were respectable and she could now see that she had not brought a failure into the world.

We drove up and popped in. Paul was not around, and I am not sure quite what happened, but while she showed me all her new clothes and the presents that Paul had bought her and boasted about the cruise they were going on, it was difficult not to feel jealous. I felt a little hard done by. I do remember that on the way home, Jeremy and I had a tremendous row, I honestly don't know what started it, but I was asking myself what was I doing married to a man who was so unreliable and so volatile?

I enjoyed my new school and to try and give us some financial stability I took on a second job which came about by accident. Trying to replace the school guinea pig that had met an untimely end, I discovered they were in short supply and there was money to be had in breeding them. I then expanded into gerbils, rabbits and hamsters. It was hard work cleaning and feeding but it brought in a small, but steady income.

My grandfather died but I just did not have the courage to attend the funeral. I felt very guilty as I wanted to go, but I knew I just couldn't see my mother. This is one of the big regrets in my life. A few months earlier we had visited yet again, when my grandparents were there, and she had caused a terrible scene and hidden my handbag and refused to return it unless I came back to live at home. I couldn't leave without it and it took several hours to talk her into giving it back. I was scared this would happen again and I would not be able to escape. To appeal to any kind of authority was unthinkable, it would bring such shame to the family. My grandmother was brought down from London to live in an old people's home close to my mother.

We got to chatting about the future one night with Ben and Sally, laughing about the TV programme 'The Good Life'. It featured Felicity Kendall and Richard Briars living a country life in suburban Surrey. Why not? Why be slaves to work, life was an adventure wasn't it? We all loved the countryside, so what part of Britain was least populated?

Scotland?

With her eyes closed, Sally put a pin in the map of Scotland and it landed in the area around Banff. None of us had ever been so far north before, so we all agreed that we would go on a fact-finding trip right after Christmas and see if we liked it.

We were enchanted with Scotland. We gazed at the lochs, and the mountains and the dells and compared them favourably with southern England. What was even better, the house prices were so reasonable, maybe, if we made a good profit selling our current house, we could even buy one practically outright. No mortgage, what a dream. We planned our migration north of the border.

1972 was 'cottage in the country' time for Londoners so it was a good time to sell. But then we discovered the council was redeveloping the area. I went down to their offices. I looked over the wall charts. Sure enough, there was a bright red line going right through the middle of our country cottage.

"Is this the proposed route for a new road?"

"Yes, it'll be a dual carriageway."

"Yes? And what about these buildings here?"

The council clerk squinted for a moment and then rather reluctantly, came out from behind the counter to look more closely at the map.

"These two old barns? They'll get knocked down."

"They most certainly are not, two 'old barns', I live in one of them!"

"Really?" A pause. "Have you got water?"

"Yes of course we have, mains water."

"And electricity?"

"Yes, that's on mains as well. And, we pay rates. The planning department must know these houses are occupied surely?"

"Oh, dear. You do seem to have a problem. Tell you what we'll do," the counter clerk was all smiles and sympathy, "we'll fill in a complaint form."

Together we filled in a complaint to say that I objected strongly to having a new highway built right through the middle of my house.

A week later there was a knock on the door and a council official stood on the doorstep.

"We're widening the road from the roundabout to the T junction and that means we must requisition this property."

"Does that mean a compulsory purchase order?"

"Yes. And that, will have to go."

"What will have to go?"

"Your 'For Sale' sign, it's illegal to sell a house when you know it's going to be demolished."

"Do you give us a fair market price?" Jeremy asked.

"Oh yes, but of course it'll be nothing like you'd get for selling to the Londoners." Did I imagine the self satisfied sneer in his voice?

They say that moving is one of the most stressful times, after death and divorce, but having your home condemned is even worse, even if you *were* planning to sell it. Sadly, I removed the sign outside, and waited to hear what the Council was going to offer us. We were young and naive and so it never occurred to bargain with them, or refuse to sell and sit tight. They offered us £8,250.00, which was only £295.00 more than we paid for the house in the first place.

I get quite angry now when I think of the money and TLC we had put into the cottage. We had opened up the original fireplace and found a genuine fire basket big enough to burn huge logs in the winter. We'd completely re-decorated, and laid fitted carpets, and these had a rubberized backing that made them impossible to lift again. I had scraped down the stairs and repainted them and we had re-tiled the bathroom.

A letter arrived giving us three months to vacate the property. Twenty years later, I took a trip back to the area, only to see Brandywine Cottage still standing. The road had not been widened, and I discovered that our dream cottage was now a council house and was occupied.

But the die was cast. We had planned to move to Scotland anyway, so why not simply bring our plans forward and move earlier?

9 SCOTLAND

Through contacts made on our previous trip, Jeremy had been offered a job any time on a large estate near Banff, together with a cottage at the princely sum of £2.00 a week!

We collected the hire van and packed it with all one hundred and eighty breeding animals, plus four cats and eight dogs. I had acquired six Cairn terriers with plans to breed puppies. I hoped to get a lot more money than I got for the small furries. It was a nightmare drive for us, but our passengers enjoyed it, for when we finally reached our destination, we had three more gerbils, two extra baby rabbits and another guinea pig.

I did not contact my mother, there had been an ominous silence from her after I had not gone to the funeral and I did not blame her. I had heard in the meantime that she had married Paul, so maybe we were square over wedding invites.

Once we arrived in Scotland, Jeremy bought himself a Ford Cortina well beyond her prime, which was all he could afford, but since he didn't fill her with anti-freeze, her block froze solid and the engine seized and then sort of exploded. Always the eternal optimist, Jeremy had reckoned "She would be OK, it probably won't get that cold."

Domino was still going, if not strongly, at least she was still going. She was no longer factory white, but bright orange with a matt black roof, boot and bonnet. In a fit of madness one afternoon, we had purchased tins of Woolworth's Household Gloss, driven her under a bridge and repainted her in the pouring rain. We got compliments on her paintwork when we stopped at the garage to fill up on the way home, but begged people not to touch, as the paint was still wet.

I was kept busy in the cottage tending to the animals, exercising the dogs and generally playing housewife. This lasted for a couple of weeks, until I decided that I must get another teaching job. However, I discovered that I was pregnant, which would not make me a firm favourite at any job interview. We'd not planned to have any family at all. Neither of us had brothers or sisters, so we were not used to crowds, and we felt strongly that we should do our bit for world population control. But we had to admit that we were pretty excited about having a family.

Jeremy started his job on the farm a couple of days after we moved in. Work hours were from 7 am until 6 pm, so he was a little surprised to find no one around at all just after seven on the first morning. Starting at seven meant that you were on site by 6.30 am, to receive the day's instructions, leaving you enough time to get to the correct place to start labouring at seven.

Score: Estate one, Jeremy nil.

The following day they were told to round up the young male calves for castration. Once the beasts were cornered, they were singled out one at a time and with the judicial use of two house bricks, all their dreams of fatherhood were, just dreams! Word must have got round quickly among the cattle, because after racing fruitlessly up and down the field for hours, Jeremy got fed up and rounded up the lot of them in ten minutes using the Landover. He was accused of depleting their body weight by kilos and given a full dressing down.

Score: Estate two, Jeremy nil.

A couple of days later the labourers were taken to a barn where the roof needed to be raised. This involved some dangerous climbing up the sidewalls, sawing down the cross beams cutting them to size on the floor and then, even more dangerously, climbing back up to replace them. After watching this performance for several minutes Jeremy made a template, cutting all the rafters first, and then constructing a forked tool on which to raise the beam. Only one man was needed to nail it into place. By mid afternoon the roof was completed and Jeremy waited for the appreciation. No praise, the job had been timed out at three days, so what was the work force supposed to do tomorrow and the day after?

Score: Estate game, set and match, Jeremy out of work.

While the cottage was attached to the job, the estate was kind enough to let us stay on at the same peppercorn rent, and Jeremy went off to seek another job. All these years later, I cannot remember just how many jobs he has had, maybe he should be in the Guinness Book of Records, but I do know he was indefatigable when it came to job seeking.

He traveled into the job centre in Banff to sign on. They offered us the dole, but Jeremy politely refused. We had enough to keep going for a while, but if they would please pay his national health stamp that was all we asked.

Undeterred, the man from the dole office turned up at the house two days later. He asked what belonged to us etc and a whole lot of other personal questions. Jeremy became angry and threatened to throw him out. However, the end product was a cheque, which arrived by post every Tuesday morning, for a whole lot more than Jeremy was paid working as a farm hand! I often wondered if the guys who laboured all those hours realized that they could get more money by signing on and lying on the sofa watching TV all day!

His next employer hired him to test and proof load cranes around the north east area of Scotland. This was much more on his level, it came with a good salary and a company car and so again, we started house hunting.

Sally and Ben had settled a few miles away, they'd had enough capital to purchase a house outright, and since Ben worked from home, I thought they were happily settled.

We found a small cottage on a quarter acre of ground, with one living room, one bedroom, a small bathroom and a kitchen with a sink and open stove similar to an Aga. We lived in the kitchen, as it was the warmest room in the house. From the north side of the house, we had a stunning view of the Moray Firth and we were surrounded by farmland. We did our monthly shopping fifty miles away in Aberdeen and wandered down to the local pub at weekends. The air was fresh, clean and we were incredibly healthy.

But the small breeding animals were not doing too well in the shed outside. One morning I found six assorted animals dead and five more deceased the following day. No sign of mutilation, no sign of illness at all. I raced to the local vet carrying my sad little parcel of bodies, but he could find nothing wrong. The answer came back from the Aberdeen Veterinary Research Centre – 'pseudo-tuberculosis'. There was no cure, as each pair of little furries died I was forced to burn their cages as no amount of disinfectant and scrubbing would alleviate the danger of re-infection.

I was more successful with the Cairns. By now, I had two males, Chaos and Havoc and six females, Storm, Tempest, Trouble, Muddle, Horror and Mischief, names I felt describe Cairns to a T. Although Cairns were quite common in Scotland, mine were silver pointed and red in colour. They also had masses of red writing on their pedigree certificates to show they were award-winning progeny.

I placed the first advert in the paper. "Cairn puppies for sale, champion stock."

The phone rang and I quoted the price as £75 per puppy. The phone rang again a few minutes later, price? £80 per puppy. Each time the phone went, the price of the puppies increased. The last puppy I sold, was destined to go and live in America, and left my unwilling hands at £250.

If I thought I was going to make mega bucks from the dog breeding I was sorely mistaken, since special foods for pregnant bitches, special pills and potions for nursing mums, and vet bills and inoculations all added up.

Jeremy worked happily for a few months until who knows what

happened. I remember getting a phone call one morning enquiring where he was. He signaled from the other side of the kitchen that I was to say he had gone to work.

"Then why is his car parked outside the cottage?" enquired the voice at the other end of the line. I had no answer to that one. Once again, Jeremy was out of work.

I was beginning to despair, but with his usual energy, Jeremy was soon off on the job trail again. He was often absent for hours on end, and one day he came home and suggested that I take a break. He'd noticed that I was looking a bit run down, so why not go and spend a few days with my mother-in-law in Bath?

We still had a bit of money put by, so I hopped on a train and returned south. I was in Bath for less than three days when Mum-in-law suggested I go back. She seemed very jittery and nervous and said that it was not a good idea to leave my husband on his own. At the time I forgot how 'fey' she was, I just felt unloved and unwanted and I boarded the train in tears and traveled back to Scotland.

Jeremy didn't seem too pleased to see me either, and I didn't see too much of him as he was always out job hunting. I felt uneasy, but I couldn't put my finger on anything specific.

Sally phoned and asked if she could pop round that afternoon. I noticed that she was looking very smart, she'd spent a lot on clothes recently, and I admired her new outfit as I put the kettle on.

"I wish you'd sit down," she said, "I've something to tell you."

"Are you pregnant again?" Shortly after arriving in Scotland Sally and Ben had had a baby boy.

"No, it's, well there's no easy way to say this, but Jeremy and I are going away together and, well, we love each other and…"

I fell rather than sat down. My world spun round and I felt sick. All I could think of to say was "When?"

"Later today. I wanted Jeremy to tell you, but he refused, but I thought you should know."

Too right I should know! How was I supposed to cope all by myself in a cottage stuck out in the middle of nowhere in the northern wilds of Scotland, with no job and a new baby to support? And no Jeremy, the man around whom my world revolved, only now, it was just the kitchen revolving around me.

"I'm not the only one. Jeremy told me about another girl he had an affair with at work in Melksham." Sally was firmly on the defensive. She stood up and left abruptly, mumbling something about having to pack.

I remembered the hairpins I had found in the bed, the kind I never used, and with a sinking feeling, I knew she was telling the truth. I lurched for the phone and rang Ben.

"Did you know about this?"

"Yes."

"Why didn't you tell me?"

"I hoped it would all blow over and you'd never have to find out."

"Sally was kind enough to come round and tell me, I didn't have to find out. How long has it been going on?"

"Since we were in England."

"What! And you knew then?"

"Yes."

"But why, why didn't you do something?" I screamed at him.

"What could I do? I hoped that it would all fizzle out and then we could get on with our lives. I didn't really think we'd all end up living near each other in Scotland."

"Why didn't you leave her Ben? Why did you put up with it?"

There was a long silence, probably the answer was that he loved her, I truly believe he did. Eventually he replied,

"Did you know Sally was married before?"

"No! Before you married her? This is her second marriage? Are you sure?"

"Of course I'm sure. She has a daughter of seven. She came to see her mother sometimes in Wiltshire and Sally was always a bit nervous that you would drop in on those days."

I was speechless. How could something so major be a part of your best friend's life and you have absolutely no inkling of it. Then reality struck home. They were leaving, both of them, today.

"She said they were going away together, today."

"So soon?"

"What am I going to do Ben?"

"I don't know Lucy, I really don't. I feel sorry for both of us."

I rang off quickly as I heard Jeremy drive in through the gates. He bounced in with a smile and gave me a hug.

"Well no luck so far, but I'll keep trying."

"Trying? Where? From your new home with Sally?"

His face turned white. "She came round?"

"Yes, and told me what's been going on."

"I couldn't help it. I do love you Lucinda. Don't you understand it's possible to love more than one person at the same time? With Sally it's a spiritual love. We're soul mates. I know we were together in a previous life and, well it's just something we had no control over. I am so sorry."

At this point I broke down, screamed, howled, rushed into the bathroom and threatened to kill myself. However, I cooled down when the phone rang. I couldn't hear what Jeremy was saying, but it got me out from behind the locked door. I sat down and tried to be as calm as possible. "I've made a decision," I said.

"Uh?" Jeremy looked nervous.

"I want you to wait until I've had the baby and then I want you and Sally to bring him up and give him a good home. I won't be able to cope as a single mother, and he will have a much better future with you two." If I couldn't keep Jeremy in full time permanent employment, then maybe Sally could.

"That was Sally on the phone just now. We're not going anywhere. It's all off. I told her I couldn't leave you, I didn't want to leave you. I must have been blind. I'm not going to leave you for a second. I'll work to earn your trust again. Oh I do love you." Jeremy put his arms around me and rocked back and forth, sobbing. If I had had a home to go to where I could find comfort and shelter, maybe I would have left then, but I had nowhere and I had no money. I was trapped.

They say that pregnancy instills a feeling of well being, of peace and tranquility women do not experience at any other time of life. It's true my country GP had told me I had a particularly bovine appearance, and I think this natural anesthetic saved me at that time. I accepted the apology. I accepted that we would stay together and I accepted that we would raise this child together, but not in Scotland, I was quite firm about that.

We had to get away, not only from this house but from Sally and Ben, somewhere warm overseas. This idea appealed to the deep-rooted wanderlust I had always subjugated, and it came with the added bonus of putting even more miles between my mother and me. After more blazing rows over the phone, we had not corresponded from before the compulsory purchase order.

True to his word, Jeremy didn't leave me for a second. He was constantly by my side as if to prove that he wasn't seeing or even talking to Sally. Once again, he threw all his energies into applying for jobs overseas. I saw a For Sale notice outside their house, but where they went and whatever happened to them I will never know. We never spoke again.

In an incredibly short time, Jeremy was offered a job in Tanzania, leaving just as soon as the baby was born. I looked it up, half way down on the right hand side of Africa, population just over 16 million, capital Dar es Salaam, chief products sisal, coffee, cotton, maize and ground nuts.

There was only one more memorable incident before we left Scotland. It was shortly after the truth came out that I woke suddenly in the middle of the night. The room was very cold and our Red Setter had dived under the bed whimpering. I saw my grandfather. I knew he'd been dead for almost two years, and if it hadn't been for the dog's reaction and the look of terror on Jeremy's face, perhaps I would have simply believed I was hallucinating. But strangely, I was not afraid and the words of comfort I received were perhaps the best I've ever had in my life.

He appeared one more time, when I was in the kitchen and Jeremy was outside in the garden. My grandfather told me to stay strong, that I had a long life ahead of me, and that I was destined to see and experience many things. It would all work out for the best and I would get through this trauma and others in the future. I wept bitterly. I still remember him as a large, portly man who would cheerfully cuddle me and let me sit on his lap. I wish now that I could meet him again, I knew so little about his life. I loved and respected him, not simply because he was my grandfather, but for what he had achieved.

He'd been made an honorary member of the National Geographical Society, been awarded medals for his work during the war and everywhere we went in London where we encountered Chinese people, they treated him with the utmost respect. He was invited to diplomatic receptions at embassies and despite his new, lowly status in life, he was obviously admired by a large number of people. Yet despite all this hero worship on my part, he held firmly to the tradition that the elder generation never broke ranks when it came to children. He never came to my rescue.

Jeremy went down with gastro enteritis and I caught it as well, or so I thought. I swigged kaolin and morphine from his medicine bottle. But the cramps would not go away.

"Do you want me to phone the doctor?"

"No, it's too early, wait until about 6 o'clock."

"Are you sure?"

"Yes, I can put up with this, and I don't want to disturb his sleep."

Dr Campbell laughed when Jeremy phoned him. "Don't be such an idiot, of course she hasn't got a tummy bug, she's in labour. Bring her in to hospital immediately!"

As he drove me into Banff, about twelve miles away, we had to stop several times to wait for the cows to clear the road. In our part of the world, you didn't have to avoid rush hour traffic, but it was wise to avoid milking hours.

Kylie Landon was born at 3.15 that Wednesday afternoon, while Dr Campbell grumbled kindly about missing his golf game. He'd been especially gentle towards me since I had told him about Jeremy and Sally, and he'd also commended me on being his only patient who used black knitting wool in his waiting room. I'd read somewhere that fathers-to-be often got jealous of the baby, so to avoid this, I knitted a black jersey for the father instead of pink or blue booties for the new arrival.

The mid seventies in northern Scotland were kind to new mothers. We were allowed eight glorious days in hospital to recuperate. My only fear was that the four other patients would discover that I was a primagravida, already 26 and far too old to be having my first baby. I put my hair in bunches and giggled along with the other mothers, the oldest of whom was 18 and having her second child. While I lay and recovered in my single room, Jeremy was packing up our few household items and finding new homes for the animals.

All too soon the eight days came to an end, probably one of the longest breaks I've ever had. I'd already scandalized the Scottish nursing sister by asking if Kylie would walk or talk first.

"But you're a trained teacher, how come you don't know?" she asked.

"Well I think I skipped all the lectures on very early development as I don't really like babies."

"And your family and their babies?"

"Ha, between my mother and me? To tell you the truth," I lowered my voice to a whisper, "this is the first time I have ever held a baby in my life."

Sister looked shocked for a moment, then probably remembered me asking for a pair of scissors to cut baby's nails at three days. How was I to know about things like scratch mittens? I would buy some immediately I left hospital. Clearly, this incompetent mother needed some advice and information.

"Remember this," she told me, "babies are made to survive and she will scream her lungs out. Don't get taken for a ride, start as you mean to go on, don't let her get the upper hand. Don't allow her to wrap herself around your little finger, you show her who's boss from the moment you step outside onto that pavement. You've got to win the battle." In 1974, Sister would have been in her sixties and I doubt if she's still alive today, but she certainly knew babies.

I resolved not to spoil this little bundle of dynamite, but Kylie didn't resemble a baby. Weighing in at seven and a half pounds, she was a miniature adult, with perfect features, a full head of jet black hair, which fell down to her shoulders and a cute wrinkle-free complexion. She had bright blue eyes, a little button nose and a delightful smile. She looked stupid in baby clothes, so apart from the baby-grows, I dressed her in dresses with matching panties and mop bonnets.

Having a daughter changed Jeremy. He became more responsible, taking one hundred per cent of the credit for producing such a perfect child. People would stop and exclaim how beautiful she was, and ask if we were we going to enter her in the Miss Pears competition.

Less than a week later we were ready to leave Scotland and Britain forever. We were to report to offices in London and fly out to Tanzania.

We visited the doctor and had a plethora of vaccinations, for about every disease on the planet, cholera, yellow fever, typhoid and a whole lot of others. Little did I know at the time that most of these are really unnecessary, and colonials living in Africa simply do not bother.

We packed up our belongings and put them into storage. I had received written instructions that the dress code for Tanzania was strict for women, it was a Muslim country and females were not encouraged to walk the streets unclothed.

Jeremy then announced we didn't have enough money for train tickets to get us to London. Great! What were we supposed to do? We'd sold the house, but the money wasn't in the bank yet. Anyhow, there would be little if anything left for us, as we actually sold the cottage at a loss, and this, in the early days of the North Sea oil boom! We'd consulted a very conservative Scottish lawyer, who'd advised us to sell.

"Who knows what might happen if you rent it out? You'll get all these Sassenachs from over the border, who will probably tear it all apart, and you will still have to keep paying the mortgage. Not a good idea at all. Better to sell it."

A nasty reminder of large piles of tarmac crept into my mind. Perhaps selling the croft was the best idea after all. We had bought for £2,750.00 and sold for £1,800.00. Our property portfolio so far was not too impressive.

Jeremy solved the problem of train fares by buying a car. It cost us £10 and was uninsured, untaxed, un MOT'd, and all it actually did was slurp petrol and fill the inside with black fumes. But it moved, and so we eventually arrived in the capital city. I never asked Jeremy where he got the car, he certainly never registered it in our name and as we only had it for four days there really wasn't time. I was just such a coward and I was scared to make him lose his temper. On the way to London, we deviated to Bath, to say a final farewell to his folks. I'm not sure how they knew we were there, but there was a knock on the door and my mother was standing on the doorstep, with Paul behind her. She was here to see Kylie. I was lost for words, I had been found out, about to sneak off abroad, although I had written to tell her she was a grandmother. It was a difficult and uncomfortable meeting, and my mother-in-law visibly bristled as she reluctantly offered them tea or coffee. Thankfully, they didn't stay long and a few hours later, Jeremy and I set out on our overseas adventure.

We abandoned the car in a suburban street, one of so many things

I am ashamed of, and found the office. I pulled Kylie behind me in her baby buggy, yes I know now that two week old babies shouldn't sit in pushchairs, but I didn't know it then. Anyway, I had precious little for her except a few outfits and a pile of nappies. They even had to show me how to deal with those before I left the hospital.

In the company's London office, we were introduced to several important-looking American men and we were told there'd been a delay, but they would put us up in a hotel and in the meantime, there was a slight change of plan. Accommodation was tricky in Dar es Salaam, so the families would be settled in Nairobi instead.

I sidled over to the world map on the wall. Nairobi? Only next door, not far. Did that mean that Jeremy would be working in one country and I'd be living in another? How could he get home every night? The American men gave me startled and embarrassed looks. I wondered just what my husband hadn't told me.

I found out soon enough. Jeremy was going to work on a project deep in the Tanzanian bush, using seismographs to locate underground minerals. Although I was deeply disturbed by this latest information about him working in one country and me living in another, I consoled myself by remembering that there were going to be lots of other families as this was a new operation into Tanzania. Also, we would be flying into Nairobi and there would be someone to meet us and help us get settled in. I had a lot to learn.

While we waited to fly out Kylie was the proverbial angel, but that was not to last, and a couple of weeks later I feared for her life.

10 KENYA

I could only cry as I looked at my small seven week old daughter lying on the sofa. I had just fed her and as before, she had been violently sick. She wasn't getting any nourishment and she just lay there staring at me with her big blue eyes, making soft whimpering noises, willing me to help her. But I didn't know what to do. How had I got into this crazy situation in the first place? Was my daughter going to die because of my reckless and foolish behaviour? Was my mother right about me all along?

We were in a small bungalow near Kikuyu an area way out in the bush, thirty miles from Nairobi the capital of Kenya. I had no friends, no family, no transport, no phone, no electricity, hardly any food, very little money and no one to turn to for help and I was trying hard not to panic. I had only been in Africa for a few weeks and I'd never traveled far from England before. Everything was still strange and unfamiliar and I was very scared.

I had Elizabeth, a twenty year old girl from the Kamba tribe, but she spoke very little English and we'd hardly got to know one another. In theory, she was my maid; in practice, she was just as helpless as me.

I dried my eyes, feeling sorry for myself was not going to accomplish anything. Somehow, I had to get to the city and find Randy the company representative, and persuade him to help me. I was twenty six years old, married and life hadn't been easy so far, so this was just one more problem to solve wasn't it?

The only way to get to town was by public bus. By now, I didn't even have enough bus fare for Elizabeth to come with me, but I wasn't leaving my daughter behind, so I grabbed Kylie and went to stand by the side of the main road. There were no bus stops, all the local buses stopped for people who waved their arms and the ancient and decrepit vehicles screeched to a halt to pick up more and more passengers, even if there were no seats left. There were as many people standing inside the bus as there were outside clinging to the top of the roof, along with the odd goat or cage of chickens. I was lucky enough to get a real seat, but maybe the other passengers made space for me, because from the incredulous looks on their faces, I soon realized that Europeans traveling by public transport was unheard of.

We arrived in down town Nairobi, certainly not the area near the

Hilton or New Stanley - hotels frequented by the tourists. Now, I had no money left at all. I eventually found the circular tower that's the Hilton Hotel landmark.

At reception, they told me that Randy was on safari, but as far as they knew, he would be back that night. I left a message for him and just to make sure, I went up to his room and knocked loudly on the door. No reply. I sat in the coffee shop, where I had the audacity to order a glass of water and watched all the rich, safari tourists as they compared wildlife notes and swapped stories of their exciting encounters with dangerous African animals. What would they think of me? I felt so ashamed. I was in a foreign capital, nursing a sick baby with not a penny to my name. It was a far cry from the private school girl, who only a few years ago, danced until dawn at the May Ball. I returned to Randy's room several times and eventually he appeared.

"I need help, I have no money, and now the baby is sick."

Randy looked alarmed. I'm sure that his job was not to go on safari and just leave all the families to fend for themselves, even if I was the only one there. He'd not come back once to see how I was getting on. I'd tried to be brave, I really had, but it was all too much. I had no idea where Jeremy was, I only had a post box number to write to in Dar es Salam, but I even if I wrote to him, there was nowhere for him to send a reply. Suddenly I burst into tears, much to our mutual embarrassment.

Randy grabbed my arm and marched us back down to the coffee shop, where I ordered several slices of cake and sandwiches and cups of coffee. It was so good to eat familiar food again. Reluctantly, Randy handed over a wad of money, with the warning that it was not company policy for him to pay out without Jeremy's sanction. A little difficult to get, since as far as I knew, he was well out of range somewhere deep in the Tanzanian bush. I was told in no uncertain terms, that Randy was doing me an enormous favour and I had every reason to be grateful to him.

I thanked him profusely and it was not until several years later I realized how I had been duped. He'd not been doing his job and yet he ended up on the attack while I ended up apologizing, it was a habit it took years to break.

I pushed my luck and pleaded for a ride back to Kikuyu. Despite not being keen, I don't think his conscience would have allowed us to travel back on the public bus service, as by now it was dark outside.

Next morning I set off bright and early, long before 8 o'clock, for the clinic Elizabeth had found close by. Close by, was her description, it was actually five miles away! I joined the end of a very long queue. If the British Empire accomplished only one thing during its long reign over the majority of the world, it was how to form an orderly queue. You have to admire the inordinate patience of the African who will queue all day in the boiling hot sun waiting patiently. They never complain, they never make a fuss. Should facilities close before they get to the front of the queue, they simply walk away and plan to return another day. They stand or sit quietly, staring into space, rarely talking to the people next to them, for they are neither close friends nor family.

I was very reassured to hear the Sister's broad Scottish accent as she processed one baby after another. When I eventually reached the head of the queue, I explained that after feeding, Kylie was regurgitating her milk and I was worried about her.

"What a beautiful baby, she's a perfect miniature adult. So, how old is Baby?"

"Baby is five weeks."

"Where's her inoculation card?"

"I don't have one."

"Why not? What jabs has she had?"

"Well, nothing, I mean…"

"But she's had her BCG of course?"

"Don't you only get that at about twelve, in senior school?"

"Not in Africa my dear, we jab them as soon as they appear. I'll do her right away."

"But wait!" I cried, I wanted to explain that I'd had TB and maybe she should check to see if Kylie should have a TB inoculation. But it was too late, Sister disappeared round the corner. I tried to follow her, but the throng of people didn't make way for me as they had for Sister. Five minutes later, she was back, and I explained my medical history.

"She'll be fine, don't you worry about it," replied Sister. "Now, let's sort out this feeding problem. We can start her on solids and I can give you powdered milk as well. It's possible your milk doesn't taste too good if you're not used to the heat."

I took her advice and I persevered, I really did, but Kylie was a European baby, and she did not take kindly to mashed up African fruits and vegetables. It seemed the more I stuffed in her mouth the more she vomited, but she liked the baby milk formulae. She never cried but I continued to fret about her state of health. She didn't seem to get any fatter, but she didn't lose weight either and she stopped whimpering and seemed more cheerful.

The following day I set off for the post office and joined yet another long queue. When I finally reached the window, the smiling black face asked how he could help.

"I would like a post box please."

"Oh dear, there is a waiting list, a long, long waiting list," replied the smiling face.

"How long?"

"Several years."

"But I need one urgently!"

"Maybe, for a small consideration?"

"How small?"

"Two hundred shillings?" Reluctantly I handed over the money.

"When can I have the post box?"

"Now." The post office clerk scrambled under the counter and re-appeared with the key.

"And I also need to have the phone re-connected."

"There's a very, very, long waiting list I'm afraid, for phones."

"But the phone is already in the house, it just needs to be connected."

"But that will be difficult."

"Why?"

"There is a long waiting list, very long."

"But for a small consideration?" I'm a quick learner.

"Ah, yes, that could be arranged." More money exchanged hands. In Africa, it was obviously all a matter of money, but the problem was that I didn't know how long the money I had wrestled from Randy would last.

The days went by. Faithfully I wrote to Jeremy every day and posted the letters on my daily trip to the post box, it was the highlight of the day. Each time I inserted the key into the little mail box door, I prayed there would be a letter, but as the days went by, it remained empty. I even wrote to my mother and all my friends and distant relatives as well, but it was a long time before I heard from any of them. I learned that it took weeks for a letter to travel in both directions and even if post arrived in the capital, it took many more days for the letters to find their way the extra thirty miles to the rural area of Kikuyu.

There wasn't much to do. Elizabeth kept the house clean, which was not difficult as there was minimal furniture and the floors were tiled. Two of the three bedrooms were unused, as Elizabeth insisted on sleeping outside in the servant's quarters, or shamba, but during the time we spent together, I think we became very firm friends.

From our initial decision to leave England, everything had happened so fast. It seemed only yesterday that I had been living a normal life, in a normal house, in a familiar country. After a twelve hour plane flight, which felt more like twelve days, the wheels touched down at Embasaki airport and as they opened the doors, I got my first taste of Africa, the sheer heat that hits you like a sledgehammer. I had never experienced such heat in all my life, it felt like walking through a gigantic oven, and I loved it. The light too was so different, here it was sharp and clear. Brilliant blue skies and a sun, which was brighter than anything I had seen before.

Next shock was the preponderance of armed soldiers at every turn. They lined the walkway from the plane steps to the terminal buildings and there were more inside. I hadn't the faintest idea what kind of guns they were clutching, but they were big and black and looked very dangerous, and the owners looked quite keen to use them too.

A hand came out and grabbed my passport. I finally had a real British passport courtesy of being married to Jeremy, living and learning and teaching in UK for sixteen years hadn't cracked it on its own! I made to grab it back, but it was only our welcoming party, Randy the American company representative.

In two minutes, he had us through immigration and customs and we were speeding towards Nairobi. More culture shocks. The houses on either side of the road were just sheets of corrugated tin and bits of wood and cardboard. Children covered in flies sat by the side of the road, and elderly wrinkled women were bent almost double under great bundles of firewood. There were younger people simply hanging around, while I wondered naively why they weren't in school. The levels of poverty, even in our poorest days paled into insignificance as I gazed at the shack lands, which seemed to stretch for mile upon mile, as we negotiated the narrow tar road, which was shared by motorized traffic, goats, sheep, and chickens alike. Pedestrians too, had little regard for the rules of the road, they wandered where they pleased, and the pedestrians themselves were a surprise. I expected them to be black, but I didn't expect the miniskirts and platform soles.

Then there were the billboards by the side of the road, advertising the familiar Sunlight soap, Omo washing powder and Embassy cigarettes. It was all so similar and yet so very, very different.

It was also a big shock to see people begging on the side of the road, something I'd never encountered before. I saw real poverty for the first time in my life, so very different from the Welfare State in England. The first time a beggar screamed at me and demanded money I froze, not sure what to do, it scared me as even though I was happy to part with a few cents, there were just so many of them, there was no way I could have given to everyone.

Randy was staying at the Hilton, while we would be staying at the New Stanley hotel only a few blocks away. We were to find ourselves accommodation as soon as possible, as we only had six days to settle in before Jeremy was due to leave for Dar es Salaam in Tanzania.

"How much do we spend on rent?" we asked.

"It's up to you really. Everything is done on a salary advance, so just tell me how much you need. It should be pretty easy, all the newspapers are in English and are filled with advertisements," Randy replied.

He dropped us off at the hotel, helped us to register, and then dropped the bombshell. He was off on safari for five days, contact him at the Hilton on Friday and he'd take Jeremy to the airport.

Where was the colonial compound I was expecting? Where were all the other families?

"Well you're the first to arrive, the rest are expected in a month, or so, you'll be well settled in by then," Randy told me. He drove off and we were left standing in the lobby of the hotel totally confused.

Jeremy left Kylie and myself in the room, and went down to the Thorn Tree Restaurant and the Long Bar, famous in literature and home to many famous and infamous old colonials. Ernest Hemingway, the Blixens, Edward the Prince of Wales, Clark Gable, Steward Granger and Ava Gardner had all been there before us.

Jeremy returned with a newspaper and the promise of a car with a driver for the following day. A driver, just for us? Yes, apparently it was quite common for all companies to have several cars and drivers to run errands for managers.

We combed the papers and ringed all the advertisements for houses to rent which we thought sounded promising. We had no idea what to expect per hundred shillings, but we were soon to find out.

Our smiling black driver cheerfully drove us round and round and round. Areas that we thought sounded not too expensive were little more than squatter shacks and I was horrified to learn that people actually paid rent to live in them! We asked our driver to take us to where the white people lived and we toured the suburbs of Karen and Langatta, where we saw small palaces, with sweeping lush green lawns but no To Rent signs.

The next day we tried further out of town, and then further and further as the days went by. We were forced to spend the majority of our remaining few shillings on hiring a car, as we couldn't keep borrowing a driver.

We began to get desperate as Friday approached. Jeremy didn't think we could afford more than a certain amount on rent and to keep within this budget we finally found a place thirty miles out of town on the Naivasha Road, next to the Sigona Golf Club and three miles from the village of Kikuyu. It was a three bedroom, stone built bungalow with a tin roof, owned by a local businessman called Mr. Karanda. It was surrounded by an attractive garden with exotic plants I'd only seen before in picture books. I was a little nervous about taking it as it seemed so far away from anywhere, even though there was a main road at the bottom of the garden.

We moved in on the Thursday night and the landlord kindly offered to phone the Hilton for us to tell Randy where he could collect Jeremy the following day.

The man from the car hire place insisted I couldn't live without an *ayah*, and presented us with his sister.

"If she does not work well, then you beat her hard," he instructed me. Beat her? Was he serious?

Elizabeth was short, round, plump, and also very shy. She had come to the city to look for work, for her home was south of Nairobi in a town called Machakos. She had never seen a real lion, which I found encouraging, and in school, they had taught her that the sea went away at night to feed and returned each morning.

We went to bed early that evening since there was no electricity and Randy was on the doorstep before seven the next morning to whisk Jeremy off to the airport. He promised to pop round later, which he never did, and I was left standing on the verandah, with a tiny baby in my arms, an African nanny I had known for a day, thousands of miles from home. I felt totally and utterly lost.

Food seemed to be the first priority and luckily, the stove worked off gas so I took my few remaining shillings and gave them to Elizabeth and asked her to buy food. She disappeared, I had no idea where, as there wasn't a shop in sight. Perhaps there was a local market?

She returned carrying some indescribable things. I would recognize them now as chicken beaks and claws and large green, knobbly pumpkins. While I didn't think I would have to worry about Kylie, who was getting good old British or Irish breast milk, I had problems forcing the food down, even though I was ravenous.

The good news was that Elizabeth brought change. I couldn't believe how much change, food was really cheap, if you could learn to eat like the locals, but I doubted my ability to do that.

The next few days passed slowly, we rose with the sun and went to bed as night fell. Kylie did not need much looking after and Elizabeth was reluctant to put her down at all. I often lay in the garden and read a book, but I was very nervous about the snakes I felt sure must be everywhere, and held a stick out behind me to tap the ground to keep them away. In hindsight, it could have attracted them instead. There were lots of insects and strange flying things, and I had no idea which were dangerous and which were harmless.

Mr. Karanda appeared one afternoon about 4 o'clock and I was so pleased to see him that I had to stop myself flinging my arms around him. Yes, he could get the electricity connected, for a small consideration. Yes, he could also suggest I go to the post office only a couple of miles away to get a post box and the phone re-connected. And would I like fresh milk delivered to the door each morning? Do planes fly?

"And one other thing…." He paused.

"Yes?"

"Maybe you will not be as safe here as you should be, you will need a guard. Don't worry, I will send Kimani round before nightfall and he will stay on guard all night."

Unsafe? A guard? It's true that I'd noticed several guards or askaris, standing around outside the houses in the suburbs, but it hadn't occurred to me that I would need protecting out here. I nodded and Mr. Karanda drove off in his Mercedes, assured that he had one cash cow tenant sitting in his bungalow just down the road. The only problem was that this cash cow, was almost totally broke, and didn't know where or when the next Kenyan shilling was coming from. Somehow, I would have to pay for both the guard and the milk.

Kimani duly arrived long after dark that night, blind drunk. He ran round and round the outside of the house banging on the burglar bars with his knob Kerrie making a terrible racket. Elizabeth and I cowered on the floor by the sofa. We were terrified, and it was only the next morning that we discovered it was our guard who had almost scared us to death.

The milk boy also arrived, carrying a real metal churn such as I had only ever seen in history books. Elizabeth took an instant liking to him, and would warble loudly "The Lord is coming to take me away," as he walked up from the front gate.

"I only wish he would," was my response, for Elizabeth's singing was truly awful and if she thought that her musical abilities would attract the milk boy, she was badly mistaken.

Yet I did have reason to be thankful to Mr. Karanda, since the following morning I woke up to see a queue outside the gate which stretched for miles down the road as far as the eye could see. News travels fast in Africa and it seemed the whole of Kenya knew that a white Memsab had moved in and surely, she must want a plethora of servants? The crowd at my gate would have been sufficient for a re-enactment of the 'Flight from Egypt', and little did they know, I had no money to pay them either. With a sigh of relief, I sent Elizabeth out to tell them that I had all the staff I needed, since Kimani, somewhat more sober, had pleaded with me to allow him to double up his duties as a night time askari with day time duties as gardener.

Elizabeth assured me that she counted herself lucky to work for me. Kimani never seemed as grateful though. He looked about seventy, but with some interpretation from Elizabeth I discovered he was only thirty five. He had three wives and numerous children, which is possibly why he looked so worn out. He would see them once every few months and seemed quite content. He saw his new job as a way to pay for another wife. I would have thought he had quite enough to cope with already.

How different it is in Africa. A man may have as many wives as he can afford, or not afford as the case may be. Marriage often takes place, if at all, after the woman has given birth to at least one healthy male child to prove she is worthy of the bride-price. Payment could vary, from one mangy goat to a herd of prime cattle among royalty, and take many months or years to pay and often leads to disputes among families.

Despite the low cost of food, the little money I had wasn't going to last too long and just as it ran out, Kylie got sick which resulted in my frantic trip into Nairobi. Thinking about it a few days later, I thought I had coped quite well under the circumstances. I'd found a clinic and knew that Kylie didn't have some weird African disease, I'd got a post box and after providing Mr. Karanda with the 'small consideration', the following day the electricity was connected and a couple of days later I lifted the phone to hear a dialing tone. I was ecstatic! I phoned the Hilton, to be told that Randy was away on safari again and was only expected back the following weekend. I was determined that as soon as my first salary advance ran out I would track him down again and demand more.

Kylie began to put on weight, and appeared to thrive. She stopped vomiting and the days passed in quick succession with only a few uncomfortable incidents.

There was a leopard in the garden at night which made me a little nervous. I freaked the first time I heard African drums, recalling old movies with boiling pots full of white men and women, and I was forced to call Kimani into my bedroom the time I saw a snake's tail sticking out of the wall vent.

At last, the day dawned when I opened the mail box to find a huge pile of letters, all from Jeremy, each one carefully re-sealed with brown sticky tape.

They had been opened and read by the censor's office, I think, in Tanzania. I'm not sure if they censored every letter sent out by foreign nationals, but after reading the first one, I could understand if they honed in especially on Jeremy's. He was missing me so much, enough to describe what he would like to be doing when we celebrated his first leave, all of which he described in lurid detail. I blushed with shame and immediately sat down to write to him and ask him to tone it down. I was so relieved to hear from him and to learn that he would be home in two weeks time for his first leave.

With my new found wealth from Randy, I decided to hire a car and do some real European food shopping and then fetch Jeremy from the airport when he flew in a couple of days later. With a new determination I didn't know I possessed, I succeeded in bargaining with an Indian dealership in Nairobi, and drove away in an elderly Datsun with Kylie lying on the back seat, no car seats or seat belts in those days!

I sat for ages in the hot car as I saw my first presidential cavalcade go by. Jomo Kenyatta stopped for no one.

I returned home with two steaks for supper, large, tender and really cheap and I gave them to Elizabeth to cook. She boiled them. I chewed my way bravely through the boot leather. I explained carefully to Elizabeth how to cook steaks under the grill and told her to do that in future.

The following day, I purchased a boil in the bag bacon joint and told Elizabeth how to cook it and I showed her how to make a white sauce and how to prepare the cabbage and the potatoes to go with it. Yes, she grilled the joint, still wrapped in the plastic, which eventually caught fire. Another meal ruined!

I did receive letters from my mother. I was so lonely and scared that once again I thought that maybe we could make an effort to get on better. After all, we were both married and I felt that Paul was a calming influence. She replied, and maybe I imagined that she was less caustic than before, but it was safer corresponding from a long distance.

Jeremy was due back and I commuted between both Nairobi airports, but no Jeremy. He wasn't on a flight the following three days either and in despair, I returned the hire car.

Two more weeks went by, no letters, no phone calls and no Randy. I did my best not to panic. What would happen if Jeremy were dead? What would I do? Randy had the return air tickets, and who knows where he was? Probably off on a nonstop safari? My imagination worked overtime. What if Randy was gored by a lion or trampled by an elephant while on one of his famous safaris? Who even knew where I was? Would the office in London remember I was here? Even if I did get back to UK, where would I go? How would I cope with no money, no job, and Kylie to look after? Most people would rush back to the safety of their families, but for me that didn't bear thinking about.

Eventually, I opened the post box and there was a letter postmarked Tanzania. I ripped it open. Jeremy and the rest of the crew had just set up camp in the night when they were surrounded by armed soldiers and accused of being in a 'no go' area. They were herded into a large hole in the ground and left there without food and water for several days, with guards whose itchy fingers caressed the triggers on their guns. They had all been released, but it had delayed the time-off rotation and he would be arriving in Nairobi on Tuesday.

Once again, I dashed into Nairobi, braving the dangers of the public transport system and haggled with the owners for an even cheaper price on a hire car. I think they couldn't quite believe that I was in Kenya all on my own, with no back up and they took pity on me. I drove away in the ancient Datsun again and commuted between airports. No Jeremy that day, nor the next and it was not until Thursday that he finally stepped off the plane.

I don't think I have ever been so glad to see anyone, and I clung to him like superglue as we walked to the car. As we drove to the bungalow at Sigona, Jeremy casually remarked that he wasn't returning to Tanzania.

"But didn't you sign a two year contract?"

"Yes, but I'll take advice about that. I think what they're doing is illegal."

"What! How is it illegal?"

"Well, a couple of the guys were arrested in Dar es Salaam last week as they tried to come home. They'd been told to say that they earned two hundred Tanzanian shillings a month and neither customs nor immigration believed them."

"My God, you're earning more than that aren't you?" I felt sick, had I taken over a year's salary advance from Randy?

"Of course I am, but they're going to pay it overseas, so no money comes in, except for the salary advances that is, but we've been told to lie about it. Frankly, I don't fancy being thrown in one of those jails, if you come out alive, they tell me your indigestion is shot from the local food."

The next day, Jeremy went into the British High Commission and chatted to one of their people, and they agreed, that the company was skating on thin ice.

For once Randy *was* ensconced in the Hilton, and Jeremy phoned to tell him he was quitting. There followed a series of phone calls, each more aggressive than the last, but Jeremy refused to budge.

So there we were again, unemployed and next to broke, but this time, thousands of miles from home with no Social Security backup. However, a small matter like this was not going to get Jeremy down, and he was off bright and early the next morning to look for work.

It's quite possible he would have found something, but we clashed with a current drive for Kenyanization and affirmative employment, and try as he would over the next few months, it was simply impossible to get a job.

In the meantime, I spent many happy hours exploring Nairobi, managing to make a Kenyan shilling stretch by shopping in the down town markets, going where no self respecting tourist would be seen dead. I never felt threatened, and I don't know if this had anything to do with Kylie, who looked more adorable than ever, or it was just sheer naivety on my part.

We visited Nairobi National Park, which is situated very close to the city, and I saw my first real wildlife. We were charged by an elephant which looked a million miles away on the photo and we drove down to the coast and broke down in Tsavo East game park, miles from civilization. We also went to visit Amboseli, gazing with awe at the snow covered mountain of Kilimanjaro standing over 19,000 feet above sea level. We also managed to explore some of the fantastic countryside including the amazing rift valley, where the land drops sheer away from the side of the road as if it had been cut with a gigantic knife. I got badly burned lying for a couple of minutes by Lake Naivasha, watching the clouds of bright pink flamingoes taking off and landing on the salt pan. We even got caught up in a tear gas attack in the city.

It looked as if we would have to leave, the money was running out fast. I should mention at this point that Randy, perhaps a little nervous about Jeremy's threats to 'squeal', had given us a fair amount of cash and our return tickets back to Heathrow. But before we left, Jeremy took part in the East African Safari Rally as a seconder, probably his best memory of Kenya.

Finally we said our sad farewells. Elizabeth and I hugged each other and fought back the tears. As we boarded the plane, I looked back for the last time at the bright blue skies and vivid colours of Africa.

If I was scared when I first arrived on the Dark Continent, I was equally scared of returning to England. I could only hope that my new experiences had made me strong enough to cope with the one person in my life of whom I was truly afraid. Going to Africa was a more adult version of running away from home, and as we flew northwards over the barren wastes of the Sahara Desert, I shuddered at the thought of seeing my mother again.

11 VALE OF EVESHAM

When we landed back in London in 1975 my shoes squished into the snow. I shivered and by the time we got to the terminal buildings, my teeth were chattering. If only there had been a way to stay in Kenya, I was homesick already.

There was no one to meet us at the airport, did I really think my mother would have been there? Undaunted, Jeremy pulled what he called the "where is my car trick?"

He approached the counter of one of the major car rental agencies and demanded to know why our car wasn't ready. I'm not sure how he got away with it, but he was so convincing, and they were so obliging, that before long we were speeding down the highway in an upgraded rental car at a reduced price. I'm not sure if the scam would work today, but in those days, and with Jeremy's personality, it seemed that anything was possible.

We traveled down to the Cotswold village to Paul's cottage, but we had only been there for less than half an hour when we realized that there was no possibility of us staying with them for more than one night. My mother began to fight from the moment we walked through the door. Had we really thought things would be different? It seemed that even Paul's influence was on the wane and he could do nothing to control her invective.

"I suppose you think it's fine for you to put your daughter into danger like that. It's a good thing that I took more care of you."

"Mum I would never let anything happen to Kylie, she's fine, look at her."

My mother looked at her granddaughter and sniffed. "Well it's no thanks to you. No one in their right mind would take a child as young as that out to Africa, but I can't say I'm surprised, you always put yourself first."

"Mum, please stop it. You know that Jeremy was offered a job and it would have been mad not to take it."

She was not to be persuaded. "And how long did that last? Must have been a really good job to be fired after only a few weeks."

"I know it didn't work out, but Jeremy wasn't fired, he decided not to go back to Tanzania and even the British consular staff said that was the right decision to make."

"They were probably shocked that you'd go out there with a baby that small. Mind, she doesn't stand much chance with you as her mother."

"That's a really unkind thing to say," I replied.

My mother managed to look shocked. "Unkind? Unkind? When it's the truth? That's the trouble with you Lucinda, you won't face the truth. You never have. You go into some fairy tale land and pretend things never happened. You may have forgotten, but I still remember all the things you did, the lies you told, creeping out of the house at night to go and meet a boy. Did you know about that Jeremy? Who knows what they got up to." My mother pointed to Kylie. "Let's hope she never gives you half as much trouble as you gave me."

Jeremy was so tempted to stand up for me and to answer my mother back, but I always begged him not to, I was so afraid it would make things worse. Most of the time, she simply ignored him anyway, and he'd walk away before his temper got out of control.

As he watched us drive away, Paul waved sadly. We had no idea where we were going, and stopped to buy a newspaper in the hope that some accommodation might be available, but it would have to be very cheap. The best we could find was a caravan just outside Broadway.

It took Jeremy a remarkably short time to find work. He still had his heavy goods driving license from the army, and this kind of job was still in demand.

Once again, I set about making a home, in the smallest space ever. It was not a large caravan, not the live-in sort, more the holiday sort of size.

Kylie continued to be her quiet, cheerful self, now quite a bit larger, but still no bother. Perhaps fate had decided that I was to be allowed two years free from parental worry, because there was plenty more to come.

The biggest problem inside the caravan was the condensation that ran down the walls. After the African heat, Britain seemed colder than ever, and I kept the heating on much higher than I should. I knitted warm clothes for all of us, as that was much cheaper than buying readymade.

The biggest problem outside the caravan was the truck, which Jeremy drove in each night to park by the van. If pets were not allowed in the holiday park, trucks were a positive no no. He had endless fights with the park owners and I knew it was only a matter of time before we would be evicted. He would park the truck out in the street, and try and sneak it in late at night, but there was no lorry park in the holiday village of Broadway, and even on the street it became a violation. I waited for the axe to fall, but in the meantime, we hunted for more work abroad.

If I knew one thing, it was that I didn't want to stay in UK. I wanted to put as much distance between me and my mother and I wanted to get back to a warm country.

It was a small advertisement at the very bottom of the page in one of the national daily newspapers.

'Plant Machinery Engineer required for new enterprise in North Africa. Phone....' Jeremy rushed off to the nearest phone box and returned with an appointment for an interview in Brighton the next day.

Since we didn't have any transport of our own, the next morning we all piled into the truck and we set off for the south coast. We parked the lorry a good distance from the offices and Jeremy changed and brushed up in a public convenience. I took Kylie for a stroll in her pushchair, which was more suitable for her now, and introduced her to the British seaside. She didn't seem too impressed, especially when the cold wind blew into her face, and this was June!

It seemed a long time before Jeremy reappeared, but it was with the news that he had got the job.

"Where is it?"

"In Libya."

"Where's Libya?"

Jeremy admitted that he hadn't been too sure of this himself, but luckily during the course of the interview, he learned that it was on the southern shores of the Mediterranean Sea, that is, North Africa. I remembered my history from college, and the maps showing Rommel's campaign and where General Montgomery had routed them during the Second World War. I had visions of wide sandy dunes, and a lot of heat and that part pleased me.

"When do we go? When do they want you to start?"

"As soon as possible, but it's not easy to get into Libya, you have to have an invite and a mentor and a special entry visa." To my dismay he added, "... you can't come for the first month, but I'm sure it'll pass quickly, and I'll write to you every day."

"Not those kind of letters please," I murmured quietly.

When we returned to Broadway that night it was to find that, reasonably enough, Jeremy had been sacked and we had been evicted. Along with the loss of the job, went the loss of our transport.

Since Jeremy's parents didn't have a car, and we had lost touch with the few friends I had had in my home town, and we had no other relations, in desperation I phoned Paul. He was only too happy to help, and he arrived a couple of hours later, packed us and our few possessions into his car and we were on our way back to the Cotswolds. Our other few possessions were still in storage in Aberdeen.

My mother was less than delighted to see us, but she seemed pleased that Jeremy was going abroad and that I was going to be on my own for the next four weeks. This was one of the very few occasions that Paul actually took control, quietly reminding my mother that this was his house after all, and he was fond of his newly acquired extended family.

In no time, Jeremy was off and I was left to the tender mercies of maternal care. Kylie was no trouble at all and for a few days my mother played with her and showed her off to the local people in the village. My daughter had blossomed even more and still looked like a miniature adult with her long black hair and big blue eyes.

The next four weeks passed very slowly. I saw how nasty my mother was to Paul and was amazed. It was the first inkling I'd had, that I was not the only victim of her fury and rages. If he upset her, she would hide his glasses so he was unable to drive. She would not allow him to go to the pub for a drink and he was not to see his best friend since my mother didn't like him. She refused to speak to him for long periods as well and she had to have her own way in everything.

There were violent rows about his younger son Dick aged about six. Mother refused to allow him to visit his father and removed all the photos of him and packed them away. Paul had previously had a good job, but had lost it and Mother insisted that he drove a delivery van to bring in extra money. He was so miserable doing this that I vowed never to try and force Jeremy into a job that he did not want to do, even if I ever had that amount of influence with my husband! I should have taken comfort from this display of continued verbal abuse aimed at someone other than me, but all I wanted to do was escape. Mother would occasionally be nice to me, only to criticize Paul and when I wouldn't agree with her, she would fly into a rage.

"Well of course you'd take his side, that's what I'd expect from you. But then you never loved me and don't pretend differently."

"How can you say that? It's not true!" I gasped.

"You took me for a ride, all you wanted was to get as much out of me as you could. And what did I get in return? An ungrateful child who lied and stole and had no morals at all. I did the best for you I could and I never got one word of thanks."

It was no good arguing with my mother, she always had the last word and she was adamant that I had been the child from hell, while she had been the perfect mother. Everything was all my fault.

Whenever I got the chance, I would go and visit my grandmother, who was still in the old age home. I apologized for not going to Grandpa's funeral and she said she understood. She told me that my mother had always been difficult, even as a child. But those were the only words of criticism she ever uttered. My mother had insisted

Grandpa's funeral be held in her home town. Granny was not well off, and I don't know how she paid for a hearse all the way from London, but my mother was determined. My mother had decided that there wasn't enough room for Granny to live with them, so that was why she was in a state home. I guessed it was difficult for Granny, miles away from all her London friends, and she was very lonely and sat in her room all day doing nothing.

I know my mother visited her regularly, but again, the atmosphere was not pleasant and perhaps it might have been kinder not to upset the old lady each time, as my mother certainly wasn't nice to her either.

It seemed like forever until Jeremy returned, bearing tickets for all of us, destination, Tripoli. I had done some research and discovered that Libya was the sixteenth largest country in the world, supporting a population of only two million. It's bordered by Egypt on the right, Tunisia on the left with the vast reaches of the Sahara Desert at the bottom.

I had once again slipped back into my dream world to escape the tensions, and had fanaticized about quaint white washed walls, little donkeys with flowers in their ears and velvety-nosed camels led by cheerful and playful brown-skinned boys. I saw the blue Mediterranean Sea lapping white sandy beaches like on all the post cards and posters I had seen in the travel agents' windows. The reality was going be very different but once again, I was going to escape the atmosphere at home.

12 TRIPOLI, LIBYA

This time the journey to the North African coast, on Libyan Arab Airlines flight 732, was much shorter than the flight to Kenya, and Kylie was no trouble at all. The three hour flight brought the usual food, duty frees and boiled sweets, but no alcohol, for the 'dry' Muslim rule begins the moment you step off the ground and walk up the airplane steps.

The minute the wheels touched the tarmac on the runway at Tripoli, all the passengers leapt to their feet and began to grab suitcases, bags and coats and fling themselves bodily at the nearest exit. This unseemly display was not for us of course, and we waited patiently for the plane to roll to a stop near the terminal building.

When I stepped off the plane, the reality was a long way from the pictures conjured up by my imagination. While I had enough sense to realize that the Sahara Desert was not rolling sand dunes down to the coast, I was not prepared to land in what can only be described as a massive building site.

Only two prestigious skyscrapers looked completed, certainly none of the houses were. Above every dwelling, steel rods stretched towards the sky, apparently this announced to the world that the owner had not finished building, and one day would add at least one or more stories to the structure.

Once again, the heat hit me and I breathed in the hot dusty air and smiled. The sun beamed down out of a bright blue sky, with not a cloud in sight.

I saw the reason for the lunatic behaviour on the plane. Queues stretched as far as the eye could see. In theory, there were queues, in fact, a seething maelstrom of humanity. Forms had to be completed in Arabic and there was one translator for each plane. People screamed and shrieked, shouted and pushed and jabbered away nineteen to the dozen in a language that sounded totally foreign.

In all fairness, the Libyans have built a superb new airport in Tripoli, and they don't have potholes in the runways any more, but in 1975, there was only one terminal building, roughly the size of a local British railway station.

"Take the passports," Jeremy told me and go to the front of the line. Women take precedence here, I'll wait at the back."

"Male chauvinist pig," I muttered as I headed for the only counter. But he was right. Like the Red Sea those many years before, a path miraculously opened before me among the crowd and I was through. This was to happen in all our time in Libya, I could go straight to the front of any crowd simply because I'm a woman!

Then a tall, good-looking Arab immediately whisked our passports away and we were guided past the huge throng waiting at immigration. We completely ignored the customs as well as we exited out by a back door. Our luggage miraculously appeared beside us. Right outside Tripoli Airport, parked in the no waiting zone was a large black limousine. One of our welcoming committee flung the door open and a bit nervously, I stepped inside.

The young man in the front seat turned and nodded at me, and then shook Jeremy's hand. I was really curious to know who this person was, but I was too nervous to ask. His minions stashed our luggage in the boot and a little to my surprise, we left them standing on the crumbling pavement as we sped rapidly away along wide, dusty streets. It was cool and dark inside the car, yet everyone was wearing dark glasses. I felt uncomfortable. You can sense power in some people and the young man in the front seat had plenty of that.

We stopped at a large building called the Beach Hotel, the largest and grandest in Tripoli. Not that it looked particularly grand. The brickwork needed pointing and the paintwork was dull and peeling in several places, but inside it was immaculate with the most expensive furnishings I had ever seen.

While the surroundings were grand, the crowd was not. I was the only female in sight, as men dressed in long nightshirts milled around and everyone talked at the tops of their voices. There were several arguments in progress across the wide reception counter, and the few European businessmen I saw looked hot, uncomfortable and nervous.

Our host had remained in the car, while one of his bodyguards checked us into the hotel. He accomplished this in record time by pushing his way straight to the front and a few minutes later we were whisked upwards in the lift, more marble tiled floors and walls, along a carpeted corridor, and into our suite.

There was a sitting room, two bedrooms with king sized beds, two bathrooms one with a huge circular bath, and an area which housed a fridge, kitchen counter and the basic requirements for making light snacks and cups of tea and coffee. The whole area was several dozen times larger than the caravan in Broadway.

I took Kylie out of her pushchair and left her to explore at ground level while I checked out the balcony for safety. Kylie was now almost a year old, but she'd not started to crawl, just being content to sit and play with things within her reach. As long as I was in sight, she was happy. The moment I disappeared from view, she would start to wail.

The view from our suite overlooked the pool, and the city. Three to four storey buildings stretched out into the distance, and they all looked in need of a good coat of paint. The traffic moved lazily on wide dusty streets between the blocks, all built in neat squares along the American system. The heat felt so thick you could almost touch it.

Jeremy didn't stay with us too long as he had meetings with Mohammed in the office. I was further impressed to hear that he had a car and driver at his full disposal. He advised me to stay in the suite, at least for the time being, and he would be back shortly.

Our luggage was all delivered safely and I packed some of it away in the cavernous cupboards, so at least I could find stuff. Just how much luggage did this hotel expect guests to bring?

As soon as I finished, there was a knock on the door. The hotel men who delivered the cot kept their eyes on the floor and refused to look at me. When I thanked them they just grunted and rushed out, which at least spared me the embarrassment of trying to explain why I couldn't tip them. I had no Libyan money.

The novelty of my posh surroundings soon began to wear off, as I waited and waited for Jeremy to return. Did I dare pick up the phone and ask for room service? We hadn't eaten since we landed and Libyan Arab Airlines were not noted for their culinary feasts. I thought about going downstairs to the restaurant, if there was one, but I was too nervous, what if I couldn't sign for the meal?

I investigated the fridge, which was well stocked with orange, lemonade and mineral water, but no spirits and no beer. I drank a couple of cans as the day wore on, but although they were refreshing, I still felt hungry.

At last I plucked up courage and went to the phone. There was a purring sound from the handset, which was a hopeful sign I thought. I pressed the button for nine, and waited. I tried pressing all the other buttons but it just purred.

By the time Jeremy returned very late in the evening, I was in tears. I was hungry, Kylie was fretful, she was hungry too, and I'd given her the last bottle of baby food I packed for the journey. He disappeared and returned to say he had ordered food from the reception desk. We fiddled with the phone a bit more, but all it wanted to do was purr.

"How long are we going to be here?" I asked.

"Not sure, a couple of days I think, and then we're going to Benghazi."

"Where's Benghazi? I thought we were going to live in Tripoli!"

"Well I thought so too, but I've been promoted."

"Already! You've only worked for Mohammed a few weeks!" I didn't know whether to be proud or alarmed. I had told everyone that I was going to North Africa to live in Tripoli, and now I wasn't. We were leaving to go somewhere else, to another town called Benghazi. This rang uncomfortable bells from the past.

"Don't fret," said Jeremy as he gave me a big hug. "I am going to start up a whole new workshop and yard for Mohammed in Benghazi."

"But where is Benghazi?" I asked again.

"Further round the Gulf of Certes. It's also on the coast, and I've heard it's a lot nicer place, more relaxed for expatriates, away from the capital and all the politics."

"Politics? What have politics got to do with it?" For a split moment Jeremy looked a little uncomfortable.

"Well it's a different way of life here and you have to be more careful."

The knocking on the door brought the food, and I was so hungry that I forgot about my fears and began to eat anything off the plates that looked familiar. A lot of the food was quite spicy and I wondered how I was going to get food for Kylie, she certainly wouldn't like much of this stuff.

But Jeremy, as optimistic as ever, swept aside all my worries. "Don't go out, or even go downstairs whatever you do," he told me as we ate like starving orphans. "They're holding a party downstairs for Leila."

"Who's Leila?"

"I think she's some kind of terrorist, or heroine, whichever way you look at it. She was the one that hijacked that plane, remember?"

"Hijacked!! What plane?"

"Well I'm not exactly sure, but they got people out of jail and she's seen as a freedom fighter and things are a little wild down there right now."

True to his word, Jeremy disappeared shortly afterwards and returned with plenty of supplies for his daughter, even though I was sure the shops wouldn't be open this late.

For the next four days I learned what it was like to be a bird in a gilded cage. The suite was indeed sumptuous, we got in lots of supplies, and we got the phone put right, so I could order from the kitchens, but I was not allowed to go outside.

There was nothing to watch on the television, unless you wanted to see men praying in the mosque, or were fanatical about football, and the radio played Arabic music that sounded screechy to my ears.

I read some magazines that Jeremy managed to find, and I finished the few books I had packed for the plane and I spent time playing with Kylie and gazing out over the balcony at the swimming pool below. I watched Arab men walking hand in hand, and urinating against the back wall of the hotel, nothing like the scenes I'd imagined in England, not a flower-strewn donkey or cute whitewashed cottage in sight.

On Friday morning, Jeremy got up late and announced he had the day off.

“On a Friday?” I asked.

“Yes of course, Friday is the Holy Day in Arab countries.” I felt such a fool and realized how little I actually knew about the world.

“So what happens on Saturday and Sunday?”

“Normal work days.”

It took me several years to get used to having a Friday off.

The following day, Jeremy announced that we were off to Benghazi. We were picked up from the hotel, this time not by limousine, but in a combi, and driven off to the docks to collect our new car, a Toyota Corolla. It had just been offloaded from the boat, and I helped put on the hubcaps and tried to wipe off some of the protective coating that covered the bodywork and windows.

We piled everything in and we were off. It’s not easy driving in a country where the road signs are all in Arabic script, and we didn’t even have a map. But, as my enthusiastic husband told me, all we had to do was keep driving with the Mediterranean Sea on our left and we couldn’t go wrong.

It was a bit nerve wracking, especially when we came to a fork in the road, but we took the left one each time as we were traveling east and hoped for the best. My imagination ran wild as usual, I had visions of driving deep down into the Sahara Desert and only being found after the vultures had picked our bones clean.

While the blue ocean sparkled on our left, inland, as far as the eye could see, there was sand, interspersed with small prickly shrubs on the undulating, flat, empty plains. We passed Al Khums, Misurtata, Certes, El Agheli, Ajdabiyah, and Qaminis, small towns close to the sea, with perhaps a few dusty one and two storey houses, a shop or two and a petrol station. Each time, we filled up two jerry cans with extra petrol, as the distances between towns was vast. We traveled for hours and made good progress as the road was tarred, although there was only one lane in each direction. In places, the sand had blown over the tar and we prayed that we hadn’t driven off course.

Eventually, after too many tomatoes, I needed to stop. There were no obvious facilities at the next hamlet we passed through, and Jeremy couldn’t explain my dilemma to the bored-looking man at the petrol station, well not without being too graphic, and that might have got him locked up!

“Never mind,” I said, “just stop at the side of the road, and I’ll hop out, choose a long, straight stretch and we’ll see anything coming, there isn’t all that much traffic.” I have since learned that no matter where you are, even in the middle of the Sahara Desert, the moment you try to commune with nature, someone appears from somewhere. This time it was an elderly Arab man with a donkey, minus flowers, who suddenly popped up from behind a sand dune, while at the same time half a dozen oil trucks came speeding down the road. I hastily leapt back into the car, nature would have to wait.

We eventually arrived ten hours later in Benghazi, hot, tired, thirsty and covered in dust. We were to book into one of the major hotels until our accommodation had been sorted out. Not more incarceration I thought, no matter how smart the surroundings, it was still a form of imprisonment.

13 BENGHAZI, LIBYA

This time, the hotel was not nearly as grand, and we had a standard room, but at least we could go down to eat meals in the dining room and Kylie was very well behaved.

Jeremy disappeared once more, leaving instructions for me to stay indoors, and went off to meet his new boss. Working hours in Libya were from seven in the morning until one, and then again from four in the afternoon until seven in the evening. It was just too hot to work in the extreme heat in the middle of the day, and everyone took a siesta waiting for it to cool down a little.

When Jeremy returned, he told me that we had been allocated a flat in one of the blocks owned by Mohammed and that the next day, they would be buying furniture, and as soon as that was delivered, we could move in to our new home.

"Are they buying brand new furniture for us then?" I asked.

"Yes, you'll love the flat, the kitchen is fully fitted, but we need bedroom furniture and a sitting room suite and dining table and chairs, but we'll get that all tomorrow."

"Oh great, I'm really going to enjoy choosing stuff! How much can we spend?" I asked.

"Well, uh, I don't know, and you, uh, can't come." Jeremy replied.

"What do you mean I can't come? Can't I help choose furniture for our home?"

"No, it seems that the men do that here, the wives don't go shopping. I will try to get nice stuff, Abubaka said we would look together in the morning."

I was a bit miffed, but I guess that Jeremy and I had the same taste and how awful could furniture be?

Our new home was in a ten-storey block of flats, with a wide marble entrance hall, two lifts and large, solid mahogany doors to the six flats on each floor. Ours was on the ninth floor, and again I was overwhelmed by the size. As Jeremy opened the door, I thought for a moment we were in another corridor leading to further flats, but no, all this was just for us. There were three large reception rooms, three bedrooms, a bathroom and a kitchen. All the rooms were large and airy, with a balcony off the main bedroom that overlooked the city and the sea. The only room you couldn't swing a cat in was the kitchen, but of course, this was where the women would be! How the other Arab ladies in some of the other flats managed I'm not sure, as there was certainly no space for two people in our kitchen.

While I was thrilled by the flat, with its pink and grey marble floors, I was not so thrilled with the furniture when it arrived. The bedroom suite was a dark, shiny wood, patterned with white curly lines. The dining room table was covered in carved birds, the chairs were large, solid, heavy, and sported more carvings than St Peter's Basilica, and the lounge suite was red velvet with gold trimmings, tassels and carved wooden arms. I gulped.

"I'm so sorry," Jeremy said. "I had very little say, Abubaka chose it all, and I'm sure he thought we would really like it, he seemed very pleased with his selection."

"I'll see what I can get to hide most of it. Perhaps a few blankets over the sofa for a start?"

A trip out into town that evening with Jeremy cheered me up. We drove into the centre in time to see all the metal shutters going up to reveal the Aladdin's caves behind. They were not there to protect the goods from theft, crime was practically unknown in Libya, but during the afternoons, and on Fridays, every shop front was an unprepossessing steel door.

Benghazi was a pleasant city, with a vibrant commercial centre and as it was beginning to get dark, the lights spilling out from the shops reminded me of Christmas. I tried not to look at the really nice furniture in some of the stores, but at least I was able to buy pots, pans, bedding, and a cot for Kylie.

"I thought you said that women were not allowed in shops," I remarked.

"Well they turn a blind eye to Western women, and remember you have me as a male escort, but until we understand what is, and what is not allowed, it's best we take it one step at a time," Jeremy replied.

I was a little alarmed at the clothing stores, the only things on offer seemed to be made of fluorescent materials, threaded with gold reminding me of road workers or cheap night club attire.

"Do people really wear all this stuff?" I whispered.

"Yes, I think so, but the only women I've seen so far are well covered from head to foot." Jeremy was right, the very few women I had seen, wore black headdresses, and long black or blue nightgowns called barricans, under which peeped either football socks or very elegant jeweled shoes. Indoors I learned, the women took great pride in their clothes, but these were never seen by anyone outside the immediate family. I also discovered the English bookshop, and I spent a fortune stocking up on things to read.

The following day we moved into the flat and while we were provided with the basic furniture, and the kitchen contained a stove, fridge and sink, there was no washing machine. For months, I washed everything by hand and took it up onto the roof to dry. Isn't it amazing what men think you need in a home? True, in our four years of marriage we'd never owned a washing machine, but in UK I could always rely on the launderette round the corner and in Kenya, Elizabeth did all the washing in the bath.

I waited for Kylie's cot to be delivered. Sure enough about ten in the morning, the intercom buzzed and a highly excited male Arabic voice gabbled on and on. I said it was fine, he could come on up. There was a deathly silence and then more frantic gabbling and more silence. Again, I invited him up,

"We're flat 93, on the 9th floor." I opened the front door and waited by the lift. Nothing happened, no one appeared. About an hour later the buzzer went again. This time it was a different voice, but also unintelligible.

"Have you come to deliver the cot?" I asked. There was a long pause.

"You there Madam? You husband there?"

"No, he's at work."

"Goodbye."

"No, wait! Do you have the cot?'

"Bed here, no man here. Goodbye."

"No, please wait, I'm coming down!" I raced down in the lift just in time to see two skinny Arabs loading the precious cot back onto the truck.

"Hey wait, that's mine, don't take it away, please bring it upstairs!"

The Arab doorman looked at me in horror as I watched the truck drive off. He shook his head mournfully at this appalling display of behaviour, but then what could you expect from a foreigner?

I went back upstairs and burst into tears. Why wouldn't the men simply carry the cot upstairs and let me sign for it? We'd paid for it, so what was the problem?

I couldn't get hold of Jeremy, we didn't have a phone in the flat, and I discovered later that very few people did have phones at home. The limited communications system was geared only to the work place.

I ran back downstairs and shouted "Inglesi" at the doorman, but he only stared back at me. I pantomimed carrying something heavy to the lift and behaved so badly I was lucky he didn't have me arrested. He just walked away.

But my extreme efforts must have had some effect, for a few minutes later, there was a knock on the door and sure that the cot was finally being delivered, I flung it open to see a cheerful, fat lady standing outside, holding a fat, curly haired infant. I could tell immediately that she was English, and so began my close friendship with Diana. Not only had I found a friend, but she also had a daughter not much older than Kylie and we spent many happy hours while our daughters played together. Well, no, that's not really true. Sara and Kylie would play together for a short time and then Sara would attack my daughter, kicking, punching and biting. Kylie had a very hard time, and I wondered if I should start the self-defense lessons this early?

It was Diana who taught me how to clean the flat, with its acres and acres of marble floors. In the middle of the kitchen and bathroom floors were holes, so I learned to empty a bucket of water onto the floor and sluice it all down the drain holes with a rubber squeegee. It was a bit like playing ice hockey I guess, as I chased rivers of dirty brown water from room to room. The dust, dirt and sand, and there was a lot of it, disappeared down the holes and the floors sparkled. Later on, I met one girl who washed everything down with a hosepipe, but I felt this was taking things a little too far.

In those first few weeks I also learned to live with the frequent power cuts. They were an almost daily occurrence as the power plant to the north of us blew off excess steam, creating an eerie wail that lasted for anything up to an hour.

I spent many miserable hours in the lift and learned to carry a book and torch with me at all times. Why not use the stairs? Nine flights, with bags and a pushchair? The temptation proved too great and I usually took a chance in the lift.

"Are there other ex-patriots here in Benghazi?" I asked Diana when I had been there a couple of months.

"Yes, dozens, haven't you met any of them yet?"

"No, where are they? How can I get in touch with them?" This was the best news I'd had since arriving.

"At the British Beach Club, haven't you been there yet?"

"No," I was really excited. "Where is it? How do we get there?"

"Actually, it's just over there." She walked over to the window and pointed to a low building on the edge of the beach about fifty metres across the road.

I could hardly wait! Surely I could walk across the road all by myself. I'd take Kylie in the pushchair. I'd been stuck in the flat for days and days and days, only going out when Jeremy was not too tired to drive me into town and look at the shops. There were no cafes and the only restaurants were in the hotels and were horribly expensive. Later I discovered that it was not wise to eat at any of them as you normally ended up with food poisoning.

Feeling extremely brave, I left a note for Jeremy, put on a long skirt, covered my head with a shawl and ventured outside into the bright sunlight. Ignoring the frosty stares from the doorman, and all the other men who were lounging around in the road, I walked past the police station and the mosque and across the street.

There was a high wire fence and a gate leading onto the beach, but no notice. I hoped I had the right place. Slowly I pushed it open and saw a crowd of people sitting on towels on the sand and they were wearing bikinis and swimming trunks! I walked right in and heard familiar words in English, and a board on the wall offering specials: 'Fish and Chips', 'Egg and Chips', 'Sausage and Chips'. For a moment I thought I was hallucinating.

I was in seventh heaven, apart from my long chats with Diana, hours of sluicing floors and hand washing, playing with my daughter and talking to Jeremy at odd moments, I'd had little contact with the world for over two months.

I amazed myself, once so painfully shy, by talking to complete strangers. I ordered a cup of coffee and began to make new friends. I have many really good friends from living in many different countries, but the people in Libya were extra special. It may have been that we were left to our own devices and the fact that we were all very well paid helped as well I think. Nothing was too much trouble, everyone helped everyone else and life suddenly took a new turn for the better.

The British community in Benghazi turned the clock back to the Victorian era and we all had a great time. There was a secret underground theatre and we put on productions four times a year. There was also a weekly play reading group and Jeremy and I become involved, and because I was seen to be organized, I became stage manager, plus the props lady, plus general secretary.

Jeremy blossomed on stage and was the leading man in several productions. A particularly memorable part was that of the murderer in 'Wait until Dark'. Before each performance, he would get into the mood, playing Black Sabbath at full volume on the stereo. I kept my distance.

On a couple of glorious occasions I was allowed to act on stage. I'm certainly not Julia Roberts, but I was certainly dismayed at the responses I got. I played the part of the simpering little secretary in 'Big Bad Mouse', dressed in large clumpy shoes, a tweed skirt and a shapeless jersey. The part required that I wring my hands frequently and whinge and whine a great deal. A lady I didn't know too well stopped me in the English bookshop and complemented me on my smart attire on stage. I didn't know quite what to think.

There were evening parties, usually on a Thursday night, where we all did a 'turn'. There were no excuses for being shy or without talent. The worst performances were usually the best, and we had beetle drives, and whist nights and fancy dress parties where the creations defied belief. There were also lots and lots of dinner parties, and I had one regularly every Tuesday evening.

Perhaps the greatest and most cutthroat pastime was the darts league. All but about five families worked on contract for foreign companies, mostly in line with the oil production or with building. The five remaining families who worked for Arab families, formed an independent team that we called the Union Jacks. We practiced like mad and every company fielded at least one team in the league. Some enterprising person had returned from leave bearing a huge silver cup and we fought for the honour of winning it in the finals. Each team had four men and two women and Monday night was darts night. Of course the venues were all private homes, and you could expect anything up to twenty or more people to land on the doorstep. Every team had a host of supporters. You were expected to feed and water all these guests, and in those days, I thought nothing of catering for up to sixty people.

We'd known that Libya was a dry country and neither of us had thought too much about it. We weren't big drinkers, that was to come later. I rarely drank alcohol, so we assumed that a few years without it would be no hardship at all.

The first time I was offered beer at a friend's house I was genuinely shocked, but it wasn't long until we realized that everyone had beer on tap and a good deal more. Perhaps peer pressure doesn't stop in the late teens, because we soon dropped off the wagon. The majority of our newfound friends seemed to be raving alcoholics and soon we too were making seventy litres of beer a couple of times a month. The more gregarious in our community, made that amount or more, every week!

But it didn't stop at beer. Wine was popular too and there were plenty of grapes to buy in season. I spent many boring hours treading grapes in a seventy litre dustbin, book in one hand, cigarette in the other. We all knew that you didn't wash grapes before treading them, nor did you remove too many of the extraneous stalks so it's quite uncomfortable work. Much to my horror, the first time I trod red grapes, they dyed my legs a lurid pink! White wine was more discreet. We also used rice and lemons, which made a very passable sake.

Many of the Central European expatriates in Benghazi made pure alcohol, which they willingly sold to other foreigners. It was always delivered in an old Johnny Walker bottle, usually black or blue label. Not long before we left Libya, one of our suppliers arrived on the doorstep and pushed his still into our unwilling arms. We were horrified. It consisted of a number of old metal funnels, pipes and a pile of marbles. I was totally against it, but Jeremy was determined to try it out. For once I put my foot down, I knew if you were caught, it was straight to jail. We left the assembled still in a spare room, and almost forgot about it until there was a knock on the gate one night during a party. A group of men was standing outside and they demanded we let them in. They knew we had booze on the premises and they wanted some. If we refused, they were returning with the police. We slammed the gate in their faces and rushed back inside.

Thirty half drunk British ex-patriots suddenly became very sober as some rushed to empty sixty odd bottles of beer down the sink, while another group were hard at work in the garden digging a hole large enough to bury the still. The young men never returned, but we waited a couple of weeks before putting down another batch of beer.

The accent was on family life and everywhere we went Kylie came too. Daytime outings during the week were usually to the Beach Club. Here the children could play on the sand, frolic in the warm Mediterranean Sea and we'd all tan furiously on our beach towels. For the more energetic, there was beach volleyball and cricket and we ate regularly at the restaurant. While Thursday night was party night, Friday saw us all heading off to the sea further up or down the coast, and most weekends we camped on the beach, swimming in the water at dawn and cooking our beef fillets on open fires and singing songs round the fire at night.

Several times a year saw us heading due south into the desert. We would head off a little to the east and discover desert roses, mica rock formations of surprising beauty, or a petrified forest, lying as if from the dawn of time untouched by man. There wasn't one ex-patriot family who didn't have a chunk of fossilized wood on the sideboard at home. From more modern times, we explored old forts and uncovered debris left over from World War II.

If I'm honest, I often got quite scared on our trips into the desert. How foolish we were I'm not sure, but apart from telling friends we were going south, I'm not sure anyone would have found us if we'd got lost, or would they have even come to look?

If life in Libya so far sounds like one big party, that was not the case. Where we got the energy to do all of the above and work as well, I'm not sure. But we certainly used every minute of each day.

When Jeremy said he'd been promoted after only a few weeks, I was thrilled, but there was still a niggling doubt as to whether he was telling me the whole truth. He was working for a family that was related to King Sanoussi, the leader deposed by Ghadaffi, but Jeremy was very enthusiastic about his job. I hoped this would last, since I had already lost count of the number of jobs he'd had in our first four years of marriage. If he walked out on this job, just what would our position be? I pushed these thoughts to the back of my mind and concentrated on running the house and looking after Kylie. At least money was something we wouldn't have to worry about for a while, since Jeremy was being well paid and all our basic needs such as rent, water, electricity and a car, were all part of the salary, the usual ex-patriot perks.

At some point I must have mentioned my teaching qualifications, for one evening there was a knock on the door and Jeremy opened it to find a smiling European man standing outside. I'm ashamed to say I can't even remember his name now, but he was the headmaster of the local British Council school.

We invited him in, I hoped he wouldn't look too closely at the appalling three piece suite as we sat drinking coffee in the lounge. I said that Kylie was a little young for school as yet, but we would certainly put her name down if there was a waiting list, as we were going to be in Libya for a while.

"No," he said, "I've not come to recruit Kylie, it's your qualifications I'm interested in. Will you come and teach at the school?"

I really wasn't keen. It took a large part of my day just to keep our enormous flat clean, I was just getting to grips with the difficulties of shopping in a foreign country which didn't stock the usual food and household items, and I didn't want to leave my baby and start work when she was less than a year old. I said I would think about it and after some general talk, our visitor left.

The following evening he rang the doorbell once more. "Let me tell you more about the school," he said. "We have a hundred and fifty children aged from four to twelve years. We follow the British schools' model and although there are limited facilities, no gym or music or playing fields, we do the best we can. There are six classes, but only five qualified teachers, and we need you desperately."

He mentioned a salary package that was extremely attractive.

"But what about my daughter?" I hedged. "She's too young to leave alone, and she's too young to put in a crèche."

"That's not a problem at all," he replied. "There are several women who would be only too happy to care for her and she would have lots of kids her own age to play with. British families tend to be isolated and scattered in various houses around the city, so most mothers get together in the mornings to allow their younger children to play together."

I said once again, that I would think about it and he left, promising that they would be happy if I started the following Monday morning.

I was tempted. Domestic life had never appealed to me, I'd had enough housekeeping as I was growing up. Also, if I had a job, then I could buy a car and I could get about and not have to rely on Jeremy.

I accepted the offer to teach the kindergarten class, and Kylie went to play at one of the impromptu playschools with the sons and daughters of the other teachers. She had a ball, with a social whirl of coffee mornings, beach parties, shopping trips and morning entertainments all aimed at the under two and a halves.

School started at seven while it was still cool, so it meant rising early, especially as I had to get her ready as well. I taught until midday when the little ones were let out, while the older children worked through until one. Then school was out for the day. It would have been far too hot to try to teach after lunch.

I enjoyed my work and it was fun to meet and educate children from all round the world. Although the school was automatically open to all British children, many other nationals also sent their children to us, since learning English was, and still is, regarded as a passport to world success. Many of the little ones I taught had very little English, and it was fun teaching them a new language. So I settled in happily and enjoyed my new job. Jeremy found me an old Beetle and although I hated it, it certainly got me around.

About a month later, I was chatting to a friend on the beach, who told me that they were looking for presenters on the radio for the British Language programmes. Would I be interested? How about going for an audition?

"Don't be ridiculous," I replied, "I'm already teaching at school, I've got Kylie to look after and I am a housewife as well don't forget."

Anne looked at me, "OK, I hear you," she said, "but I could mention that they are paying two hundred dinars per shift and that's only four hours, and it's three shifts one week and four the next, hardly slave labour."

I did some mental calculations. At that time, the exchange rate was two pounds sterling to the dinar. Seven shifts in a fortnight, times two hundred times two …

"That's five thousand six hundred pounds a month!" I exclaimed.

"Right," said Anne, "see what I mean? It's money for jam. They've accepted me and if you get accepted as well, then we can take care of each other's kids on our off days and we're really in the money."

"I'll think about it," I said.

That night I mentioned it to Jeremy. I was convinced that he would think it crazy that I should take on a second job, especially as he was being so well paid. Did we really need all this extra money?

To my surprise he was more than enthusiastic. "Go for it," he said, "I think you would be great on radio, and we can always do with more money. You can never have too much."

I agreed with that, and if I earned at that rate, the beetle would soon be living with a new owner, who just might appreciate her hermetic sealing or whatever it was that nearly burst my eardrums every time I got into her and slammed the door.

Despite the fact that teaching, mothering and housekeeping was already pretty tiring, I was intrigued. Working on the radio seemed a very glamorous thing to do. Nearly everyone listened to the station which broadcast from 4.30 pm until 7.00 pm weekdays. Unless you had a very powerful radio, it was difficult to pick up the BBC World Service, at least in the early days.

I think at the back of my mind I was certain that this would impress my mother, so I went for an audition and passed.

The production office was a large, dingy room, with shelves of audio tapes on large spindles and piles and piles of papers spread all over one of the many tables. A notice on the walls announced the running order for that night's broadcast. Opening remarks, 'The Paul Temple Mystery', followed by a DJ who would play the top ten songs of the week, followed by 'Men from the Ministry', and an unspecified music programme. There was a news broadcast at six and again at seven, and all this was held together by links from the anchor presenter and I was now one of them! My heart flipped over and I broke into a cold sweat. I had gone too far, I'd never be able to do this, I must be out of my mind! How could I speak on live radio? All the people I had met would hear me, all our new friends, Jeremy would be so embarrassed, all the children at school might listen, and I would only make a total fool of myself. If only I could change my mind.

Despite coping with a new country, a new job, a child and a husband, I was still very unsure of myself. While I may have looked reasonably calm and capable on the outside, it was all a big act. Inside I was a seething mass of insecurity. My self-image simply refused to rise any higher. But I really enjoyed my radio work and in my time there I produced a 'Brain of Benghazi' programme, introduced book readings and enjoyed my first experience of being paid not only to broadcast, but write as well, after all those years.

My only bad experience was one September 1st, Libyan Revolution Day, when I was met by soldiers with fixed bayonets who accompanied me to the studio, and did not leave my side for three hours. Colonel Ghadaffi was in town and someone had tried to blow him up. I sweated buckets that night with a bayonet pricking my neck every moment I was broadcasting on air. The perspiration ran down my face and dripped onto the script and turned it into a soggy mess and it became difficult to read. That is one story I never told my mother.

I taught myself to sew, not to my mother's standards, but it was the only way to replace Kylie's clothes and I was not going to wear the fashions I saw in the shops. Kylie loved shopping, because the Libyans love children. She would poke her fingers into tomatoes, scream when

I was cross with her, and then all the men would reward her with sweets.

I remember one shopping trip all too clearly. I had driven into town, popped Kylie into her pushchair and was making for the English bookshop. As I rounded the corner I stopped dead. A large platform with a makeshift gantry had been erected at the bottom of the main steps of the old cathedral, and two bodies were jerking and struggling as the rope around their necks tightened. Two men were just putting a noose around the third young man who was screaming loudly to the small crowd in the street. I was shell shocked for several minutes and stood frozen on the spot, before finding the strength to turn the pushchair around and walk quickly away. In the next street I sat down on the pavement and shook for several minutes. I wasn't sure how much Kylie had seen or understood, but she didn't appear distressed and I hoped she wasn't going to have nightmares over the incident.

Eventually I made for the car and drove home, only to see from the balcony, a pall of smoke over the city. It looked as if the whole of Benghazi was on fire. Jeremy didn't appear at lunchtime and it was well after dark before he finally walked through the door, by which time I was a nervous wreck.

Later we learned that several students had invaded the old cathedral building that was now being used as government offices. There was some kind of altercation and the ring leaders were arrested, swiftly tried and executed as an example to others. In retaliation, several other students set fire to other government buildings and ran riot through the streets. I didn't know to what extent it was a revolution, but it was quelled within twenty four hours.

And then I made another mistake.

14 ENGLAND

After the second year, Jeremy was due three weeks leave, combined with a business trip to England and a visit to equipment Head Office and factory.

Don't ask me why we went to stay near my mother, I should have known better but I felt so much stronger now. I was coping successfully, even becoming one of the better known ex-pats and my two years on the radio had proved I was not the wilting violet I once was. In my imagination I thought that being married to Paul for three years would have had a mellowing effect. How wrong can one be?

We only stayed for a couple of nights, but it was enough to undo much of the confidence building I had accomplished. She had not changed at all, and her vitriolic attacks continued as before. She disagreed with everything we said, and criticized everything I did. I know, I was trying to impress my mother, like a child who waits for a parent's full attention before showing off the latest achievement.

"Did I tell you I was working on the radio Mum?" I asked.

"Well you mentioned something, but I'm not really that interested in what you do."

"It's interesting work. I did a book reading, 'The Old Man and the Sea', and our 'Brain of Benghazi' was hysterical. And I've become quite a good DJ."

"It's hardly the BBC is it? I don't suppose there are many people listening anyway, that's if any of it is true. I've never been able to believe a word you say."

"Of course it's true! I taped a couple of episodes for you to listen to, that proves it's true."

"No thank you, I told you, I'm not interested in what you get up to over there with your little friends. Of course now you think you're so big and important, you come home throwing your weight and your money around, thinking you're better than the people here. If your new 'friends' over there knew what you were really like they'd keep well away from you."

I sighed with exasperation. "Mum, all this is nonsense. I haven't told a lie since the day I left for college, and I've not taken a thing that didn't belong to me for years. That was bad behaviour as a child. I'm an adult now."

"Leopards don't change their spots, never will. You will always be bad and I did everything I could to give you a good start in life and look where you are now!"

"What's wrong with where I am now? I'm a good wife and mother, I'm a successful teacher, I work on live radio, I entertain business people, I have weekly dinner parties and I have lots of good friends." I was desperate to change her mind, to get her to admit that I was not necessarily something special, but just a normal person who deserved a place on the planet.

"Well if you're smug and self satisfied about your life that's all that matters isn't it? Doesn't matter what I think." With that my mother got up and walked out of the room.

Why didn't I just accept defeat and learn to ignore her? The problem was, I still worried if what she said was true. Was there a dark side to me that I couldn't see? Exchanges like these sent my self-image crashing through the floor.

Thankfully we escaped and the rest of the time we spent in Greece, flying into Athens and then taking a flight to Volos and then we took the boat to Skiathos and Skopolos. We spent a magical week and this time there really were cute whitewashed cottages and neat little alleyways and donkeys with flowers in their ears.

There was only one bad moment when Jeremy went out drinking one night. I was aware that he had begun to drink quite heavily in Benghazi, and certainly the beer we made was very strong, we even had to decant it out of the bottle leaving the sludge behind.

It had been impossible, even with the aid of a phrase book to get a baby sitter in the pension where we stayed, and Kylie liked her routine and got very fretful if she was kept up late. I'd already had a couple of difficult evenings sitting near the waterfront, while waiting for the restaurants to open at about ten o'clock at night. The reins I'd bought, now she was motoring around at high speed, saved her life on at least two occasions, but I often received adverse comments from passersby about how cruel I was to my child, by keeping her on a lead like a dog.

I could hardly say no to Jeremy when he wanted to try out the local tavern, but I didn't expect him to be out until the following morning. I sat up all night and was in tears when he returned just before breakfast. But somehow I found it impossible to really explain how I felt. If I questioned his behaviour in any way, he got so angry and began shouting at me, making it all my fault. I simply didn't have the courage to pursue it.

When I left Libya for that holiday, I did not realize that I was pregnant with my second daughter and it wasn't until we got back off leave that the truth dawned on me. There was no question of my taking time off from work, and I waddled into the classroom each day growing larger and larger. I also had to move the chair back from the microphone in the studio and hope that a sudden frantic, internal kicking would not make me gasp while on air.

While medical facilities were free in Libya, I was not going to trust them and I was also determined that the baby would be born in Britain and so qualify for a British passport and right of residence. Jeremy got extended leave and at eight and a half months pregnant we flew home. Since I had had no one to advise me, I didn't realize that it was a very stupid thing to do. I'm sure that Libyan Arab Airways would load you on board without a murmur if you were in the final stages of labour, but it wasn't until much later that I discovered, larger, more advanced airlines generally refuse to let you fly after seven months.

I had had a couple of really nice, friendly letters from my mother, so I thought that perhaps this time all would be well.

The moment we landed at Heathrow, I began having mild contractions, which was a bit alarming. Mother and Paul, who were supposed to meet us, were nowhere to be seen. So, Jeremy pulled the "where is our hired car?" trick and soon we were speeding westwards in an upgraded vehicle for the price of a much smaller one. I really don't know how he did it.

As we walked into Paul's cottage he apologized for not meeting us. My mother interrupted to say it was because Paul had a cold, and he gave her a really funny look.

"Would you like a cup of coffee?" she asked.

"That would be great, thank you," I replied as I sat down carefully to relieve the sharp pains a little.

"I'll have a tea and get Jeremy whatever he wants, you know where the kitchen is," said my mother. "Afterwards, I'll take you round to the cottage. I hope you realize what a lot I've done for you in arranging this let. I hope you are properly grateful."

"Yes, thank you Mother," I replied as I winched myself out of the chair and went to make the tea.

This pregnancy had been very different from the first one. There was still no English speaking doctor in Benghazi, but I had consulted a nurse when in my second month, I looked as if I was already nine months gone with triplets. I had been wearing maternity clothes since the third month and I was very anxious to consult my old doctor.

It was getting dark when we drove round to the cottage at the end of the village. It was cold inside, since the heating had been turned off, but my mother told us we could buy a pile of logs the next day. In the meantime, Jeremy found the switching system for the central heating and put it on full blast.

"Did you think to turn that on?" he asked my mother.

She looked at him in astonishment. "I wasn't going to waste money if you weren't here. Anything could have happened, you might not have come over and then I would have to pay all the bills." My mother is just so thoughtful. She kindly consented to help me make up the beds, while I tried to comfort Kylie who was really feeling the cold, she was also tired and hungry. I was worried that the sheets felt damp, one thing we never had to worry about in a hot country.

Mother completed her welcome by lending us a bottle of milk and telling us that we should catch the milkman at 6 am the following morning and get onto his delivery round so we could return her milk the next day. I just hoped that we could avoid Mother as much as possible while we were in England.

The doctor I saw was not the one I wanted, and inadvertently I upset the nurse when I asked if it was possible to have this baby privately. I received a long lecture on how good the National Health Service was and why waste money, even if I apparently had plenty of it.

The doctor to whom I was referred, was a specialist for infertile couples, a problem Jeremy and I certainly didn't have. I told him that I had already had contractions and that I thought the baby was due in a couple of weeks.

"Nonsense," he replied, as he poked and prodded. "This baby is not about to make an appearance for at least another two months. You got your dates all wrong."

"I don't think so. What about the contractions?"

"A bit of imagination I should think, just ignore them and carry on as normal," and with that, he dismissed me.

But the contractions continued and I insisted on another appointment earlier than he'd suggested. He looked quite tetchy as he said that 'fake' contractions were quite common, they were Braxton Hicks contractions and I had at least another six or seven weeks until this baby arrived.

Two days later I was in bed and Jeremy sent for the doctor. Luckily, it was a locum and he was much more sympathetic. I had a gastro bug and should take it easy. He wouldn't like to say how soon he thought the baby would arrive. Anyway I should rest as much as I could, and he gave me safe medicine to take.

I was back on my feet a couple of days later, since I still had Kylie to see to. Despite the fact I was ill, and she was just around the corner, my mother showed little interest in trying to help. But we did visit, as I had grown to love Paul and I felt he really enjoyed our company.

A couple of days later as we were sitting in the kitchen, I told Jeremy that it was the real thing this time. We arrived at the local hospital and I explained that I was in labour. The sister gave me a quick examination and wanted to send me right back home.

"But this is my second baby," I gasped, "I know labour contractions when I feel them."

"Baby's not big enough to be born," sniffed the Sister, "but if you insist, you can stay in overnight."

They left me on a bed, with a bell nearby to use if I needed to call for help. An hour later I pushed it to say that I didn't want to be a nuisance, but I really was in a lot of pain. The tablet they gave me did nothing to help.

A short time later, the waters broke and I pushed the bell again. This time things were different. The nurse took one look and gasped.

"Oh God, you're haemorrhaging!!" I wasn't too sure what this meant but everyone moved very fast after that. I was taken into the delivery room and it seemed that in no time at all, the baby appeared. It required little or no effort on my part, I had no drugs, no long, hard labour and certainly no need for stitches this time round.

From the start things were difficult with Dana. She weighed in at less than five pounds, and she neither whimpered nor cried. I was left to fend for myself as everyone rushed around the baby. Eventually they all disappeared and I lay and wondered what had happened and was it a boy or a girl?

Dana was small, red, wrinkled and bald and she didn't want to nurse. By now I was exhausted, totally drained. What was wrong with me? Why didn't the doctor believe me? Why did the nurses think I was just making a fuss the night before? And what was wrong with her?

"We're not sure about this baby," said the doctor, "she has suffered some considerable trauma, and…"

"But she has two legs and two arms, and apart from looking ugly, she looks normal. She is normal isn't she?" I was trying not to get hysterical.

"Well as far as we can tell at the moment, but we don't know how she's going to develop and I hear you're taking her abroad so just watch those milestones. Remember, she was under five pounds at birth."

His words meant one thing to me. I had given birth to a baby who was either mentally or physically disabled or possibly both. How would we cope? How would this affect Kylie?

Just after I'd got pregnant, and before we even told her she was going to have a baby brother or sister, Kylie had changed. From being a happy, contented toddler, she had taken to having black moods. She'd sit for hours staring at nothing, neither answering nor responding to my questions. I had also caught her trying to climb out of the window on the ninth floor, sending me into a panic when I looked down to see the spiked railings below. She refused to understand that she was not to put her fingers in live sockets, and I had to watch her every second of the day. Were both my children going to have problems? I was very afraid.

Dana seemed to progress very well, consenting to take my milk as long as it was offered in a bottle. Oh well, I couldn't have everything I thought, as I expressed milk for not only my own but a whole number of other infants in Swindon hospital.

They released us from the hospital after five days, and my mother came along with Jeremy to collect me, this time all smiles and loving words. Did I really think things would be different? Why did I keep hoping?

I was so scared of this tiny creature, so tiny I couldn't buy nappies small enough and she was fretful and cried constantly. However, I wasn't prepared to return to Benghazi without her having her inoculations, I'd learned my lesson with Kylie. Special permission had to be granted and it was with a sense of relief, that we boarded the plane to return to our own home, even with the fears of what the future might hold for us.

15 BACK TO BENGHAZI

Dana's health did not improve when we arrived back in Libya. On average, she cried for twenty three hours each day and neither of us was getting any sleep. Jeremy would arrive home at lunchtime to find me exactly where he'd left me, in a chair, trying desperately to feed this howling infant. We were at our wits end, until at last, I decided to take her to see one of the local Arabic doctors.

The only other brush I'd had with the medical services had been six months earlier when Kylie had developed a very high fever. It was late in the evening, and Jeremy was out, I didn't know where. I paced up and down the flat trying to calm her down, but she continued to whimper. I remembered that there was a doctor living on the third floor, so wrapping her in a blanket I went downstairs and knocked on his door. He showed no interest whatsoever and told me to take her to the hospital. He was off duty and he was tired. Even in winter the temperature can drop sharply at night, and I didn't think that a trip out in the cold was going to help her fever. In the end, I sponged her down with cool water and thankfully, by the morning the fever had broken.

It was only later I discovered from one of the other mothers that even simple childhood diseases such as measles, could easily kill a child in Africa, and high temperatures and fevers result in brain damage. One of our friends put her two year old son in a cold bath to cool him down and later he lost most of his hearing and suffered minor brain damage as well. Maybe her action saved his life, but she was wracked with guilt over her actions.

I queued up in the doctor's large waiting room, the only European among a crowd of chattering barrican-covered women.

I was shown into a small consulting room, which looked none too clean and tried as best as I could to explain the problems. It seemed that the short, friendly doctor spoke little or no English, but I'm sure he could see what was wrong, since Dana continued to howl loudly. He handed me a small phial of green liquid and by holding up three fingers, and pointing to the clock, indicated that I should give her three drops, every four hours.

I returned home and placed the phial on the kitchen counter. Should I use it? What was it? I went back out, down to the local chemist, and handed the phial to the pharmacist.

"Could I give this to my baby?" I pantomimed the actions to

reinforce the English. He took it, opened the bottle and sniffed and then he shrugged. It told me nothing.

After dithering for another day, I decided to try it and ten minutes later after placing a drop of the green liquid on Dana's tongue, she was in a deep sleep. I didn't know whether to feel alarmed or relieved. I raced around the flat making beds, piling washing into the bathroom basin and washing up several days' worth of dishes. Every couple of minutes I rushed back to make sure she was still breathing.

As if in answer to my prayers, a couple of weeks later we heard that a British doctor had arrived to work at the local oil clinic, so I grabbed Dana, jumped into the car and was first in line the next morning.

With the phial of green liquid in the one hand and the baby in the other, I explained all the problems we'd had. Dr John examined the medicine.

"She's been well doped with this, she must have gone out like a light."

"Yes, but I got so desperate. Jeremy even kicked the pram across the room one night, we've not slept in weeks and I'm at my wits end."

The resulting diagnosis was three month colic, only Dana had this for almost eight months and the treatment was large doses of harmless gripe water. During that first year, she continued to be a worry, as we wondered just how damaged she'd been at birth. She got one cold after another, a bout of flu and another cold and continued to be very sickly. She was slow to gain weight and we worried constantly.

I made numerous trips to the clinic for her inoculations, but it took almost two years to complete the course of three, since every other time, she was not well enough to receive the second, or third inoculation, and then we'd have to start all over again.

We'd returned to Benghazi in June, at the start of the long school summer holidays, so I had a few weeks before it was time to return to work. By now, another enterprising mother had started a fully-fledged playgroup and Kylie was quite content to spend her mornings there, while I trudged into work lugging the carrycot into the classroom. I was not prepared to leave Dana with anyone else while she still seemed so frail, even though she'd stopped howling.

Kylie's black moods came and went and she still continued to try to escape the quickest way out of the flat via the window. In desperation, I told Jeremy that we had to find a villa and move out of the flat.

As usual, he tackled the project with unbounded enthusiasm, and returned a couple of days later to say he had found just the right place and he couldn't wait to show me.

If I thought the flat was large, I'd not counted on the size of the villa. There were four enormous bedrooms, three bathrooms, a gigantic lounge, dining room, large kitchen and several other extra rooms off the kitchen that we could utilize as the brewery. The main entrance was a large area, with screen doors and windows, and from that, double doors led into the house and more double doors opened into the main lounge. The reception rooms had French doors onto a balcony at the rear of the house, which measured forty metres long, by seven metres deep. Surrounding the villa on all four sides, was a wasteland that was not even a pretense at a garden, since water is so precious, you would never waste it by watering a lawn.

"But we'll rattle around in here," I gasped, "even with four of us!"

"Nonsense, there's lots of space," Jeremy replied. "It belongs to one of the Sanousi's and it used to be the residence for the British Consul."

"Yes, and all his staff, I bet," I replied. "There's room for a whole consulate in here."

We moved in, and I tried to fill up the place by utilizing one bedroom as a playroom, another as a sewing room, leaving a bedroom for the children and one for us. It was going to take hours to keep clean, especially after the scorching hot Ghiblis, the very fine sand storms that blow up from the southern desert. It made no difference if you closed all the windows, dropped the blinds and fastened the shutters. The fine powdered, dusty sand found its way in. The only way to remove the dust was with water.

"Why don't you employ Fifi?" asked one of the other ex-pat housewives. "I have her twice a week and she's brilliant."

It had not occurred to me to employ someone to clean my house here in Libya, but the idea appealed to me enormously, another Elizabeth, how wonderful! I asked her to send Fifi round as soon as possible.

If the name Fifi conjures up visions of a cute French maid with pinny and feather duster, you'd be dead wrong! Fifi was an Egyptian lady, married to a Libyan, a rarity, and she must have weighed in at almost a ton and moved with the speed of an elderly tortoise with sore feet. Since not one Libyan would condescend to work for a foreign infidel, Fifi was indeed a rarity. As a result, Fifi was housemaid to a very large number of the ex-pat community, and since it took her half a day to clean a house, there was no way she could come regularly once a week and not once did she come on the appointed day. She 'did' for all of us on a rota system known only to herself, but to fire her would have been unthinkable. Just as I was getting desperate, she would pitch up, all smiles and yet again, I would welcome her with open arms. We all lived in fear that she would be transported back to Egypt.

Both the plumbing and the electricity services were problems. The water was just as likely to bubble back up the drains when I sluiced it down, and I never trusted the hot water tanks they put up over the baths. I doubt if many buildings would even approach British safety standards, and loose screws on the brackets holding the tanks in place gave me no confidence at all. I took to using the shower instead.

There were frequent power surges and the main power was notoriously unreliable, with almost daily power cuts. When the power was restored, it came back with such a surge of energy, that most of the light bulbs exploded. We kept an enormous stock of spare globes.

Life was a blur of frenetic activity. There was the teaching every morning, the radio station every other weekday, Saturday through Thursday, the jam packed social life and the business entertaining.

There seemed to be a constant flow of people coming over from England, and since Libya is such a foreign country in comparison to western cultures, we always invited the visitors over for dinner and drinks. On many occasions, we warned them that the homemade beer was really, really strong and it wasn't wise to have more than a couple of glasses. No one ever believed us, and Jeremy had a difficult time returning our visitors to the hotel in town, trying to conceal the fact they were more than a little under the weather!

We improved our standard of living. I bought extra furniture, usually from departing ex-pats, though we treated ourselves to some really nice Persian carpets for the main rooms, and I exchanged the hated Beetle for a nippy little Fiat, which I christened Sarah. We invested in a state of the art sound system, only after we found a surge protector for the power supply, and our record collection soon began to rival that at the radio station. We bought a full jungle gym for the children and Kylie even had a battery operated car she could sit in and drive all round the villa and out onto the patio. By the age of four, she was adept at three point turns! We also bought a small yacht, and learned to sail on the Mediterranean Sea.

Every year we took leave for a couple of weeks, and since it usually included Jeremy visiting the suppliers' offices, we returned time after time to Britain. We'd had that one week in Greece, and that was the only other European country we were to see. I was desperate to visit the pyramids and see the wonders and antiquities of Egypt, but the border between the two countries was closed. The quickest and easiest way to get to Cairo, only a few miles from where we lived, was to fly north to Athens then south again, back to the North African coastline.

Before we returned to Libya, we loaded up with all the goodies that we couldn't get in our new homeland. The most precious was bacon and when the children were small, they made excellent smuggling companions. I hid frozen bacon under the mattress in the carrycot and when the children were older, in the cozy toes in the pushchair. When she was old enough to walk, I bribed Kylie with promises of sweets to wail and scream loudly when we reached the customs table. It worked every time, a shrieking child is difficult to ignore and extremely irritating and we were passed through very swiftly.

All those returning from leave, treated their favourite friends to a full English breakfast, with pride of place being the bacon rasher in the middle of the plate.

We had floods one year, and I spent hours rescuing the tortoises that lived below in the back garden. We also had a cute chameleon we'd take indoors during parties in case he was trodden on by mistake. He'd settle quite happily in the bedroom, clinging to a chair leg and never minded being cuddled.

Of course in time we acquired dogs, usually passed on by other families on their way home. There was Snowy a large white thing roughly the size of a small elephant, and Jeremy brought home two local mongrel dogs from an abandoned litter he'd found. We nursed them back to health, and Samantha and Rebecca became part of the family too. That was, until the night Jeremy left the main gates open at the bottom of the drive while he took the baby sitter home. He'd only been gone a few minutes when I heard the first shots. It was the dog catching brigade, or rather the dog-killing brigade. Benghazi was plagued by feral dogs that roamed the streets at night, ferreting in the forty-five gallon oil drums we all used as rubbish bins. I raced outside, but it was too late. Rebecca and Samantha stood inside the gate barking at the truck, while I was screaming at the men not to shoot, these were our pet dogs, don't hurt them! The men ignored me and began shooting, while I ducked down in the main porch as bullets flew in all directions. Rebecca was killed outright, but they left Samantha screaming in agony as they drove off, after flinging Rebecca into the rubbish bin. Samantha survived, but we sent her to live at the workshop as she was never the same after that.

Dana was only seven months old when I fell pregnant again. I was distraught. Within a couple of weeks I blew up like a balloon and looked as if I was about to give birth any moment. I tried not to panic. We were still unsure if Dana was going to be mentally challenged and her physical development was far behind Kylie's at the same age. How were we going to cope with two disabled children?

I went to see Dr John at the oil clinic, all the symptoms were the same as my second pregnancy, and nothing like my first, what was I going to do? To my amazement, he suggested a termination.

"What? Get rid of it?"

"Well you have excellent grounds for it. I can recommend a good friend of mine at Swindon back in the UK. Look, the tests are not back yet, you might not even be pregnant."

"I don't need to see any test results, I know, trust me, I know. It's happening all over again."

"At this stage, it would be a simple D and C, so go and chat with Jeremy about it and come back tomorrow when the test results are in."

There were many times when Jeremy surprised me and this was one of them. I thought he would be mad at the idea of a termination and shout and scream, and it took a lot of courage to bring up the subject.

He simply smiled and said; "It's your body, you must make the decision. I'll support you either way."

Sure enough, the tests came back positive and in some miracle of organization, we obtained an exit visa in only three days, certainly a record, and we were on a plane bound for London.

I'd first spoken to Dr John on the Wednesday, we flew out on the Saturday and on Monday morning, I was sitting in front of his doctor friend in Swindon.

"Did I want to end the pregnancy?"

"Well yes, I guess so. We'd always planned to have two children. And we don't know if Dana will be OK and the thought of a second disabled child…"

"Fine, I'll book you in, and since you're going privately, we'll do it tomorrow." It was as simple as that.

I was very nervous about telling the grandparents, but again, I was amazed at their reaction. My mother was incredibly supportive, and Jeremy's mother had a real go at him for not having a vasectomy, especially since I'd agreed to have my tubes tied at the same time.

They wheeled me in for surgery the next day and I was to have one more day to recover before flying back on the Thursday. I was discharged the next day but collapsed in the supermarket having gone to stock up on bacon and the other luxuries we couldn't get in Benghazi. However I recovered sufficiently to get back on the plane on Thursday, so in just over a week the whole episode was over.

I've watched numerous programmes and read lots about people who suffered agonies for years after about destroying life. I must confess that I still believe it was one of the best decisions I have ever made, for lots of reasons and what happened to me in later life has only reconfirmed it. It was difficult enough to cope with the two children I already had, and I'd seen too much poverty, too many children scratching in the dust, and I strongly believe that over population is one of our world's greatest problems.

Other families came and went, as we slowly climbed the social ladder, with the hierarchy being those who had been in Libya the longest. By 1979, there were only eleven families who'd served longer than Jeremy and I and that put us among the elite. But we knew we had really made it when there was a knock on the door one day, and we opened it to see three representatives of the British Embassy from Tripoli on the doorstep. While there had once been a consulate office in Benghazi, this had been closed for several years, which was just as well, since we were living in the old residence.

We were asked if we would join the committee and help plan the Queen's Birthday celebrations to be held that year in Benghazi and after a pregnant pause, would we be ever so kind and allow them to use our home to house the reception? Naturally we agreed with alacrity and immediately work began on the planning and preparations.

If my mother could hear this now, I thought, she would have to be proud of me. We were only too happy to oblige, it was difficult to keep our pride and excitement within bounds.

The back patio was an ideal place for a large gathering, but we would need to spruce it up. Groups got together with gardening equipment and paint brushes.

The official permission allowing us a gathering of more than ten people arrived and invitations went out to all the Christian ambassadors in the city, and it was open house for all British passport-holding residents. The Maltese cooks at the university baked an enormous iced cake and lots of other 'nibbly' delicacies, and two huge portraits of the Queen and Prince Philip arrived by courier from Tripoli, along with a Union Jack and lots of red and white streamers and balloons. There was quite a heated discussion about which way up the flag should go.

"It's the broad white stripe at the top," I insisted, I'd learned that at Brownies. I was prepared to set fire to the flag rather than endure the humiliation of having them hang it upside down for such an occasion in *my* house. With all the help and support from both committee members and others in the community, the venue looked fantastic on the great day.

We coerced a couple of the elder children to look after the younger children in three of the bedrooms and once again, our chameleon was brought indoors, along with two of the smaller tortoises.

Dressed in our very best clothes, I had been working frantically at the sewing machine, we waited in great expectation for the arrival of the British Ambassador and his wife, and we waited and we waited and we waited.

We had decided to use the side gate, which had never been opened in all the time we'd been in the villa. It had taken a great deal of coaxing to prise it open, but this meant that we did not have to paint the front of the villa and no one would have to walk through the jungle in the front garden and the house to get to the patio.

Other dignitaries began to arrive and, as the resident hostess I was pressed into service to welcome them. A large crowd of local Arabs had gathered outside the gate and of course, there was the usual contingency of the Morality Police outside as well.

The evening got off to a good start as a bevy of white coated waiters offered snacks and red or white grape juice from silver trays, and still there was no sign of the British Ambassador and his wife. Unknown to us, the official state car kept in Benghazi had not been used for four years, and once it was finally run to ground, there was no time to check it out. Of course it wouldn't start, so it never reached the airport at all. Our honoured guests were forced to make other plans and eventually arrived at the front gate in a bashed and battered twenty year old fiat. Nothing to compare with the smart limousines ferrying the other diplomats, with pennants fluttering and uniformed chauffeurs.

By the time the Fiat ground to a halt outside the front gate, the raucous laughter of the crowds and the loud, patriotic music ensured that no one heard them at all. They finally found their way round to the back of the house, through the weeds in the bits of garden we had not tidied up, since that part 'wouldn't show'. Sadly, her ladyship's tights were the worse for wear, but they certainly received a very warm welcome. We hastily woke up the flower girl and pushed her out to present the slightly wilted bouquet of flowers.

'Rule Britannia', 'Land of Hope and Glory', and the National Anthem were played, the cake was cut with great ceremony, and as we all raised our glasses to Her Majesty, we thought fondly of home with tears in our eyes.

As the evening wore on, people became more and more relaxed and it didn't matter how often we denied it, no one would believe that the whole assembly was slowly getting drunk on pure grape juice. It must have been the atmosphere, the music and the sense of occasion.

A couple of weeks later, Jeremy and I were approached by the French Committee, and asked to submit twelve names for members of the British community to attend the Bastille celebrations to be held at the French Consulate. If we'd felt important before, this was the cherry on the top. It was another glamorous evening rubbing shoulders with the most important people in the country. We were riding on a high, popular, in high society, and recognized as one of the main leaders in the ex-pat community. We were wealthy, our social life was a whirl and we had dozens of really good friends. What more could life give us?

But fate is a great leveler, and our nemesis was approaching.

Things had begun to unravel politically for those few remaining rich and powerful Libyan families, and Jeremy was summoned to meet Mohammed in Tripoli. There were problems with the government and his boss was going to leave the country. Since life was still good Jeremy saw no reason to leave and assured Mohammed that he would continue as before and stay and run the workshop and sales in Benghazi.

But we began to notice other small changes. All the foreign beach clubs must be open to everyone, and this resulted in hoards of young Libyan men sitting very close and leering at us as we sat with our children on the sand. We chose to visit beaches further outside the city but there was often a hassle at the barriers that manned all entry and departure points on all roads. Previously we had been treated with respect by the police and army, now, all that had changed.

I had also been worried for some time about Jeremy's drinking. He spent many evenings away, and I hoped and prayed that he wasn't having another affair. If he was, I never found out, but he often came home late. I was nervous he would be caught drinking, and he was. He was arrested after running over a local man while drunk and thrown into jail. The police were kind enough to come and tell me first, so I knew which station they had taken him to. Could things get any worse? Life never seemed to run smoothly.

In the morning, I returned to the police station again, where they said they had never heard of Jeremy. I decided to throw myself on the mercy of Jeremy's boss Abubaka. I had never met the man and had never been to the offices before, but Jeremy had pointed them out once when we'd been in town. I had to wait four hours before he agreed to see me, and I tried not to cry as I told him what had happened. I lied when I said that Jeremy had not been drunk and no, I had no idea where the company car was.

Abubaka waved me away and there was nothing else I could do but go back to school and take charge of my class. If I could stick to the normal routine as much as possible, perhaps I would not frighten the children. Later that day I toured all the police stations I could find, looking for Jeremy, but I had no luck, I had no idea where he was.

It was two days later that the company driver banged on the gate and told me to go to the central police station. Sure enough, I found my husband, by now, a very sober man. Could I bring him food and drink? Prisoners were not fed by the state, you had to rely on parcels from friends and relatives on the outside. And, he had run out of cigarettes. I promised both and returned with bags of supplies.

Despite Jeremy's Arabic being a good deal better than mine, he had no idea if he was going to be charged, had been charged, or how long they were going to keep him in jail.

Within the week Jeremy was home. He was still not sure what steps the authorities were going to take, but he blamed it all on Mohammed having skipped the country and took no responsibility for getting drunk. Later we received orders to leave Libya and we were given one week to get out of the country.

Seven days is not long to pack up over five and a half years of household goods, sell three cars, and wind up our financial affairs. We knew that we would only be able to leave with the luggage we could carry onto the plane, and one box of favourite toys.

While I was very relieved that Jeremy was back safe and sound, it broke my heart to dispose of all the things for which we'd worked so hard. I drove my faithful little Fiat to the local car mart and gave her away for almost nothing. The yacht went to friends who promised to try to send out our Persian carpets, and sadly I hugged and kissed Snowy the dog as I dropped her off at her new home.

I said goodbye to the people at the radio station and the other staff members and the children at school. From being among the admired elite, I now felt shamed and embarrassed. Sure, everyone brewed beer and everyone drank, but no one should get caught, that was the shameful part. I felt that Jeremy was making matters worse by not admitting his mistake, but blaming the politics and Mohammed's behaviour. I felt sure that no one believed him.

There were further hassles in the final week as night after night there was loud banging on the outside gates. Group after group of Libyans demanded entrance, saying they had been allocated the villa by the housing authorities and were going to move in right away. Jeremy slammed the gates in their faces, but the banging and shouting went on for hours.

Jeremy gathered in what money we had managed to get for selling practically everything we owned and took it to the bank. He filled in the deposit slip and made arrangements to have our money transferred into our British bank. The bored bank teller told him they were very busy, put the deposit slips and money into a drawer without even counting it, and told him to come back the next day.

When Jeremy returned, it was to find that no one in the bank had any record of his bank account, nor of the money he'd passed over the counter only twenty four hours earlier. It dawned on us that our Libyan money was going nowhere.

Typical of Jeremy, unlike most of the other ex-pats, he had not made a regular transfer each month, but simply let the money accumulate in his account.

Custom didn't allow me to open a bank account of course, so I'd given Jeremy all my spare money in the naive belief that he was sending it out on a regular basis. I looked at the fistful of Dinars I had collected by selling the children's clothes and surplus toys, it was all I had left. On the last night we were in Libya, Abubaka made arrangements for Jeremy to visit the bank late at night, where he received a fraction of the money we'd accumulated, all in filthy, dirty, greasy Dinar notes.

An exit visa was delivered as if by magic and on the final morning, I stuffed dozens of Dinar notes inside my bra before we set out for the airport. When I saw the newly installed metal detector, I broke out into a cold sweat. What if it picked up the silver strips in the money?

"Please let me get through," I prayed. "I'll never put any store in material wealth again, just please let me out."

I urged Jeremy to push to the front of the queue and go through with the children, being sure to put the pushchair through the detector. It would either go off and hopefully blow a fuse, or, like most things in Libya, it wouldn't function at all. It remained silent, and with sweat dripping down my face I raced through, ran across the tarmac and flew up the steps of the plane. In theory, we were still on Libyan territory, in practice, I could not believe that we'd be thrown off the plane.

16 ENGLAND

We landed at Heathrow to be welcomed by a fine, cold drizzle. How depressing everything looked. Kylie kept whining about going back to the sun, and I shivered in clothes, which were not warm enough for a cold English day.

Determined that we were not going to stay anywhere near my mother again, we hired a car and went down to Bath to stay with Jeremy's parents. After one night, we realized that it was never going to work with all four of us crammed into one very small bedroom, and although they were kind and welcoming, there was no way we could impose on them. We rented a small house in north Wiltshire while we considered our options. Jeremy was to contact Mohammed in Brighton and he would exchange the dirty, greasy, Dinars for sterling. How much he would give us, we weren't sure, but we had left very little in our British bank account.

It was important to get Kylie into school as quickly as possible, and quite by chance, I bumped into a lady who ran a small, private school and she would be happy to take Kylie, she was so impressed with the two well-behaved little ones. Personally I think they were both still in shock, but I didn't like to say so. What was more, the headmistress also had a large cottage to rent, not all that far from the school, would we be interested? We were.

I could hardly believe it when we found out that Forty Cottage was in the next village to my mother! What was fate trying to do to us? It was a lovely old, two-storey Jacobean stone cottage, with three bedrooms, a bright kitchen, lounge and dining room. It was just perfect and, it was fully furnished and had full central heating as well. We paid the deposit and moved in.

After exchanging the cash in Brighton, only a couple of days before Mohammed left England to settle in the States, we counted up what we had left. Three suitcases of clothes and assorted toiletries, one wooden box of toys, a sewing machine and eight thousand pounds in cash. It was not a lot to show for over five years hard work when we'd been earning such huge salaries. Ever optimistic as usual, Jeremy looked on the bright side and said we were young enough to start over.

1980 in Britain saw unemployment go over three million and Jeremy made it one more. This time, we did sign on the dole, but we would have to wait several weeks before we saw any benefits. This didn't worry us too much, as we felt sure we'd get work before our money ran out.

Each day fell into a routine. Drop Kylie off at school, then Dana at the village playgroup, then go buy the newspapers. Read every job advert, list them in order of preference and type up a CV. I typed solidly most days. Three copies at a time, the top one for jobs that sounded suitable, the first carbon copy for those less exciting, and the second carbon copy for those applied for in desperation. In all, Jeremy must have applied for hundreds of different jobs.

To begin with, we chose those in countries we fancied, for we'd no intentions of staying in Britain, I couldn't take the chance that my mother would try to run or ruin our lives. For over six months we applied and applied and applied for work, until our reserves were alarmingly low. It didn't take too much to slip back into careful living, but the heating bill cost a fortune and we really felt the cold.

I decided to look for work and within a few days, I was offered two weeks temporary work in one of the village schools and I breathed a sigh of relief. That was followed by a post in a school for ESN (S) children – educationally sub normal (severe) as it was known in those days. I really hated my new job. I had a class of only six children but each one was a handful. I was miserable every minute I was in the classroom and I was there for a year. I was relieved when I was not offered the permanent post, but transferred to supply teaching instead which I did enjoy.

During this spell we had one small indulgence. I took a lesson once a week at a local riding school and the children came along as well. They put Dana in a special basket on the back of an old, tired, hack which only came up to my knees, as it plodded round and round the ring. Sometimes she fell asleep, but she always enjoyed the lesson. Kylie was more of an aspiring cowboy, but in the end, the horse was firmly in charge and she had little or no effect on it at all, but she never fell off either.

Ultimately, it was impossible to ignore my mother, and we would visit occasionally. She blew hot and cold, and on one occasion, she refused to talk to me for several months. I can't remember how I upset her, but I remember she cut me dead in the street, which puzzled Kylie who cried,

"That's Granny, hello Granny! Why doesn't she say hello to me?" and she promptly burst into tears.

We saw a lot more of Paul, who popped round as frequently as he could escape. My mother was giving him a hell of a life, and I guess I should have felt vindicated in one way, but it didn't work like that. He wasn't allowed to see his best friend Lionel and even one drink at the pub with Jeremy was frowned on. If my mother guessed that he was going to defy her and go out anyway, she would hide his glasses and car keys so that he could not drive. He was also subjected to days and days of silence. Several times Paul appeared on our doorstep in tears and we would feel very old and wise as we tried to comfort and counsel him as best we could.

On one memorable occasion, he rebelled. The three of us decided to take a picnic to the horse trials at Badminton the next day. The Queen was going to be there and I wanted the children to see her. It would be an exciting day out. We arranged to meet Paul and Mother early the next morning and I'd pack up the food and we'd go in Paul's car.

Nine and then ten o'clock came and went. Their phone was constantly engaged and it was not until nearly eleven when Paul arrived. Mother had been furious that she hadn't been consulted as to whether she wanted to go. She had screaming tantrums, until at last Paul had had enough and walked out.

We had a super day out at Badminton. Kylie refused to believe she saw the Queen, since queens wore crowns, not headscarves, but all day long I knew how Paul felt; a deep fear of what he would face on his return. It had happened to me too, so many times.

How can I possibly explain what a hold this woman had over people? The misery she put us through, despite the smiling and gracious face she gave to the rest of the world. Should you tell anyone the truth, it was enough to make you out a liar and a troublemaker. In those days we were all so keen on keeping up appearances of normality to the outside world. There was one row after another, but as much as Jeremy and I tried to keep our distance, somehow we always seemed to get dragged in.

On the financial front, things were getting desperate. The money I was earning was not enough to finance all our needs and Mother kept suggesting we apply for a council house and live off Social Security, while she offered to pay Kylie's private school fees. I refused, I felt it would be giving up altogether. Paul came to the rescue and gave us the money to refill the heating oil, and we took Kylie out of the very expensive private school and sent her to my old school instead, it was still private, but much cheaper. I confess to reacting to my mother's vicious comments about allowing my child to receive a public education. I grabbed at what little pride I had.

Jeremy's next endeavor was photography. He purchased an old second hand printing and developing machine, and took pictures of local Cotswold scenes. They were very good, but sadly, they didn't sell, though I traipsed from shop to shop offering them for sale.

It was a full sixteen months before Jeremy finally had a hopeful reply to one of his job applications. In all honesty, we had turned down two jobs, one in Nigeria and the other in South Africa. About the former, we'd heard lots of tales of how dangerous it was and that all foreigners were herded into compounds. As regards the latter, we didn't approve of apartheid and would have nothing to do with a minority government rule.

Returning from the interview, Jeremy announced he'd been offered a job in Botswana, if he could arrange all the paperwork quickly.

"Where's Botswana?" We looked it up on the map. Lying north of South Africa, south of Rhodesia, recently renamed Zimbabwe, and touching on Zambia, it was crossed by the tropic of Capricorn and looked hot.

"Let's go for it," I said.

It was only a couple of days until the Easter weekend and in that time we had to obtain references, receive inoculations and assemble a host of other paperwork. We had also to get references from a Minister of the Church, or a Justice of the Peace. We didn't know either personally, but never daunted, Jeremy succeeded in persuading the local parish priest to put in a good word for us in return for a series of photographic portraits of the local church.

Jeremy flew off to get settled in and the girls and I were to follow him a couple of weeks later.

During this time, my grandmother died and I was grateful that I was there for the funeral. It was so sad to see the few possessions we gathered up from the old folk's home. I cried for a long time, as she was a dear, gentle soul and I had so very few relatives. Worse was to come. Paul told me that he had been diagnosed with pancreatic cancer. There was no cure, no bits they could cut out to stop it spreading. He was only expected to live for another few months.

Once again, I packed up and sold off what we couldn't take. Four weeks later, Mother and Paul took us to Heathrow and I clung tightly to Paul as we said our final goodbye, I knew I'd never see him again.

The children and I boarded the plane, and took off for Johannesburg and then a connecting flight to Botswana where Jeremy met us in Gaborone. Yet another country, yet another new start, but I was riddled with guilt thinking of my mother and what she was about to go through. I also felt so sad about Paul, I really loved him and it was heartbreaking that he had not had a happy life these last years while married to my mother.

17 GABORONE, BOTSWANA

Standing in Gaborone airport surrounded by 91 kilos of luggage I prayed that they'd let us in. Reluctantly the immigration officer waved us in the direction of the exit door, and once again, the family was re-united.

Before I left to fly out to Botswana, Paul asked me to write home once a week and I agreed. I wanted to keep in touch with him, as we'd grown very close, and it was the best I could do to share our experiences of another new country. That very last hug at the airport was so hard; I just hoped that my letters home might cheer him up a little.

Since my mother has returned all the letters I ever wrote home while I was living abroad, it's helped remind me of our experiences, especially when we first arrived. The reason for giving them back to me was that she wasn't really interested, and my letters from overseas were cluttering up the house. Beside the letters on the bed was every single Christmas and birthday present I had ever given her. She did not want those either.

Gaborone
11th June 1981
Dear Paul and Mum,

Sorry not to have written before, but I have been up to my eyes finding my way around and getting settled in. I was exhausted when I arrived as the children would not go to sleep on the plane, and Kylie was quite determined to stay up for the film that didn't start until after midnight. In the end, we had about three hours catnap during which the children slept on me and I kept waking up all numb.

However, we arrived at last, Jeremy was waiting for us at the airport, and I sent the children on through to him.

There is so much news that I don't know where to begin. Later I will send you the guide book they have on Botswana and that gives you all the facts and figures, but my first impression is that it's cold here.

Jeremy assures me that it started on the day I arrived, but it's freezing in the morning and one day we woke to find frost on the car! By mid morning, it's warmed up and it's warmer out of doors than in.

So it's just the climate at the moment to go down with a cold. I wish now I had brought more winter clothes, but the children don't seem to feel it as much as I do. This weather lasts for about two months, then in September it's warm again, remember it is mid winter here in the southern hemisphere.

The house we're in is very nice, three bedrooms, a lounge and a dining room, plus kitchen and bathroom of course. It is beautifully furnished and the children have been very good, mainly because they're out of doors all the time.

We are house-sitting at the moment, as the owner is in the States, until the company finds a place for us to live. But we will be here for three months.

We have a temporary maid who doesn't speak much English. The usual house girl has gone away to have a baby and this is her official replacement, so we are stuck with each other regardless, but she is very willing and cheerful. Luckily, we get on, but it's obvious she has never done this kind of work before. I had to show her how to use a can opener, how to use the kitchen sink with washing up liquid after I found her rinsing the dishes over the drain outside. I watched in horror as she went down on hands and knees with a dustpan and brush to clean the floors and carpets and introduced her to the vacuum cleaner. She shrieked and ran and hid behind the sofa. It took a lot of coaxing to get her near the machine, but once she saw what it did there was no stopping her.

Now, she is starting at 6 am and waking the whole house with the vacuum and she doesn't stop all day. I have tried to cut down her work hours, but she expects to expect to start at 5 am and only finish around 10 pm. I tried to explain as best I could, that eight hours a day is quite enough and besides having Thursday afternoons off, she is free on Sundays as well.

The main problem here is schooling. I was absolutely horrified when I arrived, and perhaps Jeremy had not been totally honest, as I understood as soon as I started teaching, the children would get in automatically. However, now is one of those times when they don't need teachers and both schools are fully staffed. I have been asked to go on supply later this term, but I won't unless they take the children too.

Kylie has made friends with a little girl named Claire, who is the same age and very bright and we are hoping the competition will be good for her. My eldest is totally disinclined to work and I could get nothing out of her the first week teaching her myself.

Jeremy has purchased a Toyota Land Cruiser for me, very old, battered and bent, with a hunting seat welded into the back bin. It took a bit of courage to climb up into it and try to drive it. I'd refused to drive it last week, until Jeremy had time to show me how. I used the company car a couple of times, but I can now swing the Cruiser round corners like a pro, helped by two things, the speed limit in town is 50 kms an hour and there's not an awful lot of traffic, so no traffic jams.

Jeremy got his work permit last Friday, it's for two years and with it, the residence visa as it all comes together. None of the hassle and delays we have come to expect in the past.

We have taken up horse riding again, but because we're watching the pennies, I only go for one ride a week, and the children have one as well. Anyway, the lessons are far cheaper here than in UK, and my first try was last Friday morning when we went for what is called an outride, or hack. I admitted I had ridden before so I went in the intermediate class, but it was not quite what I expected. We went like bats out of hell on tiny tracks with thorn bushes either side. It reminded me of the stories of racing over the African veldt.

Kylie and Dana had their lessons in the large outdoor ring and Kylie did really well and had some control over her horse at last. Dana felt that the horses were a bit big, as they don't have little ones here, but she is still keen to go.

We go to bed quite early at night, around tenish, there's no TV, but Jeremy's hours are 8 until 1 and again from 2 until 5. He likes his new job very much, selling business machines is different from the earth moving stuff, but we won't make pots of money. We have to pay a monthly water bill and also have to pay for our electricity, which is at the highest rate in the world. Most places run partly on solar power and we all have panels on the roof and of course, there are the school fees to pay as well.

Tomorrow we are going to Francistown for the weekend. Jeremy has some business at the branch office there and we are staying at the company house where the manager lives. We're leaving at lunchtime and will come back on Sunday morning. It's 485 kilometres north, so it will give us a chance to see some of the countryside.

We'll be moving to our own place in a couple of months. It's not as nice as this one, but solar powered, which will make an enormous difference to our electricity bills. In a fair sized house, it's not unusual to pay £87 a month! The only drawback to the new place is that it only has a very tiny garden at the front and a tiny one at the rear. Not a good idea with a dog and two children in this climate where a garden is very important. Still we have a bit of time to look around and if we don't find anything better then we can always move in until we do.

We were warned about the high price of electricity and we were warned about the lack of fresh fruit and vegetables. But there's loads of fresh stuff on sale and it's cheap as well. Most things come in from South Africa and things seem to be much cheaper there. You can get just about everything here, and for anything else, you just pop over the border. The trip to Johannesburg takes about three and a half hours and most people seem to go about once a month or so.

Gaborone
17 June 1981
Dear Mum and Paul,

Kylie had a terrific row with Jeremy the other day and then a long, private talk, I wasn't included and now things are back to normal. She's got impossible and I make no pretensions about knowing how to cope with her.

But in general both the girls have settled down and they love it here. It's still cold when the sun goes down, but they spend most of the time out of doors and are beginning to make friends.

Jeremy is getting to know lots of influential people, both black and white, and we are finding out as much as we can about things.

Our boxes of stuff from UK have not arrived yet. I wish we knew the name of the boat they're on so we could trace them. It seems there are big delays into Durban harbour at the moment, and then they have to be taken to a central distribution point in Johannesburg.

I put my foot through the bottom of the Land Cruiser yesterday, so now it's in the garage having a plate welded under the driver's seat. I guess it could have been a lot worse, at least it was only my foot! I still think it was a bargain buy, it cost almost nothing and it's amazing where the thing will drive, places you would never dare take a car!

We had a lovely time in Francistown and went to the Francistown Club where we had a super Korean meal. On the Saturday night, we went to a local amateur production, which was very good. I hardly saw the girls over the weekend as the nanny employed by our hosts took them over. Kylie was particularly put out, but I explained that it was our turn to have some fun. She sulked for several hours I understand, but thankfully, I was not there to see it!

In later years, when I was on leave in England, I learned not to talk too much about our *servants* in Africa. It evoked looks of disgust and on one occasion a fierce argument about the undying remnants of colonialism and how we were perpetuating the ills of that era, although in fact we were contributing enormously to the economy. The girl I had inherited with the house was cheerful and enthusiastic. She was very fond of the children and Dana had already discovered how to sidle up to 'Mrs Tebling' and get illicit biscuits and fizzy drinks that were on the list of rare treats.

Gaborone
24 June 1981
Dear Paul and Mum,

We drove over the border to have a 'look see' at South Africa. I'd never seen such a large supermarket before. It stretched for miles in either direction and had over fifty check-out points. I guess I should have guessed by the size of the car park outside, but it was truly enormous. I'd suffered feelings of inadequacy when I went back to UK after Libya, but how do you choose from seven different kinds of butter when you only ever had a choice of one before? Here there were seventy kinds of butter and just about everything else. I just stood and stared and this was Africa, the Dark Continent?

We had a shopping list, kindly provided by our new friends, and it took longer than expected to find and decide on the purchases. Not only was there the main supermarket, but a string of other shops around the edge. I guess you could buy anything there under one roof, literally, from a loaf of bread to building materials and pet snakes.

Most of the products were completely unknown to me and the stuff I had to buy was strange, much of it is manufactured in the UK, but obviously for export only.

We got directions back to the South African/Botswana border gate, and set off back home. It was about 4 pm when we realized we'd been given the wrong directions, or we were too stupid to interpret them correctly.

"Just keep the mountains on your left and you can't go wrong," we were told.

How delightfully African, we thought. But somewhere along the way, the mountains disappeared and we realized that we were traveling in the opposite direction and had covered an extra 200 kilometres. We ran low on petrol and gave a sigh of relief as we found a petrol station. Unknown to us, it's illegal to buy petrol from 12 pm on Saturday until Monday morning, and it's also illegal to carry a spare can in the boot without a special permit. This was news to us, as for our trip to Francistown, we'd taken extra fuel, since there were no petrol stations on the way. The South African law is in place to reduce petrol consumption for weekend outings, remember, there is an international embargo.

This time, we were in luck, hearing our story and realizing we were just ignorant tourists, the garage owner put in a few litres and we drove hell for leather to the border. Well this time we hoped we were on the right road, but it was little help to stop and ask the locals. Ask anyone in UK the way from Inverness to Southampton and they will have a vague idea, but here in the rural areas of northern SA no one seemed to have any idea of anywhere outside their farming community.

Thinking back, I think we only singled out the village idiots to ask for directions, especially when one replied, "Botswana? Never heard of it!"

Finally, we made it back to the border gate, but missed the closing by twenty minutes so we had to spend the night in the car!

Unfortunately Mother did not see the funny side of this as her comments scrawled at the bottom of Paul's letter were pretty scathing. She said they giggled for hours over my bad spelling. I wasn't sure what to write that would not bring down a torrent of criticism and contempt. I hesitated to tell her that once again Jeremy had been promoted and we were being relocated to Francistown 400 kilometres further north.

It was good to hear that the company was a founder member of the British School in Francistown and both children would gain immediate entry, and there was a vacant teaching post, I could start next month. I asked Mrs Tebling if she would like to come with us and she was delighted.

Through my letters, I made many enquiries as to how Paul's treatment was going and tried to sound upbeat and hopeful that he would beat the cancer. It was during this phase that perhaps I had the most frequent postal contact with my mother, though it was usually Paul who replied to my letters.

We'd settled in well in Gaborone and I was of two minds whether I wanted to go and live in Francistown. One thing I would miss was the riding, we all looked forward to our weekly lesson. I needn't have worried about that. It was typical of Jeremy that he walked in one evening and announced that he had just purchased two horses.

"You bought horses?"

"Yes, from the stables where you go riding."

"But what horses, what do you know about horses, except you're frightened of them?"

"Well I'll get used to them. I asked which one the kids rode and which one you liked best and I only paid £60 for Kojak and £150 for Calypso. Hell, we could get £100 back if we flogged them for horsemeat," he added tactlessly.

"Not in front of the children! What about tack and all that stuff, and where are we going to keep them? The Francistown bungalow has only got a medium sized garden and...and what if they fell into the pool?"

"All sorted," answered Jeremy airily. "There's a ranch outside town where they can stay. No problem.

The children were over the moon, their very own pony! How would we get them 400 kilometres north? There were no horseboxes in Gaborone, or, as far as I could discover, anywhere else in Botswana.

But fate was pushing us firmly in one direction, for a newly arrived expatriate turned up the following week, and brought both horse and horsebox to Gaborone. It would be no trouble to lend it to us for our journey north.

Jeremy had one photography commission while in Gaborone, to take a picture of a teacher in Lobatse who'd written a radio play chosen for the International Radio Festival in Milan. They published the picture in the South African TV Times.

It was time to leave, after a round of braais or b-b-q's to wish us well on our way. Jeremy's title was now 'General Manager Northern Botswana, Technical Manager and Transport Manager, Botswana'. He was regarded as the whiz kid, who could do no wrong and rushed around making himself popular and liked by everyone. I was so proud of him. Maybe this time it would work out? I really should have known better.

18 FRANCISTOWN, BOTSWANA

We moved into yet another new house owned by the company, it came with the job and it was even possible to walk to school as it was quicker than getting the car out and driving there. But hot water on tap was another matter entirely. This was accomplished by lighting a fire in a stone structure called a Rhodesian boiler outside the back door. First you had to load in the wood and set fire to it, and then it took several hours for it to get hot enough to heat the water in the forty five gallon oil drum on the top, which then drained into the hot water tank hidden somewhere under the roof tiles. The answer was to install a solar panel on the roof and this was duly done, by a plethora of builders who took days and days and, I feared, threatened to move in as well.

We had admired the pool on our arrival and the children were thrilled to be able to swim again. But much to our dismay, after about a week, it turned bright green and we couldn't understand it. When we told our neighbours Nan and Doug about this, they laughed so hard the tears ran down their cheeks. Didn't we know about Chlorine? And acid and the PH balance? No. I suppose it was stupid, but it never entered our heads that pools took hours of work and lots and lots of money to stay bright blue and sparkly.

After a few weeks Nthebeleng – Mrs Tebling, asked if her new boyfriend could come up and stay with her in her quarters. I had no problem with that at first, until he put her on the game in the shamba outside the back door. She had to go, I had the children to think of. I was really very fond of her, but I couldn't have her looking after the children while working as the local prostitute. I suggested that both her boyfriend and her customers go away, but she didn't seem too keen on that, so clutching a month's severance pay, both Nthebeleng and boyfriend departed.

There followed in quick succession a number of hopeful housemaids desperately seeking work. Some lasted a day or so, others a couple of weeks. After flexing my muscles and firing Nthebeleng, I found that easier and easier as time went on. Some drank, others stole money or clothes, some were suffering from ill health, coughing and spluttering through the day, while others didn't understand a word of English.

I was about to tear my hair out when Ester came along. She was the answer to all my prayers and she stayed with us all the time we were in Botswana. She was great with the children, liked to cook and was clean, neat and efficient. For once, I threw caution to the winds and gave her an excellent salary, hoping no one else would find out.

The ponies, or rather pony and horse, seemed happy in their new home at the Lady Mary Ranch and we traveled out to see them in the afternoons. School was from 7.30 in the morning until 1 pm and both children settled in happily, although the yellow and green uniform didn't suit their colouring at all and made them both look bilious. I was also back in the classroom and loved my teaching and the children were happy and contented. But for how long?

The next development started innocently one day after school, when Kylie wandered into my classroom with a friend.

"Kylie says she has a horse," Fiona challenged me.

"Well, yes, she does," I replied.

"Where is it? I've not seen it." Fiona was not convinced.

"We keep two of them up on Lady Mary Ranch,"

"When can I see them?" asked Fiona.

"Well ask your mummy and if she agrees, you can come up one afternoon, and maybe you would like to go for a ride?"

Fiona said no more, but the next afternoon she was back, dragging her mother by the hand. We took Fiona riding several times and she seemed to enjoy herself, it was difficult to tell, but then one day she announced,

"My mother will pay you if you give me lessons." Brilliant! This was a way to offset the expense of the horse feed and keep, as we were paying a small rent for the stabling. The only problem was, I had no idea how to teach anyone to ride. I never admitted to my children that much as I loved riding, I was very wary of the horses and I never, ever took any chances. A gentle canter was as fast as I wanted to go, and bless him, Jeremy had chosen a gem in Kojak. He was fifteen hands high, but his legs were never very good. It must have been caused by all those years herding cattle across Botswana to the slaughter house in Lobatse. Here they were reconstituted into cans of corned beef, the cows that is, not the horses. Kojak was as lazy as a horse can be, and obviously sensed how nervous I was.

Calypso the dark bay pony was a different kettle of fish, bouncy, a real go getter and adult hater. However, I wasn't scared of riding him, at only fourteen hands it wasn't too far to fall. I also had the excuse of letting the children look after him, as he was ready to kick any adult who came too close.

While I was debating what to do about offering riding lessons, we received the news that the ponies would have to be moved. The South African landowner had arrived on the ranch and wanted them off. What now? Always trust Jeremy. Within twenty four hours, he'd found a piece of land out by the Inchwe River and we could start building stables that weekend. And that's just what we did. Using an enormous number of gum poles and wood planks, and with the help of lots of new friends, we put up three stables and fenced in a large area that was to become the riding school.

I now had to find someone to look after them and, as if by magic, a smiling, young African appeared, announced his name was Hardstone and he'd take over from here.

After all this effort, it was difficult not to offer riding lessons to the community at large and there was no going back when the Headmaster called me in and asked me to set up classes for the afternoon, as this would be my out of school activity that all the teachers were supposed to do one afternoon a week.

So I said goodbye to the netball team and put up a notice offering riding lessons. I phoned a friend in Gaborone and asked her to find out if there were any books on the subject, as there was no library in Francistown. A few weeks later a parcel arrived containing *the British Pony Club Hand book*. I devoured it over breakfast, lunch and supper, even in the bath. I stuffed it down my jeans to refer to during lessons and hoped for the best.

I was still teaching every morning, but at 2 pm I was waiting outside school for the customers who all clambered into the back bin of the Land Cruiser and off we went. It wasn't long before I found that I had so many children that we urgently needed more horses. We scoured Botswana but they were not easy to find, however over the next couple of years we acquired ten more, most of which were wrecks and needed to be nursed back to health before I could use them in the riding school.

The lessons became more and more popular, and during the holidays I held adult classes early in the mornings, all children, including my own were banned, and I held tiny tot lessons for the under fives in the afternoons. Like Dana, several of them fell asleep on horseback, but I made sure that one or two of the older children led each one. News spread like wildfire that there was now a riding school - what a grand name for my appalling establishment - and we were offered another pony to buy. I accepted and Cornflakes joined the motley crew that made up our menagerie.

If the truth be known, I ran the worst riding school in the world. Lessons included interesting additions such as, 'how to fall off your horse safely onto an old mattress', and 'how to load your pony into a Chibuku Beer truck' – necessary for gymkhanas. We also cleaned tack and mucked out when half the ponies were laid off after their African horse sickness inoculations.

The traditional housing areas were on the outskirts of town, some built of stone, but most constructed in the time old methods, mud mixed with cow dung. We used to weave the horses through the small dwellings on our outrides, and the locals, always cheerful and smiling, would come out to greet us. They had so little, yet they appeared content. I came to understand that as far as the men were concerned, as long as you had a roof, food and a woman for today, tomorrow could take care of itself.

My next letter home was written in the November, still asking when Mother and Paul were coming out to see us, as they had promised to make the trip while he was still well enough. I said that I was working hard, very tired with two jobs and we had acquired a kitten for Kylie. She had set her heart on it and so of course that meant one for Dana as well.

I had hoped that life had settled down at last. What a difference to the previous year, when we'd run out of money, with no work and no future. Now, we were mixing with lots of friendly people, Jeremy was doing brilliantly in his job, making the first profits for years, and the children were happy and settled. Kylie was still a bit of a problem, but Dana was happy and looking forward to going into the reception class in January.

At last, the boxes of possessions had arrived from UK, along with the photo processor and we already had several people keeping their films for us to develop. We were beginning to settle in at last.

The only small cloud on the horizon were rumours that maybe Jeremy might be promoted and moved back to Gaborone to take over the company for the whole country. It made me feel a little unsettled, but for the moment I would ignore that and take each day as it came.

However the black clouds didn't go away completely, as another problem arose. We had of course automatically become members of the Francistown Club, a lone colonial bastion on the outskirts of town. We usually went on a Friday night, and spent a few hours in the bar and had a meal. All the kids played in the garden and pestered Mama Kim who was famous for her delicious spring rolls.

But Jeremy started visiting the Club after work more and more often and his drinking became heavier and heavier. He didn't get drunk every time we went out, but I never knew if 'tonight was the night'. I came to dread social occasions, as Jeremy got very loud and extremely aggressive when he'd had too much alcohol, and there was never any chance that I could take him by the arm and lead him out to the car. Driving was also a problem, as he'd never let me get behind the wheel, no matter how drunk he was. How we got home in one piece on those occasions I'll never know.

Sometimes he would stagger home late at night weaving the truck up the lane. I had visions of Libya all over again. If he hurt or killed someone in Botswana, the law stated the driver was liable to pay compensation to the bereaved family forever.

I never tried to reason with him when he was in this state, as he quickly turned nasty and threatened me with violence, although I have to admit he only hit me once. I would remain calm, scared that the girls would wake up, and was as docile as possible. Even the next morning I would only mention it tentatively, as Jeremy was well known for his quick temper and I was scared of provoking him. Perhaps the years of subservience to my mother made me an even bigger coward, but I was determined the children would not find out. I'd seen the embarrassment it caused other children when their parents got drunk or argued in public.

I can see from my letters home that life was quite hard, we didn't have an easy time. The electricity supply became intermittent all over town and the water was switched off for several hours a day. I had really enjoyed the heat, but was told the climate went in seven year cycles and this was the middle phase when the drought was quite severe. We'd not seen any rain since we arrived, so we thought this was the normal state of affairs.

The drinking problem came to a head late one night when friends dropped round to say that everyone was out searching for Jeremy, who'd 'borrowed' a car and was careering all over the golf course in it, and this was after he'd tried to slit his wrists in the men's loo at the Club.

Jeremy, committing suicide? Why? I paced up and down the lounge. Ester had gone out and I couldn't leave the children on their own. I knew they would bring Jeremy home when they found him.

It was several hours later when he staggered through the door and collapsed. I put a blanket over him, checked the bandages someone had wound round his wrists, stuffed a pillow under his head and went to bed. But I couldn't sleep. What was going on that I didn't know about? Life had seemed just fine, hard work yes, but we were beginning to make progress. Or were we?

The following morning Jeremy denied the suicide attempt. He said he'd just got so mad he'd punched a hole through the window and accidentally cut his wrists on the jagged glass. He was of course suspended from the Club, not for breaking the window, but for driving over the golf course. We had to pay a hefty amount to repair the damage to the fairways where Jeremy had driven the 'borrowed' car.

It was explained to everyone we knew that Jeremy had had a breakdown. He went to see a psychiatrist, the only one in Francistown of course, who said it was the backlash from months of unemployment in UK and the worry of the stability of the job here. He took two weeks off work and, on the bright side, I was unlikely to become a golf widow, no Club, no golf. After that, the drinking eased up for a while, but I was nervous about the 'next time'. It was also a strain trying to pretend, especially to the children, that everything was normal and explaining why we no longer went to the Club with everyone else on a Friday night.

At least I had work to keep me occupied. I taught at school every morning, taught riding every afternoon, helped Jeremy in his photographic lab in the evenings and held an adult lesson on Saturday mornings. Even Sundays were busy, as we held an outride, or hack for adults and tourists. Jeremy would drive the Land Cruiser to a pre-determined spot and set up a good old-fashioned English breakfast. We'd arrive on horseback, eat and then amble home and have a few drinks.

I continued to write weekly letters, addressed to Mother and Paul, but it was always Paul who wrote back, my mother never did. I tried to sound as optimistic as I could, but as 1982 dawned, it became obvious they were not coming out to visit us after all. The next few months were uneventful and it was not until June that the axe fell.

19 ON OUR OWN

Jeremy was given a choice, a return ticket back to the UK or three months salary. He was given two hours to make his decision. He came straight round to school, where I left my class to hear the worst possible news. We were both in a mild state of shock. There was very little decision to make. If we returned home, then we would arrive flat broke, with nowhere to live and quite possibly leave debts behind in Botswana. We would, once again, join the dole queue behind three million other hopefuls. It meant re-packing all our stuff and selling the horses, moving the children to yet another school and I had signed a two year teaching contract at the school, which offered a 25% gratuity.

If we stayed, we had a very small income from the stables, Jeremy could possibly find work, rents were relatively cheap and we had made lots of friends. We would stay and throw in our lot in Africa. We would cope somehow. It seemed hard, we had been in Botswana for less than eighteen months and, as before, it seemed as if each time we picked ourselves up, we were promptly knocked down again. I have no idea why the company decided to let Jeremy go, in fact I have no idea why he lost so many jobs, he always seemed to be doing so well and then came the almost inevitable parting of the ways.

I agonized for hours wondering if this was our fault. What exactly were we doing wrong? It wasn't lack of hard work, I knew that, but it was very difficult not to feel more than a little paranoid.

Just as we were reeling from this shock, disaster struck again. When I arrived at the stables next day, it was to see that Kojak had lost most of his tail and his newly grown mane.

Hardstone rolled his eyes and said the place was cursed, they wanted my horses for *muti* as it would make powerful medicine. I didn't know what to do. In all the time Hardstone worked for me, I had never really trusted him. He was too sharp, too smooth and I had to check on him continually.

The following day, things got worse. Kojak was obviously in pain, his belly was hugely distended. I walked him round and round and round while sending Hardstone off to get the vet. I knew that if Kojak was suffering from colic and lay down, then he wouldn't get up again. The vet confirmed my amateur diagnosis, but how could he possibly have colic? Horses get this from gorging themselves on too much rich, green grass. The area around here was mostly barren with small prickly shrubs. I fed my horses on horse nuts and other hard food purchased at the local farmers co-op, and hay I imported from Zimbabwe. We dosed him and he seemed to perk up a bit, so I led him back into his stable for the night. Next day he was dead. I burst into tears. It was all too much, I had worked so hard, and put so much time and effort into the stables and Kojak was only twelve years old, it didn't seem fair.

"Look Candy," said Hardstone. She had the same symptoms. This time the vet gave her enormous doses of medicine and I walked her right through the night, but just before the sun came up, she stumbled over for the last time and died in my arms.

"I'm closing the riding school and selling off the rest of the horses," I announced at breakfast. I didn't really mean it, how could I close the stables when we desperately needed the extra money? The children also burst into tears and begged me not to. I didn't have the heart to follow through, but how could we stand by and watch the rest of the horses die one by one? How potent was African medicine? How broad a hint did we need?

Since we were going to lose the house anyway as it went with the job, Jeremy went out and found a bungalow on a plot or smallholding of ten acres that would house both the horses and us. It was on the banks of the Tati River, had five storerooms at the bottom of the extremely large garden and once again, we dismantled the stables and re-built them inside our perimeter fence.

"Just anyone try and hurt them now," I muttered. I could see the stables from the house and I was damned if anyone would get close to them.

Once again, we packed up our belongings and drove across town, through a small shack-land area and into our new home. We still had two chairs and a coffee table but little else and precious little money to buy anything.

Francistown
17 August 1982
Dear Mum and Paul,

A lot has happened since I last wrote. We moved into the new house on 31st July and for the first eleven days we had no electricity, so that slowed us up and we were not able to work as fast as we wanted. We never thought the oil lamps we bought in England for 'atmosphere' would actually be in proper use. Of course they sell them here for the locals, but not quite as smart as ours!

Well I cheerfully queued up with all the locals on Saturday to buy my four bottles of paraffin. The problem was that they'd disconnected the old generator from the house, but they hadn't connected us to the mains, which for some unknown reason is a three-phase system and there are no meter boxes in the country. Hence the delay, and since only a small percentage of homes have electricity, the electricity people see no rush whatsoever.

We had all the water piping in the garden ripped up, it works from a borehole on a water pump, but something was wrong. When we lit the boiler, yes back to the old Rhodesian boiler again, the loo flushed boiling hot water and the only other place to have hot water was the servants' quarters. Jeremy went deep purple when he realized that they were all bathing in the afternoons in work time in hot water from proper taps in the baths, while we smelled very badly indeed. So he ruthlessly cut off their hot water supply and re-routed it back to us.

You should have heard the cheers when the power was connected, you'd have thought we'd never had it before instead of suffering for a mere eleven days!

As you know, we had little or no furniture. Well first we bought a double bed, Jeremy insisted that we needed a good night's sleep. The company sold us the bunk beds for the children and a friend sent down an 'old' electric cooker and a fridge with a broken door from the company warehouse. There was a little note on the truck from the technicians in the Gaborone workshops, saying they hoped we liked the cooker. It's gas and it's brand new! We were very touched, and it only took Jeremy ten minutes to fix the fridge door.

Jeremy bought some wood and knocked up some wall units, nothing smart, but two friends are off to copy his idea. Now we have somewhere to put all our books and ornaments. Then Jeremy made a refectory table from railway sleepers, all doweled, but it's so solid and kid proof that an H-bomb wouldn't destroy it. The stuff in the kitchen is on planks on cardboard boxes, but there is one built-in cupboard, so we're not doing too badly.

We have a three-piece suite on loan, also a kitchen table and a bench, I am sitting on it right now and we also have four garden chairs of our own, so we are getting very posh. We may even borrow a spare bed!

We've fenced in three acres around the house, putting in extra barbed wire to protect the equipment, and I've planted cabbage, onions, broccoli, kale, tomatoes, beans, aubergines, peppers, carrots and alfalfa, the last one for the horses. Already the shoots are showing.

At the back, we've finished the office, all painted, and this typewriter, a super electric, fell out of the back of the company junk room, pushed by dissatisfied and outraged technicians. Everyone says how upset they are that Jeremy is no longer working in the company.

The local hotel found two desks it didn't want, and I have started painting the woodwork shop. Jeremy has put an air conditioner in the lab, which arrived from a local gold mine, in return for a crate of beer, and we've taken water from the second tank to the lab. We found an old sink and water heater in the garden and Jeremy has plumbed it all in and it works beautifully. As soon as we get the electricity in there, we will take a trip to Johannesburg for four days to buy the chemicals and photo paper and the framing material is on order. We are almost ready to open our photographic processing business.

This last month I made a good profit on the stables, more than I earn teaching, so I'm really pleased. That will help fund the trip to SA.

We had a suspicious dog in the yard the other night. We thought it might be rabid as it was frothing at the mouth. Jeremy took a pot shot at it, but missed. However, it was shot on a farm nearby the next morning.

I was very excited at having my own post box key at last, instead of waiting for Jeremy to bring the mail back from the office, he was always forgetting. However, after only two days, he lost the key, so I have to apply for a new one and as it has to come from SA, it will take four weeks. In the meantime, I have to queue in the post office with the receipt slip and that can take anything up to an hour or more.
Love,
Lucy xxx.

There was only one small hurdle to overcome and that was Jeremy's application for a work permit. Since I was under contract, in theory that should allow him to stay, but you never know in an African country, where the women are still second, if not third class citizens. We had to wait a long time until it finally came through.

We completed converting the out buildings and set up the processing and developing equipment in one, a wood store in another and the framing equipment in the third. It seemed that everyone we knew in Francistown had films for processing and developing and there was certainly plenty of work.

The only problem was getting supplies, as everything had to come from Johannesburg and the extra cartage made the stock quite expensive. All we had to offer was speed, we could print and develop and return in three days, where before, via Johannesburg, it took six to seven weeks. But processing the films quickly was another problem. Our machinery was not the 'develop in one hour' sort and Jeremy was working from dawn until dusk most days.

We traveled down to Johannesburg to get supplies and I worried about the children's behaviour in the shopping malls. They shrieked with delight at the automatic glass doors, running in and out to make them open and close. They disappeared up or down escalators just for the sheer hell of it, and promptly sat down on the floor of the mall when they were tired. Oh dear! Had we raised bush brats? At some point, we were going to have to civilize them. Dana screamed very loudly when I suggested that she have a ride on a mechanical horse, saying it wasn't safe. I pointed out that it was a lot safer than her own pony, which had tipped me off the previous week. I was still nursing a broken finger.

I dragged them into the changing room in one of the larger stores and tried to pour them into dresses. They giggled. All they possessed besides their school uniforms were shorts and jodhpurs. The dresses I had made for them they refused to wear, and I was hoping that if they had shop-bought ones, this might help turn them into young ladies. No such luck.

We arrived back with half our purchases, while the rest would be on the way by train a day or so later. We continued to work from dawn until late every night. But as hard as we worked, we never seemed to make much headway, there were always so many bills, and I despaired of ever getting ahead.

Another Christmas came and went in the African heat. While it's true that the sun shines brightly, there are also cold spells. Temperatures can be up in the thirties during the day and drop to fifteen at night. While this isn't exactly cold, the comparison can be quite extreme, chilly enough to make you shiver.

I'd been writing home as often as I could. I hoped that the letters cheered Paul a little, as I guessed his health was failing. He would reply with the latest news of England and the major current events that kept us on the periphery of what was going on in Europe.

I phoned home just before Christmas as we'd not heard for a few weeks and I was worried. Sometime later, I received a letter, this time written by my mother. I can't remember the phone call too clearly, nor the content of her letter, but this is my reply:

Francistown
16 January 1983
Dear Mum and Paul,

Thank you for your recent letter, though I got the idea it was written largely in demonstration of how everyone else has made it in Britain, whereas we didn't. I was extremely upset by the phone call at Christmas and for a while I thought to hell with it, I would never keep in touch or phone again.

Firstly I phoned out of love and feeling to see how you both were, especially Paul, and to wish you as happy a Christmas as you could make it. I rang to cheer you both up and settle any worries you may have about us. I rang, even though we cannot really afford it, especially as we rang Jeremy's mum too, when Dad was ill.

However all I got was a lecture as if I was about six years old. "Have you done this? Why haven't you done that? Don't you think you ought…" and so on and so on. I did not retaliate in return on the phone, you can't argue over that distance and, incidentally at that price.

I am now 34 years old, and having been married for 11 years and brought two children into the world, I am past justifying myself to anyone except myself. I don't live the life that others live in your home town, it's not the life I want, nor would it make me happy. I have never felt happy in England, it has some incredibly bad memories for me, though Jeremy and I did try to make a go of it and coupled with the cold, it is not for me. There are some deficiencies in Botswana, but this is where our present life is, and as to the future? Who knows, we may all be dead tomorrow.

So I will leave it there, but if you do want to stay in contact, please show some love, sympathy and gentle advice to us and vice versa.

Although the words I wrote sounded brave, it was much easier to do this from a distance. I would not have had the courage to say anything directly to my mother. Her words had sliced right through my fragile confidence once again and left me feeling very vulnerable.

I gathered they had not received some letters, for I continued:

I wrote nearly every week last term and because of commitments, I gave the letters to our EX gardener to post. We later discovered that these were not sent and he kept the postage money. He was fired for other reasons and when we cleared out his quarters, I found the torn letters stuffed behind his bed in a plastic bag.

In future I will find the time go to the post office myself, and wait in the enormously long queues.

It has been the hottest anyone can remember here, almost forty degrees, and even I have been suffering, and getting lots of headaches.

The film developing is going well, but not making a lot of money as yet. The belts in the processing equipment broke down and we are waiting for new ones from South Africa. We are doing our best to cope as the ones in the other machine are on their last legs.

Our water pump blew up, so for several days, we had to collect it in barrels from the village in a wheelbarrow. Eventually, the landlord installed a new electric pump for us.

They finally solved our nine or ten power cuts every day and now we only get cut off the same as Francistown, about once a week for a couple of hours.

Kylie is getting up at six every morning and riding out on the dry river bed with one of the stable hands while it's still cool. Calypso is the most important thing in her life, I only wish she would work half as hard at school.

Dana has taken a fancy to Cornflakes, he's a bit big for her, but she is trotting round the ring on her own without holding on, extremely brave when you see the size of her, she is still very tiny and the size of the horse, very large. There was no break over the holidays, as the riding school kept going full time.
Will write again soon.

By now, we had five stable lads. I really didn't need as many as that, but every so often young men would walk up the front driveway begging for work, refugees from the Zimbabwean civil war. I didn't have the heart to send them away. So our wage bill and our food bill grew and grew.

There were lighter moments, the gymkhana with the Selebi Pickwe riding school, Guy Fawkes Night, birthday parties and social evenings with good friends.

But life was hard. The harder we worked, the less we seemed to get. Unknown to me, the landlord forgot to deliver the phone bill, since the connection was still in his name, and when two or three arrived all together, we couldn't afford to pay them all at once, so it was cut off, our last contact with the outside world. But Jeremy still kept insisting that he could handle our finances.

I got up at five each morning to give a couple of riding lessons to adults before work, and had classes at five thirty pm, after I delivered my younger customers back to the school gates.

One young lady fell off a horse, broke her arm, and had to be taken to Bulawayo to have it reset. This involved a dangerous journey since Zimbabwe was generally under siege, and you had to be desperate to try driving up to Plumtree and through the border. On top of that, it cost them over a thousand Pula for the treatment and that freaked me out. What would we do if it happened to us? Right now, we couldn't even afford the phone bill!

Two of the horses went lame and we all went down with a tummy bug. I began to think we would never make it after all. It was difficult to discuss anything with Jeremy. He would fly into a rage if I tried to talk about our future, which was beginning to look decidedly bleak.

Paul died in the February of 1983 and I heard the news from a close friend of my mother. Was I going over for the funeral? I knew I should, but I was very scared, scared of being with my mother with no one to back me up, Jeremy would not be with me. What if she took my passport? It would simply be impossible for us all to go. Money wasn't the issue as my mother offered to pay for my ticket but not for anyone else in the family.

I asked for time off from school, but got nowhere. I was firmly told that if I left to go overseas then there wouldn't be a job waiting for me when I got back. I couldn't believe the Headmaster could be so mean, but he convinced me that he would tear up my contract and that meant no 25% gratuity, and I'd been hoping that would solve a lot of our financial problems.

There was another problem, Jeremy had started drinking again, not at the Club this time, although they were prepared by now to let us back in, but at some local dive. If he had trouble holding his own with proper canned or bottled beer, then he certainly couldn't handle the 'sour after three day' local brews.

I didn't know what to do. Dare I leave the children with their father? Could I trust Ester and the stable boys to keep the horses alive? Did I call the Head's bluff and go anyway? Could I afford to go? Even with a free ticket, there were going to be lots of other expenses. The answer was no to all of these, so I never returned to say my final farewells to Paul. My mother never forgave me.

I continued to write every week but she never replied. I did get letters from her friends in Ireland, but even when we eventually got the phone re-connected, she refused to talk to me. I felt very low. There was no one I could confide in, there was never any time, and if I had been worried before, it was compounded now.

Somehow children always sense when you are down, and the girls became more demanding than ever. The weather continued in the low forties, it was impossible to sleep at night and every mosquito south of the equator, equipped with pneumatic drills, made a beeline for me. I was covered from head to toe in bites, which constantly itched.

One night we were working in the lab when the dogs started to bark. Jeremy went to investigate and disturbed several men in the house who were making off with most of our belongings. We immediately phoned the local police who apologized profusely but said they were unable to come as they had no transport. They might make it out the following day and in the meantime we were not to touch anything. We then phoned friends, who rushed over, one couple transporting two very reluctant policemen. They were adamant that they could do nothing as it was dark, but an ex Selous Scout from Rhodesian army days took Jeremy off to track the perpetrators. I couldn't believe that anyone would have entered our house when we were on the premises. Ester was sleeping in the shamba, there were five stable boys living in quarters in the back yard, and we had three dogs! I also found it difficult to believe that the children had slept through the whole thing, even when the men had turned on their bedroom lights and emptied their wardrobe.

The thieves were eventually caught, not by the police but again by trackers from our community. Amazingly we were able to reclaim some of our possessions including two very expensive cameras. The men were given long jail sentences, but I never felt quite as relaxed at home after that. It had become common to see men from the Matabele tribe in Zimbabwe coming over the border to steal and raise money to buy guns to defend themselves against the organized genocide from the Shona tribe, led by President Mugabe.

Still we battled on. Jeremy turned his hand to making window frames for one client as he reckoned it wasn't so very different from making picture frames. I think we must have framed every last piece of paper and every photograph in Francistown by this time. There was one funny event when Jeremy had a run in with a local photographer. He had taken a series of pictures of his girlfriend sitting naked in the only flower bed tended by the Francistown Town Council in the main high street. In each picture she was missing a head, and the aspiring David Bailey was incensed. He accused Jeremy of sabotage, and even showing him the absence of heads on the negatives would not convince him otherwise.

That winter was cold and we scoured the plot for wood to burn in the stove at night. We also had the stable lads foraging in the bush for wood to heat the Rhodesian boiler, but as often as not, we had to make do with cold water.

Our African dream was about to come apart after all. Finally, Jeremy said that perhaps it would be wiser to move south and get a 'proper' job. I agreed, but was heart sore at the thought of losing the stables, we'd put so much time and effort into them. On the other hand, Kylie would only be able to attend primary school for a couple more years, and since there was no high school for her to go to in the neighbourhood, it would mean boarding school, in either South Africa or Zimbabwe. I wasn't keen on that, even if we could afford it. We could only just about afford the reduced fees at her present school, because I was teaching there.

Jeremy bought newspapers and began to apply for jobs all that summer. The months went by, and then he had a reply from a company in Johannesburg. Would he go down for an interview? As the children and I set off to walk the three miles to school the next day, Jeremy was speeding down the Gaborone Road dressed in the one and only suit that we'd retrieved after the robbery. He returned two days later, with a firm offer and proceeded to dismantle the lab.

"We're off to Johannesburg," he said cheerfully.

"But how can I just leave?" I asked.

"Nothing to stop you," Jeremy couldn't see a problem.

"But I'm under contract, I'll lose the gratuity and what about the horses? I can't just abandon them!" I was close to tears. "Can't they wait for you just a few more months, to give us time to sell up properly? It's almost September, we could leave at the end of November."

"I start next Monday," Jeremy replied. "Can't turn down the chance. Got to take it while we can. I may never get another job. So, are you coming with me or not?"

"Let me stay until the end of the school year and then we'll join you." I didn't feel too brave about staying in Botswana by myself, but I couldn't see any other answer. At least it would give me time to sell the riding school as a business and who knows, perhaps the money would help us get properly settled into a new life in South Africa. All thoughts of our previous doubts about living in a country with cruel apartheid laws flew out of the window, we were like a drowning man clutching at straws.

Jeremy duly departed on the Sunday, luckily he left the Land Cruiser behind, and I tried to carry on as before. It was less than a week later when I had the landlord on the front door step. Did I realize that Jeremy hadn't paid any rent for the last six months? No, I only knew about the phone bill and that had been paid. I was given notice to leave the house, but in all fairness, I could leave the stables where they were for the moment.

The children and I moved into a house in town, house sitting for a guy who had gone on long term safari. Ester came too, I would have preferred her to keep an eye on the stable lads, but she freaked out about staying on the plot without us. I tried to sell the photographic equipment and most of it went to Zimbabwean escapees, who bartered with me until the price was worth little more than peanuts.

While the population of Francistown was thrilled to have a riding school, it seemed that no one else was prepared to run it. I reluctantly took the decision to split it up and sell the ponies off as best I could.

The children were typically impossible. They objected strongly to their cosy world being turned upside down and gave me a very hard time. They missed their father, and although we'd arranged to speak to him every Wednesday evening on a neighbour's phone, they were often out, and we would sit outside the empty house and hear the phone ring inside. We knew it was Jeremy and we couldn't answer it and talk to him.

A few close friends gave me moral support and friendship, but I was very depressed. I kept asking myself what we had done wrong to deserve all this, was it our fault? Had we made the wrong decisions? I pulled myself together and was reasonably cheerful at half term when I left the children with a friend and went down to attend an interview to teach at a very upmarket private school in Pretoria.

My current Headmaster gave me a glowing reference and my only problem when I arrived was what to wear. I had nothing at all suitable for an interview at a posh establishment. I was looking at possible outfits in a large chain store when they asked me if I wanted to open an account, if I did, then they'd let me have my first purchase for free. I promptly opened my first clothing account and walked smartly out of the shop clutching my new interview outfit before they changed their minds.

The house that Jeremy had rented for us was truly enormous and stood on a ten acre plot.

"You can bring the horses down here," he announced brightly. But I'd already seen the horses in the area and our rag, tag and bobtail crew would be the laughing stock of the South African horse world. I decided that as we were moving, it would be best to begin a new phase altogether and try to simplify life. We couldn't afford to keep the horses just for pleasure and our own use, so perhaps it was time to start over. There was no way I could teach anyone to ride in South Africa with no official qualifications and no insurance either. They would not be impressed to see a copy of the British Pony Club instruction manual stuffed down the front of my jodhpurs.

I approached the large imposing buildings of my new school in great trepidation. I'd got so used to living in the bush that I'd built up a resistance to noise, and the slightest loud sound startled me. Here was the real world again, the real 'first world' that was. I thought the interview went very well since they offered me the job on the spot. They particularly wanted me because I'd been trained in vertical streaming and the integrated day, and they wanted me to introduce all those principles into the Standard One class, ages 8 and 9 year olds, starting in January 1984.

This time I hoped most of the children would speak English. In my present class in Francistown I had 32 children, only 6 of whom were fluent in my mother tongue. The rest were Norwegian, Turkish, Indian, French, Dutch, Spanish and a large number of Motswanas who only spoke Tswana. I had to admire the determination of their parents, who would regularly sell a cow at the beginning of each school year to pay for the fees. They saw the benefits of sending them to the English school, rather than the local village school. It was through education that their children could get ahead. Exactly how I had felt when I had been in college! I hoped that hard as life had been in Botswana, I could settle back into the modern world again.

It was heartbreaking to watch them pull the stables down piece by piece, and sell off the horses. I tried to find good homes for them, but it wasn't easy. I wrote up the end of term reports, packed our personal items into a few cardboard boxes and packaged the rest to be taken to customs. I sold the Land Cruiser, since Jeremy had bought a car for me in Johannesburg and would drive it up to collect us. By this time she was leaking oil quite badly and I had to make my sales pitch very upbeat to get rid of her at all.

My 25% gratuity went into the bank, and just as I breathed a sigh of relief about the financial side of affairs, a host of tradesmen beat a path to the front door. Being a small town, everyone knew exactly when I was going to get paid, and now was the time to pounce. By the time I had settled up every one of Jeremy's debts, there was practically nothing left. Why hadn't I seen this before? How could I have been so blind?

The last day dawned and as Jeremy arrived in the car to help take the boxes down, I dragged two wailing children down the garden path, pushed them into the car and gave Ester a tearful farewell hug. And the car? It was an enormous Mercedes, at least fifteen years old and not the sort of thing I wanted at all. Jeremy was obviously very pleased with his purchase.

"But you must drive an expensive car, for your image and the children's," he said. "Life in Johannesburg is all about image, what you earn, your house in the right area, the clothes you wear and what you drive." He neglected to tell me that the power steering was defunct and you needed biceps like Popeye to steer the Mercedes round corners. Navigating round multi-storey car parks became a nightmare!

Living in Botswana and living in Johannesburg was going to be as different as chalk and cheese and I wasn't looking forward to it.

20 JOHANNESBURG & PRETORIA

Once installed in the new house, as Christmas time was the long summer holidays, we had a few weeks break before the school year started. We wandered around the local places and I made full use of my clothing accounts, stocking up on stuff to wear for teaching. I wasn't too confident that my homemade clothes would stand up to scrutiny in this upper class establishment, but I did make quite a few outfits for the children. I found that I could open accounts at lots of other clothing chain stores, it was so easy to do and difficult to resist the nice clothes they had on sale. I gasped at the cost of the uniforms for the children. They had both been accepted at the same school at a cost of 10% of the fees and free lunches. Once again, I thanked the day I'd decided to become a teacher, it had certainly paid off.

I went to open a bank account and had great problems, as they were unwilling to let a married woman have her own account. I knew though that I could not trust Jeremy with money, I wanted to have control over what I earned. I tried four different banks before I was successful. I was rather incensed that I had to take Jeremy into the bank so he could sign and give his permission for this.

There'd been a long silence between my mother and me, but each year at Christmas, I would have corresponded, after all, it's the time to forgive and forget. But I have no correspondence at all before March of 1984, by which time, we had settled into the regular routine of daily life.

Jeremy left early every morning, while I packed the children into the car and drove to school. I was right; it would have been preferable to have a younger, smaller make and model of car. I would park the old, rusty and cumbersome Mercedes at the far side of the car park, in the hope it wouldn't draw too much attention. But I was considered worthy of attention, or rather amazement. Chatting away about our family, I was met with incredulity.

"You mean you were just left in the bush with a baby that age?"

"Well, uh, yes, but it..."

"Your husband left you alone in a strange country with no money?"

"Yes, but it wasn't..."

"Were you really in a tear gas attack?"

"It really wasn't too serious..."

"How did you manage with all those Arabs?"

"They were quite friendly and..." I began to feel a complete oddity. I'd not thought too much at the time, it was all part of life and I had been brought up to do as I am told. I know now that Jeremy simply replaced my mother. But surely these teachers were the descendants of the tough *Voortrekkers* who tamed wild Africa! Why were they so surprised by my stories? I'd never really discussed our experiences with people in England, so I've no idea if they would have reacted in the same way. I soon learned to keep my mouth shut and fit in with everyone else.

Dana's class teacher told me that after testing her, she thought she would experience some severe learning problems later on at school. This I found surprising, since she had seemed so bright. Kylie could read fluently but she was battling with Maths.

Children coming from Botswana were automatically put down a year, to give them a chance to catch up, so Dana was repeating her reception year, much to her disgust. Kylie should have gone into standard one, but since I was the new standard one teacher, they placed her in standard two.

The rules were strict and it took the girls a while to adjust to being ladies, but children are adaptable and soon they were making friends and coping quite well, or so I thought.

I wasn't earning very much and we were certainly not living the high life, but we had enough to get us by. Once again, I asked Jeremy if I could handle the household accounts, would he give me some housekeeping money each month? He flatly refused, saying it was his job to handle such matters. He was not going to hand over his hard earned money to anyone. I thought this was more than a little unfair, since I had just lost all my gratuity paying off his debts, but there was no reasoning with him, and every time I asked if he had paid the water or lights account, he flew into another rage. I kept quiet and hoped for the best.

I was also unhappy knowing that he had no life insurance and certainly no pension either, but I consoled myself by thinking that as we were still in our thirties, there would be time enough for all that later on.

In my letter home in March of that year, I said that I had waited to calm down before I wrote again, so I guess there had been another blow up before Christmas. I mentioned that our new school reminded me of the school I had attended in Dublin, tall imposing buildings in manicured grounds with 400 pupils, about half of them boarders. It was, and still is, one of the very best private schools in South Africa, with a high standard of education.

Kylie was having individual tuition in Afrikaans to help her catch up, her Tswana was of little or no use to her here, but her half term report was not good, and after constant battles at home, I told her teacher to put the pressure on at that end as I was exhausted trying to make her do her homework each evening.

Since there had been hints that perhaps she wasn't well, I took her to the doctor and they booked her in for a tonsillectomy and she made me so proud being so brave about it all. The child could drive me mad, behaving like an angel one moment and a fiend the next.

At school, both children loved their swimming lessons, although Kylie was a bit miffed after being the best swimmer in her year in Francistown, now she didn't even make the team. Her diving improved and Dana also progressed well, working hard on her backstroke and crawl but she resembled a cuddly, flying worm when she tried to dive.

Reading that letter again from March, I had asked my mother to put some money in the bank for us, as we were overdrawn in our English bank account. I mentioned that I had written to the building society and asked them to transfer funds, but they had replied that our account was empty. This was strange, since I'd left money in there. I also asked what had happened to the money left to me by my father's mother. In one of his letters, Paul had told me that I had been included in my paternal Grandmother's will. My mother made no reply to this and I realized that this was the second inheritance, which had 'gone astray'.

Jeremy settled happily into his new job and although he occasionally came home blind drunk I tried to live with it, but the next disaster came from quite a different quarter. I was called into the Headmaster's study.

"We will not require your services after the end of this year," he announced.

I gasped. "But why? What have I done? I thought everything was going so well."

"It's not written into your contract that I need to give you any reason. It is written that I need to give you one term's notice and that's what I'm giving you. Thank you, you may go."

I walked back to the staff room and told everyone I'd been fired. I think they were as shocked as I was. It had never happened to me before, to Jeremy, yes, many, many times, but never, ever to me. What had I done wrong? This worried me more than anything else and after thinking about it for a couple of days I asked the school secretary for an appointment for me to see the Headmaster – it was that kind of school.

I didn't get my appointment that term and only met him again in September. I pleaded with him to tell me why I wasn't required the following year, I would accept it, but I wanted to know why. If they did things differently in South Africa, wouldn't it be kind to tell me? I'd taught in five other countries before this and no one had ever had a bad word to say about my teaching.

He refused to budge, even when I appealed to him as a man of the cloth, he was a priest as well as Headmaster, he stood firm and I got nowhere. I even rang the Bishop of Pretoria and explained what I was going through, but that had no effect either.

In the meantime, I began to look around for another job and I also persuaded Jeremy that we really didn't need to live in a house on a ten acre plot, how about a nice bungalow closer to the shops? I was hedging my bets if we couldn't afford a car for me, as Jeremy's transport was supplied by the company, I would have to cope without one during the week.

I discovered that since the Department of Education wouldn't recognize my teaching diploma from UK, I could only get work in a private school. That really cut down my options, but I applied for every vacancy, even if it meant traveling miles each day.

In the meantime, I also had to find a school for the children. I'd been told that they wouldn't allow Kylie to progress into the next class as she wouldn't pass the annual exams. They were however happy to have Dana, at the full rate of fees of course. Even if we'd had the money, I wasn't going to send one child to private school and the other to a state school. We visited several in the area, and decided on a really good primary school. It had a very good name, a nice atmosphere and best of all, it was free.

My mother went ballistic when she heard that her grandchildren were not going to attend a private school from the following January. No matter how I tried to explain that we simply didn't have the money, she refused to listen, and I guess that is one reason why the next letter is dated November 1985.

I got a position in a small private school on the outskirts of Pretoria, a class of twelve children with normal to high IQ's but they all had learning problems. The fees here were almost as high as the smart school in Pretoria, but my salary took a big drop. Once again, we were on a tight budget.

I came to the conclusion that many of the other children, whose mothers were not working, must have received huge chunks of money from parents and family members or they had all won the lottery. I found it very difficult to explain to our children why we didn't drive around in Mercedes and BMW's, and why both their parents had to work. I believe Jeremy was on a reasonable salary, he refused to tell me how much, but we didn't live the high life, entertain or take expensive holidays. Where his money went I don't know, but mine was spent on the weekly food and stuff the kids needed but not necessarily everything they wanted, including two more sets of school uniforms, paying the maid and petrol to get to and from school. I still enjoyed my teaching, the staff was friendly and much more relaxed and apart from the headmistress, who was a bit of a religious nut, we all got along fine.

However, while I was still at the posh school in Pretoria looking for a new teaching post, I had told the drama teacher about our underground theatre in Benghazi and my work on Radio Libya. Her husband was a popular announcer on the radio, having worked before on radio in the UK.

"Go for an audition at the SABC," she suggested.

"No! I could never do that, surely." I was shocked at the thought. I was a teacher, that's what I'd been trained to do.

"Don't know if you don't try," she said. I thought about this for a while, and remembered the enormous amount of money I'd earned on the radio in Libya.

So, I phoned the South African Broadcasting Corporation and put my name down, heard nothing and forgot all about it, until one day they called me in for an audition as a continuity announcer. I did very badly as I knew next to nothing about South African or current world affairs, in fact I did so badly that the sound engineer fell off his stool he was laughing so hard. I think that maybe it was the page of Afrikaans I was reading when I didn't know a word of the language. So having failed that, they sent me off to the drama department. The producer was rather underwhelmed, but because I had written my own scripts, he said

"I don't think you're any great shakes as an actress, although I will use you. Go home and write young lady, you have a talent. Go home and write lots more, it's good stuff." After all these years I was being told to write! I went home floating on a cloud. I'd always wanted to be a writer, I remember the family discussions before I left school and the "get a proper job" reply.

But gradually I came down from the clouds. Fine to be told you have a talent, but putting it into practice was another thing, and making a living from it, something else again. However, there was nothing to stop me from trying, at least part time, especially when I replaced the letter 'n' on the typewriter. The drama teacher phoned me the next day.

"I hear you had quite an audition with Jack yesterday," she said.

"Well I think so, yes, I'm not sure I was all that good," I was trying to be modest.

"He seemed to think so, so listen carefully. There's a competition for a one hour radio play, I'll bring the rules and a booklet on the layout to school on Monday. Give it a go, you never know."

I studied the accepted format for a radio play and I read through the rules carefully. Well, maybe it might be fun to try, I had plenty of ideas, but as soon as I'd finished writing, I threw it in the bin. Unknown to me, Jeremy rescued it, took it in to the Broadcasting Centre and a few weeks later, they phoned me to tell me I had won. I was so thrilled, I wanted to frame the cheque and not spend it!

I was hooked. If someone thought I could write, then that's what I would do. I got up at five each morning and scribbled until it was time for breakfast. I scribbled again in the afternoons and I bombarded the SABC with a wide variety of plays and morning stories. Not all of them were broadcast of course, but I always got constructive criticism and they put quite a few on air, which kept my enthusiasm intact. I was often invited into the studio when the plays were recorded and I got to meet many of the most famous faces in SA and once or twice, I got a small part in them as well. The extra money was a great help, but there were a finite number of plays which could be broadcast by any one person, I was aware of that.

I thought of the overseas market and wrote to several British magazines asking if they would be interested in articles about our life in South Africa?

"Absolutely not."

"Thanks, but no thanks."

"None of our readers could relate, sorry." I was not deterred by these replies. I bombarded the local South African magazines with stories about the 'Queen's Birthday Celebrations in Libya', 'The Day we Broke Down in the Game Park', and so on. Many were accepted and I opened a post office savings account and began to plan for the future.

I was asked if I would like to contribute a weekly column in a free newspaper and I happily accepted. They published my photograph at the top of the column each week, not my most flattering angle, and I found it most disconcerting when complete strangers pinned me against the baked beans in the supermarket to agree or disagree with what I'd written. I decided the 'fame' route was not for me, I'd just make do with the fortune part.

Back in the real world, we'd moved into a sensible sized bungalow outside Pretoria and we were making ends meet, until yet again, Jeremy lost his job. I can't say why, it just happened, yet again. He was soon off on the job trail, while I sadly drew out my hoarded cents from the post office to keep us going. True, it only took a month and he was driving around in another company car, for another earth moving plant company. I don't know how he did it, but he could sell skyscrapers to the Bushmen.

Then one night, he arrived home extremely late and extremely drunk. He tried to drive the car through the gates, gave up, staggered up the front path and walked into the plate glass sliding doors to the lounge. On this occasion, he did wake the girls up, dragged them out of bed and tried to play with them, although he could barely stand upright. He scared us all, but the only way to handle it was to play along for the moment. Eventually, he flaked out on the couch and we all slunk off to bed.

I lay awake for hours and decided that enough was enough. I couldn't live in this constant state of fear, wondering when he was coming home and in what state, worrying if he'd had an accident, for he was certainly a danger on the roads to himself and everyone else. I couldn't trust him to hold down a job either, we had no security.

The next morning Jeremy walked into the bedroom to find me packing a suitcase.

"Where do you think you're going?"

"I've had enough, I'm leaving, I can't take this worry any longer. I'll cope somehow."

"No, please don't go, I'll do anything it takes, I love you and would never do anything to harm you or the girls," he pleaded.

"Last night you involved them as well, that's what decided me, you dragged them out of bed and they were very frightened." I continued to pack.

"I don't remember last night. I'll stop drinking, go on the wagon, I promise" he replied.

"You've said that before and it lasts for a while and then you begin all over again. This will only be until next time. You've broken too many promises in the past."

Much to my amazement, he went straight into the study and looked up the phone number for Alcoholics Anonymous. I heard him talking and when he came back into the bedroom, it was to ask me to go with him to an AA meeting that night. This time he meant it, he would give up alcohol for the rest of his life. I paused, was this the breakthrough? I had never seriously threatened to leave before.

We went to a meeting that night, but unfortunately, it was conducted mostly in Afrikaans and meant little to either of us. At the end of the session, one of the members suggested we attend a different, English-speaking group that was not too far from the school where I taught.

We went there on the following evening, and the second group was much larger, but this time I was not allowed to stay with Jeremy, though he begged me not to leave him. I was steered firmly into another room, for partners of alcoholics, the Alanon group. Much to my amazement, I saw two other people I knew there, but it was an unspoken rule that you didn't ever mention this in the outside world.

I heard the most horrific stories about drunken behaviour and I began to wonder if I'd over-reacted. Jeremy certainly didn't drink at breakfast and he wasn't drunk every day either and, as far as I knew he wasn't hiding bottles in the toilet cistern and taking nips throughout the day.

We continued to attend for about a month, but then Jeremy announced that he was fine now and was not going to go any longer, as he didn't need to.

"Let me take it one day at a time," he said, repeating the international credo of AA. "I've not touched a drop for five weeks and I'm sure I can handle it."

I wasn't convinced at first, but then Jeremy attended a work seminar, led by a motivational speaker who had conquered his drink problem, re-evaluated his life and started over. He certainly motivated Jeremy, as my husband told me proudly one evening. He'd ordered coffee at the bar and when the guys teased him Jeremy replied that like their star speaker, he was also an alcoholic. I have to give Jeremy his due, as far as I know, he never slid off the wagon, and he kept his promise not to drink.

I put the suitcase back on the top of the wardrobe.

Pretoria
30 October 1985
Dear Mum,

I am feeling extremely old now with an 11 year old daughter. The little darling turned that age this week. She didn't want a party, so instead she chose to take a couple of friends on a camping weekend to the nearest warm water spa. The outcome was that she was insufferable for two solid days, while father and I grovelled like slaves to do her every bidding. When we were not erecting tents, we were stuffing them full of ice cream and hot dogs, or cooking over a hot stove under the burning African sun. Still, she seemed to enjoy it, but at the end, Jeremy and I were burning with ill-concealed fury, for we didn't want to demoralize her in front of her friends. At the moment she has an eminently desirable friend I'm encouraging, who is keen on schoolwork. This is a country where every child is motivated to an incredible degree because they have to pass the Matriculation exam, the equivalent of the old School Certificate. The reason for this is that there are no low category jobs for whites, so, if they don't do well, they are stuck working on the railways and living with mum and dad forever! The whole outlook is very different here.

Obviously the thing I'm most excited about is the newfound talent I've discovered, or was it there all along? I've had two stories accepted for broadcast, two plays, including the one from the competition, with three articles for one women's magazine, seven for another one and another play for Springbok Radio. I submitted a radio play to the BBC and they didn't want to take it, but the stuff I sent to a woman's magazine in UK came back saying they were sorry they couldn't use it due to lack of space, but that I had a gift for writing. I am most pleased by that, as I know the British market will be much harder to get into, as the competition is so fierce.

I have also written a children's book, which I hope to submit to a publisher in the UK when the term finishes. Two of the stories from it have been broadcast on the children's programme here, and Jeremy has drawn illustrations for it.

The culmination of all this is that the SABC rang me and asked me to submit test scripts for the Black Radio Education Service. I did this and was awarded a contract for 26 programmes on 'Health in Man and Animals'. I rushed home and wrote the first six, it took me three days to write each one, before they rang again and told me they were all too long. So back I went and cut them all shorter. Then they rang again and asked me in for a meeting. One script on hygiene I had written from the point of view of a hungry fly and it caused an uproar. I offered to re-write it, but they said no, it was to be assessed by a panel of nine black Africans. I was invited to the discussion and introduced as Mrs X as they didn't want to prejudice the findings. But the panel raved about the script and it was accepted. I am so relieved.

Now that summer is here, we are camping some weekends to get away from the city, and we've planned visits to the snake park, the zoo, crocodile farms, wildlife parks and so on. There's plenty to do. We're lucky that we live half way between Johannesburg, where Jeremy works (I omitted to say he was on his second job) and my school in Pretoria, as they're about 50 kilometres from each other.

Kylie is repeating a year at school, so I'm pleased that she's moved since none of the kids at her new school will realize she failed last year.

Dana slaves away as usual, she is so thoughtful, "Mummy, you look tired, can I make you a cup of tea?" But every week she loses some vital piece of school equipment or clothing and in desperation, I'm considering teaching her how to steal from lost property!

I love them both so much, but how do you cope with children who are so very different?

If I thought any of the above would impress my mother, I was dreaming. But now I was beginning to write in earnest. By sending the children away on Activity School during the school holidays, I was able to tap away from dropping them off at seven in the morning, until I fetched them at five in the evening. While they had a fantastic time going to the zoo, roller skating, taking part in beauty pageants and making models of the Titanic from papier-mâché, I was writing as if my life depended on it.

The first week, I wrote a play and ten articles and in the second, two stories for the children's programme and all of them were accepted for broadcast.

We all returned to school in the January of 1986. My reply to the few letters from my mother assured her that we had seen no signs of riots and no African townships in flames. There was an embargo on the news in South Africa, but life in the white suburbs continued as if nothing was happening. Mother had told me that I was irresponsible bringing them up in a dangerous country.

By the end of the year, I had completed my children's book and handed it over to an agent who said she had excellent contacts in the publishing world in Europe. I sat back and prayed.

There was no chance of me getting big headed by having plays and series broadcast on national radio. Even when I received a copy of the magazines with the articles under my by-line, the family was less than impressed. They would glance at them briefly, and say "Very nice, can I have an ice cream?"

It came to a head one Friday night when I had a phone call to say one of my radio plays was to be broadcast that night. I looked to see if I had a spare audio tape, and told the rest of the family, expecting them to be as excited as I was.

"But you promised to take us to the drive in tonight!" they wailed.

"We can go to the drive in tomorrow night," I replied.

"But we want to go tonight!"

"Tomorrow will be just as good," I said firmly. "Tonight is the only night we can hear the play on radio."

"Why can't you put a tape in?"

"I'm going to tape it anyway, but I have to turn the tape over half way through and I can't do that from the drive in." For once I stood firm, but a few days later when they broadcast 'Wicked Witch and the Silence Spell', I was being wheeled into the operating theatre for a dental procedure and I missed it altogether.

Having moved from the plot to a sensible bungalow near the shopping centre, we moved again a year later, onto a film set on a farm nine kilometres into the countryside. There were about 20 cottages on the farm, all wooden with cute, Swiss style, balconies. The children had a lot more freedom and there was a horse they could ride, a swimming pool, and several other children from their school to play with, and, most importantly, the rent was cheaper. I would take the children to school in the mornings on my way to work, and another parent picked them up in the afternoons, so it worked out very well.

At the beginning of the year, I was given a hefty pay increase, which was very welcome, but it came with a sting in the tail. Instead of teaching the small reception class, I was given the older children in Standard 3 and 4, mostly strapping great boys of 11 and 12 years old. This meant lots of preparation, more marking, and longer hours.

The parents of one of my pupils, owned and ran a small zoo and each week, without fail, he would bring an assortment of animals and reptiles, usually poisonous, into the classroom for 'nature' lessons. I grew to dread Wednesdays!

At the same time, the SABC asked me to write two more series for radio. I was running ragged, trying to balance all the balls in the air, but I didn't dare turn anything down, as Jeremy had left his job. Why he left, or if he was fired, I don't know, but he announced that we were not making headway and the only way to amass a lot of money was to be self-employed. He became an art dealer.

Jeremy knew as much about the art world as you could write on a postage stamp; but the market was currently being flooded with cheap, but expensive to buy, oil paintings from the Far East. A gallery in Johannesburg was importing these by the ton and Jeremy was selling them on a stall in major shopping malls.

Maybe I'm a snob, but from being Area Manager, to something not much above a stallholder in the local market, was a big drop in image. On one particular occasion, I had to stand in for him when he got a tummy bug and I hated it. I just hoped and prayed I didn't see anyone I knew, and if he was selling in our local mall, the children avoided him like the plague.

I went down with a medical problem and they said I might need surgery, which, in a country without a National Health Service could cost a fortune. Along with losing the job, we had also lost the medical aid (insurance). I took handfuls of painkillers and battled on.

The children had a huge number of activities in the afternoons after school, I'm sure they tried everything on offer. There was the country dancing, replaced by the modern dancing, extra Maths and swimming lessons, the girl guides, sports practice, drama lessons and ballet. To add to that, Dana began violin lessons, with a quarter sized instrument we hired on a monthly basis. She joined the Pretoria Youth Orchestra at the age of seven.

Remembering how I'd not been allowed to give up the hated ballet lessons, I made minimal fuss as they changed from one activity to another. Unfortunately, each change invariably meant new equipment and, or, new uniforms. However, if they were to discover what they really wanted to do, or if they had some amazing, hidden talent, I wasn't going to stand in their way.

Jeremy's career in art lasted only a few months, and then

thankfully, he got another job with yet another earth moving plant company, along with a company car, medical aid and a regular salary. I breathed a sigh of relief, as I began scripting two more educational series for SABC radio.

Although I was happy to take credit for my radio plays that were broadcast on the 'A' service, the equivalent of the old BBC Home Service, I asked that they put another name to the 'drama/educational' programmes aimed at Black Africans. I genuinely hoped that the advice I packed into these dramatized stories would help uplift impoverished communities, or at least improve lives in some way. So I suggested they use a fictitious African name when they were translated into the eleven black languages spoken by indigenous South Africans. I was flattered to learn that some well-known people acted in my radio plays which gave me much needed confidence.

I was having big problems getting time off school to attend script conferences in Johannesburg. These meetings, held in imposing board rooms in the SABC in Auckland Park, involved the producers and people from various government departments, who discussed content and ideas for each of the series. Occasionally I took unpaid leave, but on one occasion, I phoned in sick. I felt very guilty as I sloped off in the car, but I was not confident enough to give up either the teaching or the writing.

Some of my early articles for magazines, reflected some of our experiences overseas, and I was approached by Radio Springbok, an independent arm of the SABC, to write and record my experiences in Libya. I enjoyed being on radio again and I recorded seven programmes for them.

The longest Jeremy had been in any one job, apart from our time in Libya, was eighteen months and I couldn't rely on him to bring home a regular pay packet. It's true that as soon as he *left* one job, he was off looking for other employment, but there was always that gap in between, when he'd walk in the door and announce he was through with this or that firm.

"How much have we got in the bank?" he would enquire. That's not what he meant, the correct question should have been "How much have you managed to put by?" It seemed that as soon as I had a couple of thousand Rands in savings, I would have to raid it to pay rent, water, lights and food.

Jeremy changed jobs again and this time, part of his area included Swaziland, which meant that he was away for a night each week. This I didn't mind, as it gave me more time to write. It was difficult to work in the evenings, as he would, understandably, want me to keep him company in front of the television.

Each time I wrote home, I tried to sound upbeat about yet another new job for Jeremy. To be fair, each new job, was better paid, further up the promotional ladder and held more responsibility, but the uncertainty kept me on my toes. I guess I shouldn't have said anything at all in my letters, but then that's how I am, I've always been quite open and honest.

We moved again, this time to buy a house of our own south of Pretoria a few kilometres away, but we were still receiving threatening letters from the bank in UK, which had handed our debt over to some collection agency. I was worried sick about this, as the amount was now over £250, but with the exchange rate at three to one, there was little chance of us paying it back since there were restrictions about sending money out of SA. I wrote and asked my mother if she would send a letter to say she needed our support as her only family members, this was a sure fire way of exporting money abroad. She refused, saying that she would not participate in any fraudulent activity.

My mother insisted that we had left a mountain of other debts behind in UK as well, and if this is true, then I'd certainly been unaware of it. But perhaps I should have expected that might be true after my experience in Botswana. Like the proverbial ostrich, I hid my head in the sand and refused to accept the truth.

The new house had a third wing, with its own exterior door, so for extra income we let it out to a young Welsh girl. I was glad of her company the nights Jeremy was away in Swaziland and even more so, when he announced that "It's not working, I'm going to set up my own operation in Swaziland." I discovered the truth much later. They had indeed fired Jeremy, but in return they had given him the franchise for their products in Swaziland.

Much as I didn't want to be on my own, I couldn't see a way of removing the children from school, giving up both my job and the writing and leaving South Africa. I had little faith that this latest venture would prove any more successful that the ones that had gone before, but there was no stopping Jeremy once he had an idea in his head.

I rationalized that if I tried to clip his wings, my brilliant, charismatic husband would wither up and die. For years, I had been totally dominated by my mother and it never really occurred to me to put my foot down and say no. Even with the children, I was far too lenient, fearing that I would alienate them. All children say things like "I hate you," when you refuse them something, but I took such threats very much to heart. Despite all my apparent success, I was still very insecure, had little confidence in my abilities and was always apologizing to people for my inadequacies. When I was in the classroom, or recording on radio, this was not apparent, but inside, I was still a seething mass of jelly.

Jeremy duly departed for Swaziland and life continued much as before, only now I worked every evening, only taking a couple of hours off to give quality time to the children from five until seven each night. In the afternoons, they were under strict instructions not to disturb me and my train of thought, except for fire, uncontrollable bleeding, snakes, or drowning in the pool!

After a succession of maids, I found Agnes, a gem, the children adored her and she took over the running of the house for me.

One incident brought me up short. I had asked Dana to make me a cup of coffee.

She paused for a moment and then said, "Mummy I am your daughter, not your servant." She had a point. That had been such a large part of my upbringing that I automatically passed on the behaviour.

"You're quite right," I replied. "Would you like me to make you a drink instead?" From that time on, I thought twice before I asked to be waited on. On another occasion I snapped and said "Why did you never run away from home like most children?" They promptly burst into tears.

In May of 1988, I gave in my notice at school. I wrote home that Jeremy was doing very well in Swaziland and I'd been offered an in-house job working on a television series. Like a fool, the glamour of TV had blinded me and I had a lot to learn about moving from one medium to another. With radio, you can let your imagination soar, dive underwater or take off for the moon, neither costs anything, all you need are a few boxes filled with gravel and some sound effects. With TV, your feet are firmly on the ground and it's a minefield writing to a set budget. I had to learn quickly how much it cost for a camera, cameraman, sound equipment, tape, mileage and so on. It was a tremendous thrill to see my name glide up the screen at the end of each programme, but as usual, the children were not too impressed, and Jeremy was away in Swaziland and never got to see the programmes.

In my new job I was now earning five times my teaching salary, and I still had my radio work as well. Perhaps this was the financial breakthrough we needed, but I was badly overdrawn. Jeremy was sending no money from Swaziland.

My bank manager called me in 'for a little chat'. I was shaking when I walked into his office and then the tea and biscuits were brought in. Was this usual for people with enormous overdrafts? A sort of softening up before foreclosure? My hands were shaking as I showed him my contracts and the amount I was expecting in. He was all smiles, and he was kind enough to understand that corporations like the SABC took a long time to pay. However he was more interested in what I actually did and how a single woman had so much going in and out of her bank account, and what overheads did I have? Only electricity, the phone and a whole lot of paper and typewriter ribbons. I could also have added Jeremy as a very large expense.

I was further encouraged by a letter from the BBC, rejecting a play, but complimenting me on my writing and would I submit further work, perhaps with fewer characters? I'd assumed that British radio play budgets were larger than we had in SA. But for me, an endorsement from the greatest broadcasting service in the world, was akin to receiving the Nobel Prize for literature!

My children's book was also rejected as '*not being strong enough for the British market*', but I accepted that as fair, for I'd been out of UK for so long, I guess I'd lost touch with what appealed to the mass market there. But I also got a shock when I turned on the TV one day to see an American comedy featuring a creature that was so like the hero in my children's book, it was uncanny. There was no chance of it being published now.

On the television series, I was first asked to script and pre-produce the programmes, then I moved to production secretary and then assistant director out on location. This was work I had never dreamed of and I thoroughly enjoyed it. I got to see many rural places and learned a lot about village life in Africa. My production work opened up a whole new world for me. We made programmes on medicine, productivity, toothpaste, manufacturing telephones, photography, power stations, pollution at sea, and distance education. I wrote about bakeries, banking, nation building, tourism, diets, meat, margarine, aluminium, marathons, birds, splitting the atom and crime, to name but a few topics. I wrote a series on 'what to do in an emergency', legal information, modern classical music, top athletes, religion, lifestyles, pollution at sea and underground minerals. I became a walking encyclopedia of little bits of useless information, but remembered nothing in any great depth, for once a script and its production was over, I concentrated fully on the next topic. I was guaranteed to bore anyone at any cocktail party I was invited to.

In September, I became the proud owner of a second hand computer. This would make re-writes so much easier, but it took me a long time to get to grips with it. The word wrap problem freaked me out, for as I typed, the sentence disappeared off the screen, where the hell had it gone? Whatever buttons I pressed, I simply couldn't get it to appear again. When deadlines loomed, I rushed back to my faithful typewriter. Things seemed to be going well, but would it last?

21 SWAZILAND

Jeremy suggested that as he was trying to build a new business up from scratch in Swaziland, would I take care of all the bills at the South African end. This wasn't exactly a new idea, as I'd been paying most of them anyway, but I felt that this time he just might succeed if he had no other financial commitments, and could plough all the profits back into the company. Since I was working all hours the money was good, as long as the work came in.

But Jeremy got a bit diverted in Swaziland and became involved with planning the 21st birthday celebrations for the new King Mswati III. This involved a thirty two act concert with international music artists such as Eric Clapton, Labi Siffre and Joan Armatrading, along with a host of popular South African artists, such as Sipho Hotstix Mabuse, Mango Groove, Stimela and Brenda Fassie.

As Concert Venue Director, Jeremy was quoted in the papers as saying: "Swaziland could become the next rock Mecca in southern Africa, with at least two major concerts a year." He continued. "This could easily be achieved should they pass the acid test of the three day music festival at Somhlolo Stadium from July 21st to 23rd. The concert is being held for the benefit of the Swazi people, through the King's Trust and is not being staged as a 'sanctions bust' for South Africa."

Most days, pictures of the preparation for the concert made the front page of the Swazi newspapers and the inside pages of the South African ones. I was never surprised to switch on the news and see Jeremy being interviewed about one arrangement or another that had been made for fans to attend the concert. It was a massive undertaking, and I got roped in as well and helped co-ordinate some of the arrangements between Johannesburg, London and Mbabane. Jeremy handled the press conferences in Johannesburg; remember what an excellent salesman he was? He generated hype, interest and excitement and on the days before the event, more than 25,000 South Africans flocked across the border.

As a thank you for all their hard work, committee members were allowed a free stall in the 'Swazi Village' on site, and Jeremy had decided we would also make a quick fortune selling hot dogs. I struggled under the weight of several dozen boxes of rolls, frozen frankfurters and bottles of tomato sauce and mustard. Over the three days, I guess we only sold about three dozen, and made a financial loss, and I never got to meet the King or Eric Clapton although I had been invited to receptions for both of them. I was just too busy.

The children and I returned to our more mundane life at home, while there was talk of Jeremy traveling on with the crew to Mozambique. I asked him not to, as the civil war there was still simmering and in fact, Eric Clapton's car was fired on in Maputo, the capital, while racing through red traffic lights to keep up with the escort cars.

I should have guessed that Jeremy would not have been able to settle after all the hype and excitement. This, he had decided, was the new career for him, forget engineering, it was going to be organizing international concerts from now on. He'd got to know many of the British sound and lights crew and unknown to me, was planning to move in a new direction. I first heard of this when he announced that he was taking on the management of a heavy metal band called 'Iron Mask', they were based in Johannesburg so, could I liaise in the meantime?

To add to everything else, I now had a rock group on my hands, five young men ranging in age from 19 to 36 years old who squabbled constantly, never agreed on anything, and often did not turn up for band practice. I visited dozens of clubs around Johannesburg and Pretoria with a demo tape trying to get them bookings. I found myself in lots of seedy places, but I wasn't too successful, as most of the clubs were too small for that kind of music. We did get them a regular gig and a recording session, but a couple of years later, they broke up after a huge row, and they all went their separate ways.

It was Christmas before Jeremy and I were able to spend any time together again and I was astonished when Jeremy announced that he was not going back to Swaziland but would now stay at home. Obviously I was pleased, but I was also worried. He never returned to collect his clothes, or the household stuff we'd sent back with him on his weekly trips over the border. As to what happened to the vehicles, or the office and workshops and plant equipment and his employees I'll never know. He simply refused to discuss it and I backed off, secretly glad that he was going to be sleeping at home, since our Welsh tenant had left, and I was a bit nervous on my own at night.

To prepare him for his next new career, Jeremy enrolled for a two week course in television production at the University of the Witwatersrand. I was extremely angry about this, for if anyone should go on the course, I felt it should have been me. I was working in an industry in which I had had no formal training, learning from my own mistakes as I went along.

And then Jeremy had a series of meetings with promoters who wanted to bring Bollywood stars to South Africa. We did organize and manage a few quite successful ones in Johannesburg, but I noticed that Jeremy was excellent in delegating, to me of course, and I seemed to do most of the work, such as the phoning and typing while he attended the meetings. I'm not sure how I juggled everything, but the crux came the following March.

I had less work coming in and I was so worried about the future and about the finances, that I could sit for hours and peer at the screen without being able to string two words together. The more I worried, the worse it got, for by now I had very little money in reserve. I became an estate agent, but I was hopeless at it, I did not have Jeremy's selling skills. But the concert business seemed to be picking up and then more scriptwriting came in, so it was goodbye to the estate agency after a couple of months.

We did organize and manage three Bollywood concerts, one in Johannesburg, one in Swaziland and the third in Gaborone. This kept us extremely busy and Jeremy hired a PA to help with the arrangements. While they concentrated on the first two, I was left with the Botswana one to manage. Luckily it was holiday time, so I packed the children into the car and drove them off to stay with friends and I continued up to Gaborone to oversee the stage construction and the seating and ticket sales, and the hundred and one other details.

I was upset, since Jeremy had taken his newly hired PA to Mozambique and when I had phoned through to his room, she answered, and told me he was just in the shower. Warning bells rang loud and clear and I was sick with worry. Perhaps I had papered over the cracks with his first affair, but the veneer was very thin and my trust was severely tested. When he eventually came on the phone, I told him I did not want her traveling to Gaborone and if she did, I would not be responsible for my actions.

Unfortunately, he argued that she had been a tremendous asset on the tour, and had even traveled airside on the baggage carousel to ensure the equipment was landed in Maputo. But I didn't care. I was not going to work with another ex-friend who was 'innocently' in my husband's hotel room while he was in the shower. I wanted her fired and I didn't want to discuss it any further.

In the end, all three concerts were a great success and I could add Indian music to my list of new experiences, and possibly more infidelities as well.

Flushed with success, Jeremy organized a local music event in Johannesburg which was a flop, and then we lost everything in organizing another Bollywood concert in Durban when the promoter's cheque bounced after I had got confirmation with the bank that it was good. But we had paid suppliers and we were not going to get our money back. We sued and won, then the debtor appealed and lost again, but we never received a penny and financially we were back to square one.

In answer to my prayers, a flood of radio scriptwriting work came in for me and I was back at the keyboard again working all hours. I computed that over two and a half years, I had written non-stop, but the producers had said that they really needed to use other writers as well, so I was put on the back burner. I was so grateful when it all come flooding back the next season and I now had three regular fifteen minute radio programmes being broadcast each day. While I had found it difficult to write on 'spec', now they dangled a cheque at the end of the contract, my creativity reappeared as if by magic.

I began writing more for television. Several production houses approached me, since the SABC had made it a condition for awarding some of the contracts, that I was employed to write the scripts. It was just as well I was so busy, I didn't have time to think about Jeremy and his PA, they were still seeing each other, though he denied it vehemently.

I'd been writing to my mother infrequently, but secretly hoped she wouldn't reply. While she has kept my letters, I certainly didn't keep the few she wrote to me. They were full of criticism, vindictive remarks and comparisons about how badly we were doing compared to every other inhabitant on the planet. I dreaded opening and reading them, I would usually end up in tears, and every bit of confidence I had built up would drain away. I never wrote the unvarnished truth, but I did tell her the main news, such as the concerts, and the writing and how the children were doing. I wrote about everyday life and the animals we had collected, but never once did I receive any encouragement, only complaints and criticism. At the same time, I saw mothers on television whose sons were condemned on death row, sticking up for their offspring, and I saw other mothers and daughters laughing and smiling together over coffee and it hurt, it hurt a lot. Jeremy and I may not have been the average couple, but then we were hardly on the police wanted list either, well not quite.

The concert front went very quiet so Jeremy finally admitted defeat and went off to find a job. It took him two weeks and he was selling insurance. He then got involved with people who I never met, but it all sounded very shady. I didn't realize at the time that the large sums of money Jeremy brought home, were commission on insurance policies and if these lapsed, the commission was returnable. We looked for another house to buy and found the perfect one within a walled complex, complete with heated pool, sauna, tennis court and centralized servants' quarters. We planned to move in after Christmas 1990, and I promised myself that I would take three months off. I was absolutely exhausted and close to burn out. We didn't see much of Jeremy, he was putting in long hours and spent more time poring over paperwork when he got home.

We moved into our new designer-built home and three months later, we had to move out again. The money Jeremy was expecting to pay for the house never came in, and he finally had to admit that this was yet another venture that was not going to be a success. We had sold our house, so we rented a bungalow and to make matters worse, a project I had spent hours on was cancelled.

It was while we were in our designer house that my mother phoned me, a rare occurrence. She was beside herself and very worried, as Paul's eldest son Andrew, had written to say he wanted his father's money as he was entitled to it. Apparently, Paul had left my mother very well off and she was scared that she was going to lose everything. I could only advise her to see a lawyer and tried to comfort her as best I could. In the end it was all sorted out as Paul had left everything to my mother quite legally, explaining in his will that he had bought and paid for a house for Andrew and he considered that fair. As far as I know, he left nothing to his younger son Dick, who was born outside his first marriage and with whom he had very little contact. My mother refused to have the child in the house and always referred to him as "Paul's little illegitimate b******."

Most people felt very unsettled, times were changing in South Africa. There were very few advertisements on television and the SABC cut back on new programming. Most of the old laws had been repealed and there was a new sense of unease, maybe even fear, as previously 'safe' white suburbs became new venues for large numbers of black people who would sit outside your house, or lie on the grass chattering loudly. Prices soared in the shops and a trolley of groceries, which had cost R40 eight years ago, now climbed to almost R400.

After a couple of workless weeks, I panicked and rushed off to sell insurance. Frankly, I wasn't very good at it, certainly no better than I had been selling houses. The insurance company thought I would be very successful, since I had taken dozens of those psychometric tests and the bottom line was that I was a survivor. I didn't feel much of a survivor then, I was struggling to pay the bills.

Once, when Jeremy had still been living in South Africa, I had arrived home to find Kylie in tears. She walked in after school to find the sheriff in the house itemizing the furniture to sell to recover outstanding debts. I heard that my daughter was quite amazing and ordered him out of the house, but it scared the hell out of her. It scared the hell out of me as well, as I'd had no knowledge of any outstanding debts. I paid them off, needless to say, once again, raiding my hard-earned savings account.

So, in a way, it was a relief to be in charge of all the household accounts, at least I knew where we stood. Sincc Jeremy had returned to South Africa, I continued paying most of the bills, and I made sure the electricity and water would not be cut off.

If I thought life was bizarre before, it became more so. Jeremy seemed to be doing well selling insurance and of course he was expecting huge commissions. On a trip to the coast, he decided our future was to buy a yacht and sail around the world. He saw the perfect boat in Durban and the deposit, taken from my bank account, changed hands. I wrote the following letter to my mother, partly to convince myself this was a good idea, but it was always difficult to dampen Jeremy's enthusiasm. It was like trying to hold back a tidal wave with a sieve.

22 DURBAN HARBOUR

C/o Yacht Club
Durban Harbour.
16 February 1993
Dear Mum,

By now you will be freaking out at the address! I'm sitting here on the water writing to you by hand! Perhaps I'd better start at the beginning. We found the boat we liked last year and we're paying for it in instalments. The contract of sale states that after we paid 50% of the purchase price, we had the right to live on board. We paid that by the end of November, leaving us as poor as church mice, so we piled up the car and came down in the middle of December for three weeks. December here is the start of the long school holidays, the children get five weeks off school and it is like having a hotel ready at any time, for which we don't have to pay or book. The previous owners moved off the boat on December 7th. They were an older couple, but he's had a heart attack, so they wanted to return to UK.

We arrived on the boat, expecting to feel cramped, claustrophobic and confined, but much to our surprise, we discovered that 43 foot is really a lot of space. We also discovered that a human doesn't really need all those many possessions either, well certainly not a bathroom each!

We had a quiet Christmas, still broke, and when it came to return to Johannesburg, the girls were in tears because they were leaving the beach, the local talent, the dinghy and the 'water beds'. I was a bit sad, as we'd never lived in anything we'd owned half of before! The price of a boat this size is equal to the average three bedroom house, but it also has the advantage of being a good investment. People seldom lose money on them and if you sink it, then you claim on insurance. If you sink yourself at the same time, well why worry about losing the investment?

We returned to Johannesburg on 4th January as school started two days later. Jeremy and I talked it over in the evening; would it be possible for us to live on the boat, would it be feasible, would it save money? By Tuesday morning I'd decided against the whole idea, by evening, when we'd done our sums, and discovered that we would save R3,000 a month just to sit on the boat in Durban, we decided to go for it.

I did not include in the letter that there was a knock on the door that afternoon. It was the landlord's representative, the rent had not been paid for three months. It was the only bill Jeremy was responsible for, I paid all the rest. This was the catalyst for thinking I might be better off four hundred miles away from unpaid bills. I also described the boat, how the girls were in a new and better school and how cheap it was living on board in the harbour. I had also been given another contract by the SABC. We were just waiting for Jeremy to finalize some big deals in Johannesburg and then we were off to sail round the world!

There were things I did not tell my mother in letters. For example the first cheque that Jeremy gave me for housekeeping bounced. In the first couple of weeks on the boat, I was flat broke and didn't even have enough money to buy bread. The SABC work would not pay out for several weeks.

But then I got a lot of work from a department of the local council in Durban, and again, by putting in the hours and again, going out on location, I was able to pay the bills. Life was not easy on the boat, we were moored a long way out in the harbour, and had to travel to and from land by dinghy or ferry.

As to Jeremy's work in Johannesburg, did I believe it all? To this day I don't know. I see in a letter written in March, I told my mother that he was asked to present a paper on technology transfer, to Parliament in Cape Town. He told me the Czechoslovakian Ambassador had come to his office and they had arranged a meeting with the Deputy Minister of Trade and Industry. Jeremy did show me a few letters from well known and highly placed people, so I knew there was at least a grain of truth in what he was telling me. He had lunch with the leader of the second most important political party in South Africa, and he was mixing with the important politicians in Pretoria. His PA cum secretary also told me of important, hush, hush meetings, as she often went with him. It still sounded a bit fanciful, but then I thought of Conrad Hilton and Bill Gates and dozens of others who had started small and built huge empires.

Yet, at the back of my mind, I wondered if it was all a Walter Mitty dream. Was there any substance to any of this? Considering I had researched hundreds of different topics for programmes, why couldn't I grasp what was really going on? If I questioned Jeremy too closely, he would fly into a rage and tell me I was too thick to understand it all, and anyway he didn't have time and he'd come down to relax over the weekend and not talk business. At least he did have the money for the, at first 'weekly', then 'bi-weekly', then 'monthly', flights to and from

Durban.

We battled on, which was frankly hard work when I was holding down more than a full time job. Kylie was going through a very rebellious period and Dana complained bitterly when we had to douse the lights at night as the battery levels fell. She needed to study longer, or her marks were going to go down. The only source of electricity we had on the boat, was from the wind charger connected to the battery.

I was at my wits end about how to handle Kylie. She announced that she was going out one Saturday and would only be back around 3 am. I turned purple, and said the dreaded word "NO!" I would come and fetch her at midnight if her friend's boyfriend could not detour and bring her home earlier. But teenagers don't have mothers, they sort of manifest themselves from waterfalls, or rosebuds or perhaps from behind the candied fruit counter at Sainsbury's, but they do not have mothers. Mothers may drop teenagers a block or so from the desired venue, as long as they make a rapid exit without squealing the tyres in their Mercedes or BMW's and drawing unnecessary attention to themselves. If mothers only possessed an aging Nissan Sentra called Squeak, then they better stay way out of sight.

The owner of the ferryboat had also been giving her the eye, so Dana informed me, under strict instructions 'not to tell'. This put me in a difficult situation for if I ever needed emergency help, such as storm damage or sinking, he'd be the guy I'd call for help. Fortunately Kylie told me about the problem herself and I was able to talk to her and give her tips on handling the situation.

I was beginning to unravel bit by bit and this was compounded in August when Jeremy announced that he would not be able to wrap everything up by the end of the year and it may take another twelve months at least. He would only be able to come down once a month from now on, as time was so critical with so many deals on the boil.

Relations between us were decidedly strained. I just couldn't get though to him and he wouldn't listen to my concerns. It was tough living on the boat and too, the atmosphere in South Africa had changed, from our point of view, for the worst. No one felt quite as safe as they had before. There was great excitement about the first democratic elections to be held the following April, and previously, we had both decided that we would be out of the country long before then.

On one video shoot, we were locked indoors while the street outside was filled with rampaging mobs. They were toy-toying, chanting and throwing stones, overturning rubbish bins and smashing shop windows, and I had no idea where the children were and if they had got back to the boat safely after school.

Days continued without wind and the batteries got lower and lower until they were completely flat. I didn't know how to start the engine and would frankly have been afraid to try, but it was the only other way to charge the batteries. Eventually I had to have them taken off the boat and recharged properly on shore, but it took three days and in that time we had no power. We couldn't pump water into the header tank and there were no lights. The children were not impressed.

While I was searching for pennies to pay for the batteries, it was discovered that Kylie needed to wear glasses and that was an extra expense, since we had no medical aid at all. VAT went up from 10% to 14% and the prices rose again, but somehow we managed.

We had a nasty time when the boat next to us broke its anchors in a storm, and was swinging wildly in all directions. As usual, there was a high wind, the sea was much too rough for the dinghy, even if I could get it to run, and we were marooned on the boat all day, as they used the ferry to try to stabilize our next door neighbour. The following few nights I had nightmares about us breaking anchor and whizzing all over the bay causing huge amounts of damage to the million dollar catamarans across the channel. My imagination ran wild.

I thought up all kinds of outings that were low cost or free to entertain the children in the holidays. We went to the High Court and listened to part of a murder trial, we went on a trip round the sugar mills and I got permission for the children to visit some of the places where we had been filming.

By now, Kylie was 18 and Dana 16, and both of them were there in the Yacht Club the day I ran into the ex boat owners. I was surprised to see them, as I knew they'd gone back to UK, but the elderly lady was furious. She shouted loudly that she would have us evicted if we didn't come up with the remaining money on the boat in three days. It was obvious now that Jeremy wasn't making the regular payments he'd promised. It was so humiliating, especially in front of the children.

I phoned Jeremy in a panic, and he managed to get a mortgage on the outstanding amount and the funds were transferred in time. Jeremy handled it all very calmly and I relaxed a little, as we now had two more years to pay off the boat. Even a pessimist like me thought this was possible, since we'd paid the debts incurred from the aborted concert in Durban, plus put money into the boat.

In June, I was able to write home about something I had always dreamed of, the words; "My publisher took me out to lunch." My second book had been accepted. It was only a science text book for ten year olds, but I was so proud when the six complimentary copies arrived and I sent one to my mother. Surely this should impress her? She denied ever receiving it and later accused me of lying to her about it. At least, I thought, this would provide me with a pension since Jeremy didn't believe in retirement policies or even life insurance. We wouldn't need anything like that of course once he made his millions, would we? But the millions were a long time coming, that's for sure.

Jeremy flew out to Mauritius for more meetings and called in to see us on the way. This time his plan was to set up a factory making solar panels, a sure fire winner worldwide. He was still having high powered meetings with all kinds of important and well known people, but nothing was finalized. At the same time, he won an award for being in the top 100 of insurance sales in the country and in the top 10 for the insurance company he worked for.

By now, he and his partner were living in a small flat in Johannesburg, and as far as we knew, working all hours of the day and night. We saw Jeremy less and less frequently, but I consoled myself that it would not be forever.

Jeremy came down to the boat for a weekend and repossessed the lap top, arguing that as I had a computer at work at the council department offices, I didn't really need it. He also dismantled and removed the phone, while in tears I begged him not to. It was my only link to the outside world and a great comfort if the sea was rough; as I could reach the port authorities if I couldn't raise the ferry on the radio. It all fell on deaf ears. Even simple things were difficult like taking the water barrels to the tap on shore in the dinghy, returning to the boat and then pumping the water by hand down into the holding tanks. We used the Yacht Club for showers and the occasional snack, but it was often difficult to get to shore if the weather was bad, then we were marooned on the boat. I spent a lot of time looking out of the office window to see how strong the wind was and listening to the weather forecast a couple of times a day.

I began to get very weepy which alarmed the children. They tried in turn to comfort me, and then shout I wasn't being fair. I went to the doctor, and he gave me some tablets to calm me down on the understanding I was not to drive. In desperation, I phoned my mother and begged her for a ticket to go and stay with her for a couple of weeks. I just needed to get away, anywhere and it shows just how bad it was that I should run home to Mother, instead of trying to run away.

With lots of "I told you so's," she reluctantly agreed to fund the ticket and in early September, I landed at Heathrow. If I was expecting lots of tender loving care, I was going to be badly mistaken, but I tried to close my ears as I slept in a proper bed, turned electric lights on and off, and revelled in the hot water in the bathroom. But there was no getting away from the invective, no matter what room I was in.

"Funny how you come running home the moment there's a problem, isn't it?"

"Mum, it's more than a problem, it's not easy living on the boat, and everything is unravelling. I just need a short break, especially from the kids."

"What can you expect, the way you've treated them, uprooting them every few years. They've had no stability in their lives, but then you're hardly an excellent example of how they should behave are you?"

"They've had a lot more stability than most, at least they have parents who are still married. Most of the people I went to school with around here are divorced."

"Nonsense, none of the children around here have suffered at all. They still go to the same school and have the same friends. They haven't been dragged all round the world."

"I hardly think that our kids have been dragged around all that much, they only attended two secondary schools."

"Oh you never do anything wrong do you? You're just perfect, that's how you see yourself, how you've always seen yourself. You're such a wonderful person. You didn't even come home for Paul's funeral. You were quite happy to let me face all that on my own."

"Mum, I've told you a million times that I couldn't and I've given you the reasons."

"Oh yes, I forgot, there's always reasons why you do everything. You always have some excuse or other, but then no one can believe a word you say."

There was just no hope of ever discussing anything reasonably with my mother, or asking her for help. I must have been mad to come back. On the flight over I had imagined rational conversations with her, I needed some sane advice. One problem with moving around as we did, together with the long hours I worked, is that I didn't have a girlfriend close by to confide in, I had no one to talk to. The child in me was crying out, but there was no one to hear me.

A few days later, Jeremy turned up on my mother's doorstep. He'd flown over to open a branch of his company in London, since everything was going so well. Would I go to London and help him choose premises? I was between a rock and a hard place. I sort of believed him, but there were very loud alarm bells ringing in my head. At the same time, my mother was getting impossible and I couldn't stand the constant criticism, and constant verbal abuse. She was doing me more harm than good.

Jeremy and I traveled to London and found a house for him to rent and purchased an elderly car and I returned to South Africa. Jeremy had wanted me to return to England on the next plane, but I refused. Kylie had only two months to go before she took her final exams and I was not going to disturb her education again. If she didn't sit for her Matric, then she would have nothing on paper to show she'd been at school for twelve years.

The children were very alarmed when I told them that Daddy was now living in England, but consoled them with the news that we could keep in touch on the phone, and with Mandy his secretary in Johannesburg. I didn't have the courage to liaise with Mandy, so Kylie phoned her on a weekly basis from the call box in the Yacht Club. There was never any news, until one day Kylie handed me the phone and said,

"Mandy wants to talk to you."

"Hi, Mandy."

"Lucy, I thought you should know that I'm not working for Jeremy any more. I've not had any pay, there's no money in the account and I know that the payments aren't being made on the boat mortgage either and they are very overdue. They've threatened to re-possess the boat and if I were you, I'd leave that bastard. He won't take my calls, and I think you should also know that he was wildcatting it around Johannesburg after you left for Durban. Sorry, but that's how it is. I've got my rent to pay as well and I can't sit around waiting for something to happen. Also there were people who came to the office and removed all the paperwork and everything and sealed it all up, so there's nowhere to work anyway. Sorry." And she hung up.

Despite Jeremy's past record, I was totally shocked. I had been left with two children in South Africa, a country we were all praying would not break out into civil war, on a boat that would be taken away, leaving us nowhere to live. What was I going to do?

I phoned Jeremy, but all he would say was, "It's not a problem. Mandy's wrong, I left plenty of money in the bank. Anyway, forget all that and get on a plane, bring the kids to England."

"But I can't! I don't have the money for plane tickets, Kylie starts her exams in a few weeks and I've got work I'm committed to."

"Well if that's more important, what else can I suggest?" Jeremy paused and then continued. "Look, I'll send you tickets."

"If you've got money for plane tickets, I'd rather you paid a couple of months on the boat, so I know we'll have a roof over our heads for a few more weeks."

"No point in throwing money away if we won't get it back."

"But I can't just walk off the boat and abandon it..." just then the money ran out and we were cut off. Of course we could just walk away and leave everything behind as Jeremy saw it. He'd done exactly that in Botswana and again in Swaziland. For me, it was not an option.

I examined my priorities. I arranged for a friend who worked nights on the local newspaper to boat-sit during the day, to make sure they did not re-possess it while we were not there. The next step was to throw myself on the mercy of the bank manager. I knew which bank had taken the loan, but that was in Johannesburg and I had to deal with the people in Durban. I was in luck, the manager I spoke to was the old type Afrikaner, whose credo was to care for, and protect women. Admittedly I lied, when I said that I had no idea where Jeremy was, and it was more than a little humiliating to say that he had just walked out and left us, but for the most part it was true. The tears and the hankies were also quite genuine, as I explained that the boat was not a rich man's toy, but our home. I told him the children and I lived on it, and that Kylie was taking her Matric soon and I didn't know what to do except sell the boat as soon as possible, say in December, and in the meantime, could we please have a stay of execution?"

It was a nerve wracking few days while I waited for the reply, but thankfully the bank agreed. Now, all I needed to do was sell the boat and see what to do about getting the children and myself back to England. It didn't seem possible we could stay on in Durban. A close friend collected boxes of our possessions each day with the promise to store them until we could send for them.

As the exam season approached, I managed to negotiate with the marina manager that the boat could be brought round and moored on one of the walk-ons. This meant that we did not have to travel out by dinghy or ferry. The girls had been ecstatic about this, as we also had a water supply we could use directly instead of collecting it in barrels once a week. It gave them a lot more freedom and chance to study, but they were less than thrilled about going to live in England.

"But your father is there," I said, not totally convinced myself that it would be the right move. I had never even considered splitting up from Jeremy. I had always believed that "you made your bed and you lay on it."

Along with the Christmas cards, which arrived in our pigeonhole in the Yacht Club, were three plane tickets from Durban to Heathrow, we had three more weeks left in South Africa. Even though it had been twelve years since the girls had been in England, they remembered enough to make them quite sure they were not going to like it. It rained on the day we left, which suited our mood exactly.

23 LONDON

Jeremy was waiting to meet us at Heathrow and we drove to the house we'd found together a few months earlier. He'd bought beds for the girls, but there was little furniture in the rest of the house. After the sale of the boat, I had managed to keep about five thousand pounds and like Pavlov's dogs, I found myself giving him half of it to buy second hand furniture for the girls and also to buy food. He had been living on the dole and trying a bit of selling on the side, but it was quite obvious that all the wheeling and dealing had come to nothing. He explained away leaving us in South Africa, by saying he was afraid for his life, there was a contract out on him. I really found this very, very, very hard to believe.

It took three weeks to get Dana into school, and I trailed around with Kylie trying to get her into tertiary education, but it seemed that as we'd only just returned to the country, either we would have to pay for her tuition, or she would have to be resident in England for two years to get it for free. She began to look for work and so did I. I had one last contract with the SABC and I spent precious pennies on a computer and printer and sent the scripts to SA by courier.

I trailed round every production house within commuting distance listed in the '*Writers' and Artists' Year Book*', and although a few people were interested, I realized that it was going to take time to break into a new market, more time than I had money, even if there were lots of positive comments about my show reel.

I widened the field and applied for work at the local supermarkets, as a barmaid and even chambermaid at the local hotels, but there seemed to be waiting lists everywhere. By now I was in my mid forties and up against pretty young things with a lot more energy and eye candy appeal than I possessed.

Kylie was soon fed up with hanging around the house most days, and she answered an advertisement for au pairs in America and only three weeks after landing at Heathrow, we were back there, hugging her goodbye as she departed on a plane for California.

In the meantime, Dana wasn't enjoying school and was uncommunicative and miserable. I was also depressed, with the grey skies and frequent rain. I suffered badly from Seasonal Affective Disorder.

There seemed to be a constant stream of visitors coming to see Jeremy, often saying "About that fiver you owe me Jeremy..." I found myself reaching for my purse, but stopped just in time. These were not my debts and for once, I was not going to pay them.

I began to feel genuinely frightened of Jeremy. He would spend the majority of the Social Security or Benefit money on buying paints for Dana, and then sit, and copy her paintings. He could see that I didn't believe his plans for a big future any more, with a new job, in a new country.

I went to Relate and spoke to a counsellor. Was there a life without Jeremy? Was there life for me after Jeremy? Could I do the unthinkable and leave? I only knew that in Durban, I'd been able to earn a living, here I was tied to a man I no longer loved nor respected.

My mother came to stay for two nights in London, but she was no help. I couldn't talk to her, she was simply full of criticism and just too thrilled to have been proved right all along.

"I told you it would all go wrong didn't I? But then you never listen to me, you never have," she said as she watched me prepare supper.

"Yes, it all went wrong, and you were right. But what I need now is advice. I'm worried about the future. I can't get work and I've tried lots of places."

"Well of course you can't get work in London, I could have told you that. If you tried Bristol or Cheltenham then it would be much easier."

"No, Mum, there are lots more production companies here in London, they're all listed in the '*Writers' Year Book*'.

"Then why ask me for advice if you're not going to take it? All you do is contradict me."

"You know that's not true. I could really do with some emotional support from you."

"What have you ever done to deserve support? You've always gone your own way, you don't care about me and after all I've done for you. You're just an ungrateful child. I told you you'd always be bad, you always have been. You never deserved a mother like me."

I breathed a sigh of relief when she departed on the coach bound for home. She saw someone she knew on the bus, and rushed off without even saying goodbye.

I contacted Durban. If I returned would they have work for me? They replied immediately, and the answer was "Get on the next plane back, we miss you, plenty of work as soon as we can make it happen."

I said nothing for a couple of days, but then Dana climbed on my lap, put her arms around me and said "Mum, I'm not happy here, I miss Kylie, can't we go back to SA, please?" I thought about it for another day or so, had another session at Relate and made up my mind.

"Jeremy, Dana and I want to go back to Durban, will you come with us?"

"I'll never set foot in that country again, but you go if you want to."

Not once in the time it took to spend most of my remaining pounds on Dana's ticket, the ticket Jeremy had sent for me was a return ticket, and pack our suitcases, did Jeremy ask us to stay. After twenty three years, it was such an anticlimax.

"Look, we've been married for so long, we can't let it end like this. I'll go back to South Africa until the end of next year when Dana has finished her Matric. She's worried that she's not doing Maths and English and all her other subjects here in England. Let's see how it goes in that time. It will give you time to get settled in and get a regular job."

"If that's the way you want it, but I'll never go back to South Africa, never." And so the die was cast. Tearfully I packed up the computer and delivered it to the airport to be sent unaccompanied luggage and then, on the spur of the moment, I did something totally out of character. I walked into a travel agent, put £200 on the counter and asked if it would take two people to Paris.

"Yes, but when do you want to go?"

"Tomorrow," I replied. Since we were now in the northern hemisphere, I was determined to show Dana a bit more of Europe and I had always wanted to see the capital city of France. I consoled myself with the thought that it could only help improve her French, one of her Matric subjects.

"Oh, and throw in a trip to Versailles as well if you can," I added. "We can stay in a cheap pension, that's OK." They probably thought I was mad, but the next day, Dana and I were sky borne, heading for Charles de Gaulle airport. We had a fabulous four days, and for a short while, despite the cold, we forgot all our problems and behaved like any other tourists.

Now I was about to return overseas, to stand on my own two feet for the first time. It seemed the only solution, but I was quite terrified.

24 DURBAN AGAIN

I didn't have the courage to phone my mother before I left England, I just couldn't take the explosion and the added guilt. I knew she would be furious, but I felt bad enough and being such a coward I needed all the emotional strength I could muster. I couldn't afford for her to pull me down even further. I also knew she would try and change my mind. She wanted me to stay in England. This would not be for my benefit, but for hers alone. My mother's wish was for me to live near her, not for us to be friends, oh no. She wanted me there so that I could run errands, clean her house and wait on her hand and foot. Even if I complied, she would not give me an easy life. Every time I spoke to her she wouldn't waste a second before telling me what a failure and a problem I was. The more distance there was between us, the better.

I had ordered a taxi to take us to the airport, but Jeremy sent it away when it arrived. For a moment, I thought Jeremy was going to ask us to stay, but no, he said he'd drive us to the airport. It was a very sad farewell. Dana and I were both in tears as we walked down the air bridge and onto the plane. At the back of my mind was the thought that perhaps I could get enough money saved to return with more independence and perhaps persuade Jeremy to settle in a steady job and we could live a more normal life, just like other people. True, we'd had some amazing adventures, but I was now 44 years old and the future, with no pension, no job and nowhere to live frightened me. We hadn't even kept up our British National Insurance contributions, and I knew that elderly people in England struggled even on a full old age state pension.

The Durban heat hit us like a warm, moist blanket, welcoming us back. Africa was in our blood and wouldn't let go too easily. The sun shone out of a clear blue sky and we felt we had finally come home. Of course nothing much had changed in the three and a half months since we left and our friends were waiting for us in exactly the same spot where they'd waved us goodbye. When we arrived at their house I was astounded to see Squeak sitting in the driveway.

"But I thought you were going to sell her!" I exclaimed.

"We knew you'd be back."

"You couldn't know that," I said.

"Yes we did, we knew you'd see sense one day, it just took longer than we expected."

"But did you make the payments for her hire purchase?"

"No, they can wait a couple of months I'm sure."

I couldn't impose on friends' hospitality for long, and I checked the newspapers for somewhere to rent. First, however I had to phone my mother. That was a phone call I'd prefer to forget and possibly most of the ones since as well. If she had been angry before, now she was beside herself. I felt a lot braver and safer several thousand miles away and as I put the phone down that was another hurdle over and done with. I promised to write and tell her how we were doing.

I had left a little in the bank but it was a struggle to find a place to live. Finally I found a one bed roomed flat across the road from the yacht harbour. I got Dana back into school, buying her another set of school uniform, took up work again and over the next year worked very hard, even managing to upgrade to a better apartment. We started with cardboard boxes and plastic picnic plates, celebrating the first time we could afford a bottle of squash – that brought back memories! Meals were served as first and second sittings as Dana and I took it in turns to use the one large plate. The boxes I had packed off the boat held mostly bedding, clothes and books, but every bit helped. I did have bad days, and I remember crying my eyes out the day I had enough money to buy a second plate so Dana and I could eat at the same time. It broke the first time I put food on it!

I re-financed the car and began to pay off the Johannesburg phone bill that Jeremy had left unpaid but was in my name. My credit card had been cancelled since Jeremy had not paid in the money he owed me for a purchase a couple of years ago. Obviously the statements were sent to the Johannesburg address and he'd assured me that the account was settled and I had believed him!

A couple of weeks after we had arrived back I received a phone call at work. It was Kylie calling from the States. She was very unhappy in her new job as an au pair, could I please send her a ticket so she could fly back to South Africa? I was devastated. I had barely enough money for food and there wasn't a chance that I could find the price of an air ticket. I promised to ask for an overdraft, but suggested that she used her return ticket and go back to her father in London.

I went to the bank and tried to borrow the money, but looking at my recent track record, especially with the credit card, they turned me down flat. I briefly considered going to a moneylender, but rejected this as the interest rates were truly appalling and there's no safety net in SA, no dole, no social security, and people who can't pay their bills are out on the streets, it's as simple as that. I wept bitterly, for I wanted her to come back so badly, even though I didn't have the money to feed her.

Kylie used her return ticket to England, flew in to Heathrow and took the train up to Scotland to join her father, where he was now settled with yet another good job. I prayed that this time it would work out and when we returned at the end of the following year, we could settle down like a more normal family. Also, Jeremy would have been in UK for the two year period, so maybe I could get Dana into tertiary education and, in the meantime save for Kylie's college fees.

Dana's birthday was at the beginning of May, but although she haunted the Yacht Club all day, there were no birthday cards from anyone and no phone calls. I went over my budget and bought her a cheap tape recorder in a desperate attempt to cheer her up, but it was difficult not to get depressed.

Durban
21 May 1994
Dear Mum,

This will be a short letter as I am feeling very miserable and I don't want to be too depressing. There isn't much news. I had a letter from Jeremy the other day. I still love him so very much, but as I said to him in my letter, I feel like a moth attracted to the candle flame I know is going to hurt me. At the moment the future looks so bleak. I can envisage years and years sitting here all alone in one room struggling to make ends meet. I feel so old. Jeremy and I were the perfect couple, this was never going to happen to us. I feel so alone. I know you will never contact me again and you will never forgive me for not phoning before I left. I was in such a state and I just couldn't handle it. I knew what your reaction would be. I know you have not forgiven me for not coming home when Paul died, you mentioned it so many times when I was in UK, but you didn't know that the number of times I wrote and begged you to come and stay with us was also because I needed you. I know I have never come up to your expectations and I never will. I'm sorry I am not the daughter you wanted and that my success in SA is worthless because it's not success in UK. I can't even talk to you because I was so loyal to Jeremy for years and never said anything. For years you refused to talk to Jeremy, or even ask about him, and now he's been to stay with you and you welcomed him and even lent him money. You can't understand that I need the sun. I just shrivel up and die under a grey sky and I hate the cold. I have no one to talk to and I feel very alone.

The only thing I can cling on to is that I can pay my way. I am working half day filing and this brings in a regular income and a script has been accepted and I'm waiting for papers from Pretoria before I can start the contract for nine programmes for the SABC.

Dana is very happy, she is away this weekend in Margate with a friend and her family, they are staying in a beach house. She has promised to study as exams are not too far away.

Well I can't think of anything else at the moment, the mood in the country is still good, the level of violence is right down and we all feel much safer.

I hope you enjoyed your trip to Holland. Please don't tell Jeremy I wrote a depressing letter, as I have already got the blame for messing up his work and being a worry. I can't take any more blame. For once, can't you be supportive and show some love?
Love Lucy xxx

Dana and I battled on as cheerfully as possible, but it was difficult for a teenager to accept a much lower standard of living after everything she'd been used to. Since I was blacklisted by the phone company while I was paying them off, my boat sitter friend asked me if I minded him putting a landline phone in my flat. It was a brilliant idea, and I was so grateful. The bills came addressed to him at the Yacht Club and I paid them. The only problem was keeping Dana off the phone, as we needed to keep the bills very small. I hit on the idea of asking for a lockable phone and I kept the key in a sealed envelope when I was out. This was only to be opened in an emergency, such as fire and break ins, but in the meantime, all her friends could phone her. Dana was not too impressed, but at least we were in contact with the outside world.

I phoned my mother. Big mistake, if I thought she might have forgiven me, I was totally wrong. I got the blame for leaving my husband, was probably an adulterous wife and perpetrator of all other crimes on the planet. I was not going to get any support or sympathy from that direction. I refused to defend myself. I had written to her asking her to be gentle and understanding, but I would have had more response from a brick wall.

I phoned Jeremy, but he was equally cold and unforgiving. I was out on my own and very aware of it.

Durban
8 June 1994
Dear Mum,

I didn't answer your letter as soon as I got it, as it crossed in the post with mine. As you will know by now, I've had bad flu and took to bed early every evening and at the weekends, so that I could continue going into work in the day time. It's not fair to say I've not written, as I promised you, I am doing my best to write as often as I can.

I've not sent Kylie's clothes back to UK because she hasn't asked me to, and they are only fit for the bin and much too light for UK as they are small tops and shorts and Dana has swiped the best of them anyway.

Obviously Dana would prefer to have her own room, so would I for that matter, but this is all I can afford at the moment and Dana understands that. I know you and I never lived in anything as small, but then sadly, I didn't have a house to sell that was provided by the man I promised to love, honour and obey. Everything I have now, the little that is, I have worked hard for.

I still don't know if the pain of living without my elder daughter whom I miss very much, and the husband I still love to bits, is better than the fear and worry of constantly running away from creditors and people knocking on the door asking for money to be repaid and having the utilities cut off. I guess I can cope with that when I have an income, but it's hard and I am still tired and very unhappy. I wonder if it's easier if your partner dies? I sometimes think so. Yes, it's final, but at least you are spared the fear of wondering if you've made the right decision, or wondering if they will find someone else and how you will feel about that. I would never have believed the trauma and pain a separation could bring. I don't want a life with any other man. At present I can't live with Jeremy and I can't live without him. To add to all that, I am completely on my own. I don't get support either financially or emotionally from any of the small family I have, and I've only had one letter from Jeremy. Each Friday in the Club, I hope and pray he or Kylie will phone, even for two minutes. If only I could afford to phone them.

I am quite frightened as I've taken the step to have a phone put in, courtesy of a friend, and I have instructed a removals company to collect the tin trunks that Jeremy left behind with his secretary; apparently she took them to Port Elizabeth. The removal company upped their quote from R300, to over R400 and it may be more. But I'm scared to leave it, or we will lose all those precious things I packed into them, like the family photograph albums, the medals the kids won for swimming and dancing, the rosettes from their horse riding days in Botswana, and my collection of Harrison Ainsworth books; maybe I could sell those? There will also be the mementoes you gave me belonging to my father and pics of my grandparents as well, and of course my precious sewing machine. I'm looking forward to opening it all.

Dana has settled down well at school, and she starts her work experience tomorrow and I think she's a little nervous. We will have to raid my wardrobe this evening to find her suitable clothes.

Sadly the money Jeremy promised to put into my account for the Johannesburg phone bill has not materialized, and Dana lives in the mistaken hope that her outstanding child allowance he said he's drawn, and her birthday present, will arrive soon.

She has been asked to the Matriculation Ball at the boys' high school, and I'm smiling bravely as I will have to scratch around to get a dress, shoes and pay for the hairdo.

I am still doing about fifteen hours a week in the filing office. I remember you were so proud of Paul when he took a lowly job, I hope he would approve, even if you don't, but it is honest work. I am also writing a few articles for a corporate magazine and there is another shoot coming up. The SABC made a mistake with my money and so I won't get a cheque from them until the end of July, and you can add another eleven days for it to get to Durban.

I would phone you if I had the money, but Dana and I know that it's there for incoming calls only. At least you know you can get hold of us at any time. I do promise that if I can't cope, then I will send Dana back on her return ticket, even if I can't afford one for myself. I won't let her suffer in any way. I will remind her again to write, but I suspect she will be very tired after a full day's work in the real world, and she has two art projects to do in the holidays. I must try to get her the materials for those too.

Give our love and regards to everyone and if you speak to Kylie or Jeremy, please ask them to write to us.
Love Lucy

The letter before and the following one home, tries to refute all the criticisms that were thrown at me. Like an idiot I answered all the points quite reasonably, hoping for some support from somewhere! At no time did my mother offer me any help, neither financial, practical nor emotional.

Durban
8th July 1994
Dear Mum,

I asked you to be gentle in your letter and you went for the jugular. I howled for three hours after I read your letter. I know you're angry, but can't you understand? You don't think it was good for me to come back to SA, but can't you trust me to know what's best for me and for my daughter? I feel the main reason for your anger is because I'm not living close to you, which is what you feel is best for you.

I hope that when, and I'm sure they will, my daughters choose to live far away from me, I will be disappointed naturally, but I will still give them all the encouragement I can. That way, I will be a comfort to them, not a retributive force that scares them away.

Yes, there is some truth that I love myself, but then we all love ourselves more than we love anyone else, that's normal, or so the psychologists would tell us. But I do love my family, and as I told you in the last letter, I miss them terribly. If there is one thing I hope for Jeremy, it's that he stays successfully in this job. Sadly, his record for this is not good and even if I had waited a week or so more, I don't think that would have made any difference. We had to leave when we did, as Dana's return student ticket expired at midnight on 19th April, so we left it until the last minute. As for Kylie, she told me that if the family au pair thing did not work out, then she would extend her ticket to SA. In the end she didn't have enough money for this, but if she had arrived on the doorstep, I would have made a plan, of course I would. But I didn't have the money for the air ticket, at no time did I deliberately reject her. I understand you've told her that I don't want her, and this is not true.

I will never convince you, but I know in my own mind, that I intended to stay in UK if it was going to work out, and I would never have left Dana behind with Jeremy. He has no idea how expensive teenagers are to feed and clothe. When Dana and I first discussed coming back here, she said that she took neither Jeremy nor I into consideration, but decided on what was best for her. I told her that there was no way I would come back here if she didn't want to, I never forced her at all.

To say money is my god is silly. It's not pleasant having the sheriff at your door and it's scary when summons arrive and believe me, that's happened more than once or twice. I only want enough to cover the bills each month, I don't ask for much more.

It scared me in UK that I couldn't get any kind of work and it left me feeling very vulnerable. It wouldn't be easy to get back into teaching, did you realize that I only ever taught in UK for a total of eight terms? Also I've not been in a classroom for over eight years.

Yes, I am feeding Dana and myself, we're having stew tonight and we also have spaghetti bolognese, tuna fish bake, cheese and egg pie, bacon and eggs, steak and onions, fish pie and omelettes, cold meat and salads, corned beef hash and so on. We only occasionally have beef burgers and fish fingers as Dana likes them so much. You may remember, both daughters now tower over me, so I guess I've not starved them.

And she's not suffering too badly either. I queued for three hours last week to get free tickets to a concert in the City Hall with the Natal Philharmonic and we went and had a great time. No, I have not come back here to have a wild social life, where did you get that idea? As for you not coming to SA, so what if you're not interested in this country? That's not the reason you would come surely, but the fact that you are my mother and we are your family. We came home every time from Libya to see you and the Bath grandparents, not because we were particularly interested in UK.

Maybe I am fit for better things than filing, despite a private education, but I'm not ashamed of it, and not too proud to take work where I can find it. I would have done any work in UK as well, but there was nothing, and I trailed around all over the place. I remember you knitted jumpers in Dublin and you did the insurance thing as well and you did that to survive for me, I am doing the same for my daughter.

I am also writing for another magazine and they are very pleased with my latest article, an investigation on why drugs are so expensive in SA. They have asked me to expand it and make it a bigger feature.

I'm glad you enjoyed your trip to Holland, I had a letter from Kylie so I know you have seen them and you took her shopping. She wrote a long list of all the things you got for her. Sadly, I can't give as much to Dana at the moment.

She also phoned us last Friday, Jeremy said she could as he was away in Germany, but I wish she had waited for cheap time as the call must have cost him a lot. She sounded a bit down, as she said she was quite scared sleeping there alone when Jeremy was away, but she does enjoy the food and the band and the nightclubs. She told me about the electronic drums, the hi-fi system, the music, and all the new clothes they have bought. I rather wish Jeremy had not bought a set of drums, but paid for the hi-fi system he'd asked me to buy. I'm still paying that back on my credit card and they are taking R400 a month out of my bank account for it. I was told that his secretary was given instructions to sell it, but where the money went I have no idea, possibly towards her unpaid salary?

I keep hoping that Jeremy will suddenly become responsible, I do love him so much, but instead of the drums, if only he had taken out life insurance for the kids, or paid you or his friend, who I now know paid for our air tickets home, or a training course for Kylie, or even sent Dana the birthday present he promised her.

Kylie says she is looking for a job, but I do wish she would get some training behind her, even if it is a basic computer course. She could then work as a receptionist or in an office and take it from there. She mentioned that Jeremy suggested she go for a job as a bookkeeper, which puzzled me a bit, can she do that without any training? Also, Maths is not Kylie's strong point.

I may have given you the impression we were in one room, but there is a small hallway, a bathroom, a kitchen, main room and another room off that where they have enclosed the balcony. Obviously I will try to get something bigger when I can afford it.
Love, Lucy xxx

How much of the child is crying out in these letters written by a 44 year old woman? Perhaps my state of mind shows a lack of maturity, but it proves that the constant abuse over four decades and more, had undermined me completely. This was compounded by the fact that I no longer had Jeremy to rely on, to provide emotional security, and for the first time I was completely on my own. I had no choice but to be as brave as I could. I was so desperate for approval, and why was I wasting my time trying to repute all her nasty comments in her letters to me? I must have known they would fall on deaf ears.

I continued to write for the magazine, articles about the homeless and those living in squatter shacks. I believe these helped me to feel less sorry for myself. There were so many people out there with a lot less than I had.

I joined a group for single parents, and a counselling group that was free, which took a lot of courage on my own. I learned that men had emotions too. With Jeremy, nothing was ever a problem. He was seldom down, and he hid all his negative feelings so well; that I judged all other men solely by him. Slowly, very slowly, I took the first tentative steps learning to stand on my own two feet. While friends constantly told me that I had been supporting the family for years, both emotionally and financially, I had never believed them, but maybe they saw something I didn't?

Dana had settled in well and I managed to give her a small allowance as things improved. She was mixing with a nice group and doing normal teenage things. The crowd went off to the mountains for a weekend and Dana was quite surprised that I agreed to let her go.

"You're seventeen now," I said, "and if you want to get up to mischief, you don't have to travel to the Drakensburg to do it." In the event, I was invited to go with them, as the parent they most wanted along as chauffer and chaperone, but I declined due to several pending deadlines. I guess it was a compliment, in a backhanded sort of way!

There was one thing nagging away at the back of my mind, my tax. I remembered that I was due a tax rebate from a couple of years before. Since Jeremy had always worked out the tax and the SABC and the Municipality taxed me 25% at source, it was most unlikely I had run up any debts with them. But I was sure that I should register or something. I went to see an accountant and we worked out a deal that he would get my rebate for me, then sort out the rest up to date, and I would pay him from the money I got back. His phone call a couple of days later informed me that yes, a cheque for five thousand Rand had been issued last year and was collected by my husband.

"But how could he do that, how could he cash it?" I asked.

"Not difficult, you both have the same surname and he may have paid it into his bank or even got a retailer to give him a cash portion, they know a Receiver of Revenue cheque won't bounce." So that was gone as well.

It took me until early September to pay for the trunks to be delivered and Dana and I were very excited as they were carried up in the lift. They were all securely locked and I didn't have the keys, so we decided to break them open. It took quite a while, but when we finally sawed through the locks, and looked inside, we couldn't believe it.

My set of encyclopedia Britannica was there and a wall carpet from Libya, but nothing else we recognized. There were some plastic filing trays and a few rags and toys we'd never seen before. No photograph albums, no medals and certificates, no precious toys to be kept for the next generation, no Harrison Ainsworth books, no sewing machine.

Something died in me that night.

To lose all the photographs of the girls as babies and our record of them growing up was incredibly painful. A piece of the past was gone. It was impossible to replace. Dana and I went to bed and cried ourselves to sleep.

As I was making inroads into the debts, the lady in the flat upstairs told me she was leaving. She had a much nicer flat, on the ninth floor, which actually received sunlight in day time, had bright polished and sealed wooden floors, and the rent was only R50 more a month. I jumped at the chance, but there was a catch. She'd bought a bed, a couch and a cabinet on hire purchase and she couldn't afford the payments. Would I take these over? I sat down and scribbled down the figures. It was going to be a very tight squeeze, but I took a chance. The best thing about the new flat was the extra bedroom. Dana would have her own room at last. There would also be more space for Kylie if she decided to come over later on. She was still living with Jeremy in Scotland, working as a waitress during the day and studying at night, at least, that was the plan. From her frequent letters, I suspected the clubbing was more important than the studying.

My newly acquired girlfriends came to help me move, and other friends both kind and tactful asked me if I had room to 'look after' some furniture for them as they were short of space. We had taken another step towards independence.

Work wise I was back in full production, and in many ways my work saved my sanity although it's not the glamorous life people think it is. It's just damned hard work, with early mornings and late nights and often, impossibly tight deadlines.

Eventually, much to my dismay, Dana's birthday present from her father arrived. It was a violin. Our new flat was bigger, but not that big, and I begged her to practice between 2.30 and 5.00 in the afternoons. I was afraid that we might have complaints from the other tenants and find ourselves out on the street. Were the walls as thick and soundproofed as I hoped?

As 1994 drew to a close I had work coming out of my ears. I was still scriptwriting and directing/producing, and I was also writing for three magazines. One of my SABC producers came down to Durban, took me for a very liquid lunch and gave me another contract, and I was also writing articles for inserts published in the daily newspaper.

I also won certificates and trophies for my work at the annual '*National Television and Video Awards*', which were held in Johannesburg, but often I had neither the time, nor the money to attend.

We filmed Her Majesty the Queen and Princess Anne, on their visits to Durban, and since I was now writing speeches for the Mayor, I was invited to meet HRH Prince Charles at a reception for him in the Town Hall.

We had a quiet Christmas, with supper at the Yacht Club on the night before, but we gave each other a stocking. I was so touched, that Dana thought to give me one. On New Year's Eve, we followed tradition and went out on boats into the harbour to welcome in 1995. I was on a forty foot cruiser while Dana and her friends whizzed around in a small power boat. At midnight the flares lit up the sky and fireworks blazed, yet it was a strong reminder of how alone I still felt.

We did hear news of Jeremy, from Kylie, who still wrote regularly and phoned when she could. She told us that her father had bought a ten roomed house on eight acres with two tumbledown cottages in a village outside Glasgow. Kylie was not moving in with him, but staying in the house where they were. It sounded very impractical and just how was Kylie going to cope on her own? If Jeremy was travelling a lot, what about frozen pipes in the Scottish winter? Ten rooms were a lot to heat, and expensive too. Still, I guessed that was not my problem now. Jeremy had bought Kylie a car and she had passed her basic driving test and her advanced test, so at least she could get about.

Dana and I did something I had never been allowed to do while I was living at home in England. We went to rock concerts. There was a rush of stars coming to perform now that the apartheid days were over, and we saw Cliff Richard, Roxette, Wet Wet Wet, Whitney Houston and Tina Turner.

I had a call in the April to say that Kylie was coming out for a two week visit. Both Dana and I were very excited, but at the airport, we almost walked past her. She had put on so much weight and she didn't look at all well. She had a really great time, as there was a lot to do in Durban. She went dancing, attended a concert and there were picnics on the beach and sailing on the boats and we visited all the sights.

She was quite adamant that she was going back to Scotland and I said that was fine. I only asked that she not go back and then decide to return within a short time, as that would be a waste of an expensive air fare. I was quite worried about her, especially when she showed me pictures of her friends and the nightclubs she was going to in Glasgow. The friends all looked very rough and I wondered if they were out on parole. In fact our boat sitter friend asked her which borstal they'd escaped from! She was not impressed. I also had a strong suspicion that the guy she was so keen on was married, but she said that her father was encouraging her. Surely that couldn't be true?

It was a couple of days before she went back that she let it slip that Jeremy had a girlfriend and he stayed over nights with her. I was devastated. OK, so I should have expected it, but it hurt a lot. To make it worse, she was married with two children. Another alarming piece of information was that she had persuaded Jeremy to start drinking again, after seven years on the wagon.

I wanted to talk to Jeremy about Kylie, but since he had moved, she was sworn to secrecy and told not to pass on either his phone number or his address. He had deliberately broken contact with us and we had no idea where he was.

Kylie flew back on a Tuesday night in May and the phone rang two days later on the Thursday. It was Jeremy, the first time we had spoken in almost a year. He simply informed me that my eldest daughter would be on a plane to Durban, landing on Monday at 18.00 hours and he suggested we be there to meet her. He hung up. That was the last I was to hear from him for almost twelve years.

I'll never know what happened between father and daughter, but I do know when Kylie arrived back in Durban the second time, she was very angry with the world, and especially angry with me.

Even with two bedrooms in the flat, the girls had to share and it was a tight squeeze. Dana resented having less space and they squabbled constantly. I was quite firm in that Kylie must study something and work part time, exactly the opposite to what she had been doing in Scotland. She really felt the loss of her car, it seemed that Jeremy had borrowed it and been pulled over by the Police as it was found to be unroadworthy. I assured her that Durban Transport busses would probably be a lot safer, and perhaps we could share Squeak on occasion.

Since the academic year runs from January, she could not enrol in a course immediately, so I suggested she get a job waitressing or something similar that would help her to save for the fees. I would feed, house and clothe her. I was still getting on my feet financially, but if we all worked together, she could start her course the following year.

1995 went quickly. Dana was in her last year at school and she passed her Matriculation and we enrolled her in the Technical College, where she was offered a choice of three courses. Kylie booked her course to start the next January and worked at various restaurants and got lots of tips. There were frequent explosions throughout the year, the result of too many people in too small a space, and the remnants of a break up in the family.

Neither of the girls heard from their father at birthdays or Christmas, and the only news we had of him was from letters Kylie received from mutual friends in Scotland. It seemed that Jeremy had lost his good job in Scotland, had then worked in a garage, but all the cars had been wrecked one night, and that he had gone 'underground' and taken on another name. Now, even the last address Kylie had for her father was no longer valid.

The chances of me returning to UK as soon as Dana had finished school, were simply not an option any more. I would stay in South Africa.

By Christmas, both girls were waitressing part time for extra money. To see them on the day itself, I had to eat out, while they served me! We had graduated to a rented television, a cheap stereo and a couple of nicer pieces of furniture.

I had kept in regular touch with my mother and I wrote every few weeks. There was a kind of truce between us, I think, reading what I wrote back to her, but each letter from her, which I have not kept, always contained several criticisms and innuendoes about how I was still such a failure. But I simply ignored the barbs and kept writing regularly. I'm not really sure why, but it seemed the right thing to do.

At last I received my first royalty cheque on my book, for the princely sum of £4.50! I had no idea what to expect, since they'd paid me a R4,000 advance for it, but I opened a UK bank account and deposited my first, small cheque. It was to be the beginning of my emergency fund in hard currency, a small amount to be sure, but a start!

My mother still refused to believe that I'd received money from my publishers, it was just another example of my over-active imagination. Was she surprised that I had an imagination, when I considered how much of my childhood had been spent in a fantasy world, where pretend life seemed more normal than the real one I lived in?

In the early months of 1996 I got a phone call from Jeremy's ex business partner Richard who was now in Cape Town. I was not listed in the telephone directory, but he had seen my name on some credits on the television and tracked me down from there. He was looking for Jeremy, did I know where he was?

"No," I replied, quite truthfully. I had not spoken to him in almost a year and he had moved on from his last known address. I was horrified to hear that when Jeremy left for UK in 1993, he had left debts to the value of over a quarter of a million Rand, all of which his partner had to repay if he wished to retain his license to market insurance. I remembered that he had two disabled children to support. This was the first time I realized just what Jeremy had done. I felt sick. There was no way I could personally help him myself, I was just getting on my feet and had no spare money. Then, I reasoned, it wasn't my debt, or was it?

Then it struck me. Could I be held liable for this and all other debts Jeremy might have simply ignored before he got on the plane? To pay back over a quarter of a million Rand was not an option.

Richard had employed a private detective in UK to track Jeremy down, but so far no luck. Apparently other people were also looking for him, his ex partner was not the only one.

I tried to phone my mother in law that night, but all I got was number unobtainable. I phoned directory enquiries, but was told that her number had been changed and that it was now unlisted. I asked if they could phone her, tell her who was calling and ask her to receive the call; but they refused. Another lifeline to my old life had been severed. I discovered later that she had had several threatening phone calls from South Africa, from people trying to find out where Jeremy was. She was very frightened by these and went ex-directory.

It was now that I began thinking of divorce. Not because I wanted freedom to get married again, but as a protection against what we were all trying to salvage. I approached a lawyer friend and asked about the logistics.

It was not a cheap procedure. You could pay the earth to get a divorce, first the solicitor's fees, then the attorney who represented you in court, and of course a lot depended on the settlement.

"There won't be any settlement," I observed gloomily. "Jeremy won't have a penny to his name, and even if the courts ordered it, can you imagine the problems I would have trying to get any kind of alimony across six thousand miles?"

"Then put in for one Rand, it's a loop hole in the law and should he win the lottery and you get to hear of it, then you can claim. It keeps the door open." He also told me that although it was most unusual, I could handle the divorce myself. I could even buy the forms at the local stationers and he would help me fill them in.

That seemed simple enough, but the real problem was, how would I serve the papers? You can't divorce your spouse without telling him or her about it.

After queuing for hours in the court filing office and queuing again for the correct revenue stamps, I sent off the relevant papers to Jeremy's last known address. Like a homing pigeon, they came right back.

I phoned the nearest police station in Scotland and asked them if they could visit the cottage on the off chance that Jeremy was still there. They were kind enough to do this, but the place was deserted, only piles of bills inside the front door. I then asked them to recommend a firm of lawyers who could serve the papers and they were equally helpful with this.

I sent the papers over a second time, with a letter of explanation and asked how much it could cost to try and find Jeremy. I also added that with the rate at five Rands to the £, I was working on a tight budget. They were really amazing and worked in conjunction with the police to keep costs down. Enquiries were made with neighbours nearby and they also visited his girlfriend, but she said that she also had no idea where Jeremy was. We'd reached a stalemate.

I went to court to explain the situation. I've seen lots of TV programmes showing legal stories, but I'd never expected to feel quite so over-awed. I explained the situation, and the judge said he simply could not award me a divorce, I had to serve the papers on someone. He said he'd accept delivery to Jeremy's mother and the last known girlfriend.

I sat with the papers for several weeks. Could I do this to the mother-in-law I'd loved so much? I couldn't even phone her and talk to her, but there seemed no other way, the judge had said to serve both of them.

When I went to retrieve my file from the records office, they'd lost it, and I began to wonder if my prospective divorce was jinxed. However, they phoned me the following afternoon to say the file had been found.

Again the papers traveled north over the African continent, to the law firm in Scotland and to another legal company in Bristol whose speciality was serving summons. They both came back duly signed and stamped.

By this time it was early 1997 and when I was given a court date of February 14th, my heart dropped. What an anniversary on which to remember your divorce! As I sat there, watching one marriage after another dissolved, I almost turned tail and fled. Once again I climbed into the witness box, while the same judge examined my papers.

"I'm sorry, but these have only been stamped by a solicitor's office, they must be authorized by a public notary." He saw my face. "I'm really sorry, but if I say yes to the divorce now, then later, if your husband wants to make a claim he can, and if you remarried, you could be accused of bigamy. I'll give you a date for next Friday, which should give you enough time to get them notarized," and with that, he went on to the next case, another 'instant' divorce.

This time I used a courier company, horrified at the costs, it would be another £68 for this stamp of approval. As I entered the court room the following Friday, I decided once and for all, if it didn't go through, then I would give up and stay married.

Someone, somewhere heard me, for after a ten minute hearing, Jeremy and I were no longer married. I was later told that I had made legal history in South Africa, in handling my own divorce, coupled with the fact that I had a husband overseas I couldn't trace.

Life continued as before, although I had met someone else who was fun to be with, made me laugh and was the exact opposite of Jeremy in every respect. We began to spend a lot of time together.

Dana was thoroughly enjoying her college work and to supplement her weekly violin lessons, for which I refused to pay, she went to work at the Natal Playhouse. I was quite envious of her job, for although it was not well paid, she saw all the important performances, such as the Bolshoi Ballet, which I couldn't afford to go and see. At last she was getting a large slice of culture.

I pitched for and got a series on national television, and made some really interesting programmes, on teenage drug use, half way houses and fishermen. It didn't pay a lot, but at least it kept the funds rolling in. I was also offered a part time job lecturing at the local Technical College in Video Production Theory. What a joke, I thought, I've never had a lesson in this in my life! But perhaps the practical approach of working in the 'real world' was what they were after?

I almost panicked on the first morning as I stood in front of 70 teenagers, and several mature students, some of whom were older than I was. But I guess once a teacher, always a teacher and it all came flooding back.

I interviewed many top political people including Nelson Mandela, and filmed at many events attended by world leaders and I kept writing home, I guess I was hoping at last to impress my mother with what I was now achieving.

I was continuing to make progress and was even offered an overdraft by the bank, although I didn't need one! When I reapplied for my credit card, and the bank gave me a gold card, I felt I had finally made it! I paid off Squeak, possibly the longest car hire purchase deal on record, managed all the college fees, and most of all, I was finally out of debt. I took an almost childish delight in paying all my month end bills promptly knowing that I still had money left over in the bank.

As the tension decreased, the children got on with me and each other, and Dana's twenty first was held at the Yacht Club, when, unknown to me she had invited seventy five people. I'd suggested fifty as a good number, I wasn't a millionaire, but she reasoned that lots of people wouldn't turn up. Every single invited guest did and a couple extra. The Yacht Club staff glared at me, they probably thought I was trying to feed extra from the buffet when it was charged at so much a head.

I had a setback in 1998, just when everything seemed to be almost perfect. But then fate waits for that moment to throw in the curved ball. On a visit to the Royal Show at Pietermaritzburg, I took the opportunity to have my eyes tested. I'd not been able to see as clearly as before, but I'd not had the time to check it out. Perhaps the young assistant was a bit flustered, because without thinking she blurted out, "You're going blind!"

I burst into tears. Who cared if I was standing in the middle of a huge crowd of people. While life had been a struggle, I had always taken my health pretty much for granted. Apart from a broken tooth, and a few bouts of minor ailments, I had never given my health a thought.

But fate hadn't finished with me yet. I'd had a routine test done the previous week, as all the adverts told you to do as you got older. There was more bad news, they discovered suspect cells on my cervix. I was devastated. Although there is free, or almost free medical care in South Africa, it's worked out on a means test. I knew I didn't qualify for this and I had no medical aid cover, as it's incredibly expensive, and usually comes as part of the employment package. I was self employed.

I could see me landing right back to where I started in just a couple of weeks. There was also the question of my new relationship, a widower who had nursed his late wife for five years, I couldn't expect him to go through that again.

Suddenly, out of the blue, he asked me to marry him. No, not because I could be put on his medical aid, I'd not told him about the cells which were crumbling away inside me.

My first response was "why?" He came up with the right answer.

"Because I love you and I want to spend the rest of my life with you."

I told Dana the next morning and she gave me a big hug, and said

"Go for it." I couldn't have asked for more support. Before I could stop her, she grabbed my cell phone and rang Kylie to tell her, although I would have preferred to broadcast my own news.

"I hope you said yes," screamed my eldest daughter, "you'll never get another chance at your age." Thanks, all it takes is kids to make you feel really good!

My second marriage is totally different from my first. Michael opens the bills and pays them. I can trust him and his two children got on well with mine at first. I kept in touch with my mother and we invited her to the wedding but I was not surprised when she didn't come. It's a long way and she was in her seventies.

Not long after our wedding we took a trip to UK. I had not been back for twelve years so there were plenty of people to see. Things seemed neutral with my mother and Michael but I was nervous when we arrived at her front door. I had told him about the bad relations we had, but I had no idea what to expect and I was not sure how he would react either, he comes from a very 'normal' family.

At first things went well. We climbed up in the roof and brought down stuff my mother wanted to sell, cleared out the garage and took unwanted rubbish to the dump. And then she started. Michael was horrified at the way she spoke to me and told her so. She was a bit taken aback, we were in her house as guests. I begged Michael not to say any more.

We explored the countryside, but got stuck in Oxford waiting for the 'park and ride' bus and we were late back to dinner, which I was going to prepare anyway. Mother was steaming when we arrived even though I had phoned and explained the delay. We took her out for a meal and she told us about her unhappy childhood and the storm subsided. She was disgruntled at the fact we were leaving to see other people, but generally the visit could have been worse.

Our second visit a couple of years later was to help her celebrate her 80th birthday. Before we even left South Africa there was trouble.

Mother did not see why we had to hire a car, even when I pointed out that Kylie and her boyfriend, Michael, Dana and I plus Mother would not fit in her car, and we would be making multiple trips to the restaurant which would waste a lot of time. Tactfully, I didn't add that Michael had no intentions of being reliant on Mother to ferry us around either. In the end we ignored her protests and went ahead and the occasion did not go off too badly although Mother was not particularly friendly and did not relax the whole time we were there.

I took this opportunity to visit May who still lived around the corner. My mother had not spoken to her for several years. She was now a widow and the stories she told me of the cruel and unkind things my mother had done to her made me gasp. On one occasion when they were going away on holiday together, Mother refused to collect May at her house, although May was quite blind by then. So she had to phone a neighbour to help her round to my mother's house with her suitcase, even though they had to drive right past her house on the way out of the estate!

Christine was there at the time and said she would never forgive my mother for making May cry, something that happened frequently, and she was glad that they were not in contact any more.

Still I persevered, and our third trip was the worst of all. To begin with, Mother said she was not prepared to make up the spare room for us, that it was too much trouble and if we wanted to see her then we would have to book into a nearby bed and breakfast. With the South African Rand exchange rate to the pound soaring, this was going to make quite a dent in our budget, but we agreed, at least we could escape at the end of the day.

We had lots of other people to see, and we started up north and travelled south. I phoned my mother from Scotland to say we would be arriving at the end of the week and she went ballistic on the phone as she expected us to visit *her* first. She was totally unreasonable, even when I explained we were traveling north to south and we were also visiting Michael's family who lived half way down England. When I disconnected the call I was in floods of tears and I now knew what to expect.

When we arrived Mother was really rude, constantly praising Jeremy, they were great friends now, comparing him to Michael, and she was vitriolic and nasty. She reminded me that I had always been maladjusted and was surprised that I had managed to snare a second man.

Michael kept his temper as best he could but the crunch came when we decided to go into town. We had borrowed a car and promised we would not transport any animals in it as our friend was allergic to dogs and cats. Mother wanted to take her dog as well, Michael refused, and they had a terrific argument. Michael did not give way and the result was that we went to town in stormy silence in our friend's car without the dog. We couldn't wait to escape and as we boarded the plane to South Africa I breathed a sigh of relief.

For the next few years life ran smoothly, except for my occasional calls home. We had bought a lovely house and we worked hard to pay off the mortgage quickly as we were both now in our fifties and no longer young! It's scary retiring when you still owe money on your house. Two of our children were busy with their tertiary education and two had already departed for England seeing no long term future for themselves in South Africa and as each of them finished, they too jumped on a plane bound for London. It was difficult to kiss and hug them at the airport, we would miss them terribly, but I had promised that my children would leave me with my blessing and no recriminations. They were free to find their own destinies wherever that might be.

Before leaving I had tried to warn my girls about their grandmother and how she often caused trouble between other people. I tried to explain her behavior, but frankly words failed me. It was only a few months later I had a message on my cell phone from Dana. She was with Mother and wanted to know "why your mother hated you so much." I could only reply that I didn't know, and that my mother picked a fight with most people. Dana said she was shocked at all the bad things I had done when I lived at home as a child. I cringed, what was my mother telling her? Her version of events would be very different to mine.

Sometime later, I had frantic messages from Kylie. She and Dana had gone down to the Cotswolds to see their grandmother and within half an hour they were at each other's throats. It was Mother and Dana against Kylie. Later my daughters had the most awful row on the way back to London and I wondered just how much misery my mother was deliberately causing now. She really enjoyed watching people fight, and I've seen her smiling when two people are screaming at each other. She was happy to sit and watch.

I flew over to England to see Mother and the girls, separately, and hopefully try some damage control. I could not believe how Mother had changed. She was quite charming, a totally different person. I had spoken to her doctor and explained that mother was getting a bit muddled with her pills, and I hinted strongly that she was not easy to get on with. I got the impression that her doctor was well aware of this and I suspect that Mother was on some sort of tranquillizers.

I slipped easily back into the role of housekeeper and while I was there, spring cleaned the kitchen and helped her sort out paperwork.

I'd only been back in South Africa for a few days when I had another phone call. This time Mother was freaking out about the tax man. It seems that she hadn't put in a tax return since Paul died in 1983 and they were now demanding an enormous sum of money from her. She sounded so lost and lonely that I offered her as much money as I could spare if that would help her out, and pleaded with her to consult a bookkeeper or an accountant and I would pay for it. She insisted that it was not her fault, it was all down to the tax department who should have told her she needed to file a return. For the first time, I wondered just how savvy my mother was with money.

A few weeks later I heard the front door open and close in the middle of the morning. I was writing in my study and somehow I just knew what Michael was going to say. He'd been made redundant, his company was downsizing. I could hardly equate this with Jeremy's job hopping, since Michael had only worked for three different companies all his working life.

We both knew that it was going to be almost impossible for him to find another job, as the affirmative action in South Africa was in full swing and all the managerial jobs were being offered to black people.

However all was not lost, as he was able to reinvest his pension money, and I hit on the idea of sub contracting pre-production and DVD copying work to him rather than pay outsiders. I was now independently running my own company and very busy. It worked well for several years and we paid off the house and even put down a deposit on a small flat in Spain as a bolt hole in case things blew up in Africa. We did not want to be a burden on the children and it would be a good place to retire. With the high levels of crime in the country, we did not want to grow old and frail and not able to defend ourselves if and when we were targeted as victims.

Although we had no intentions of leaving Africa for a good few years, as my retirement age approached I was getting less and less work. I took on an African and an Indian partner to meet the new legal regulations, but even that was not enough, as unfortunately most of my work was now for the provincial government who had to follow the rules. Maybe this was our wake-up call, and although it broke my heart to leave, we put our house on the market and began to pack up. It took another year to sell but at last we were ready to leave. We had both been in Africa for so long that it was a huge wrench to go, but it was the wisest thing to do and as the last days flew by, I was convinced that we would become just two more victims of crime before we reached the plane. Would we make it in one piece?

25 SPAIN

My mother sounded very pleased that we were coming home, but less pleased when I said we were making for Spain and not England. I explained that I would not be able to phone her too often as she complained bitterly when I called her via Skype on the computer, as in the early days the link would drop frequently. I told her that we did not intend to keep our little flat, but would look around for something bigger when the money from our house sale was transferred. I was amazed to learn that my cousins from Wales were living close by, the same couple who had taken me in when I was a teenager.

I made a visit to see Mother not long after we arrived in Spain, and it was a visit from hell. Wild horses would not drag Michael back, but he phoned me via Skype to her landline every day. I couldn't understand why our calls were cut off so frequently and blamed the poor internet connection, until I saw my mother holding the other remote phone with her finger on the disconnect button. She was very scathing about husbands who could not manage without their wives for a few days.

The girls too phoned daily, using the free calls on their mobile contracts, and Mother was so incensed that I had to keep my phone on silent in my pocket and slip out into the garden to answer it.

I simply tried to ignore her nasty comments about me, my husband and my daughters, who, according to her, had achieved nothing in life. When she started criticizing her neighbours and I refused to join in, she called me Mother Theresa and I just burst out laughing. Not a wise thing to do. If she had been on happy pills before, she was not on them now.

I took her into town and I was amazed to see how mobile she was when she thought I wasn't looking. I cooked a meal for her, in fact I did all the cooking and cleaning while I was there, and because I had prepared something in the microwave, time twenty minutes instead of the oven, time an hour and a quarter, she gave it all to the dog.

She had always had a dog, but like every canine she ever possessed, he made frantic efforts to escape. It dawned on me that none of our animals had ever run away, and remembered the fruitless hours I spent as a child, often in the pouring rain, trying to catch my mother's dogs and bring them back home.

I thought long and hard when I returned to Spain, and I sat down to write a long letter explaining how I felt, how I loved her, and wasn't there some way in which we could make a permanent peace? If I thought this would help I was sadly mistaken. She informed me she had shown it to a psychologist or psychiatrist and their verdict was that I was psychotic. No, I didn't really believe her, I felt quite normal, but again my confidence was undermined. To show me that I was totally in the wrong, she photocopied the letter and sent a copy to Jeremy, one each to the girls and made sure all the neighbours read it as well.

I decided to admit defeat, there were, thankfully still several hundred miles between us, and I did my best to put her out of my mind once and for all, while we house hunted for a larger place and settled into our new life. The transition was harder than I expected as I had always been so busy, and now I was just another pensioner looking out on the world from the wrong end of mortality. What was worse, I lost the inclination to write, the one thing that had always saved me in the past. Gradually we met new people and began to take part in social activities until one day the phone rang.

It was Dana and she was in a state. Mother had told her that she had a new son and he was the world to her. He was arranging for her to move to the West Country and he would sell her house and take care of her since her family ignored her. Who was this guy and what were his motives? Did he really care for her or was he just after her money?

I immediately phoned Mother and sure enough I got the same story. Much as she had hurt me I was still her daughter and my imagination saw her marooned in a caravan at the end of a muddy field, denied her medication and being starved to death. I did the only thing I could do and jumped on a plane.

When I arrived I met Dick, Paul's younger son. I was quite prepared to get on with him, it was quite a novelty to have a step brother after all these years. But we did not connect at all. He told me that when Paul had died, Mother had not bothered to tell him, so could he really love her so much now? Then he contradicted himself and said they had always been close and she had wanted to adopt him. That I knew was not true! He reassured me that he was not after her money at all, as Paul had stipulated in his will that everything my mother possessed, would be shared equally between the two of us. This I learned later was another lie.

Mother was in her element as she described all my misdeeds and faults to Dick and made me cry. It was a terrible visit, a real nightmare. She told me how wonderful Dick was driving up from the West Country almost a hundred miles, with no reference to the hundred miles I drove to the airport, and the flight over the Pyrenees, and another sixty miles in a hired car when I landed at the other end.

Dick stayed overnight and departed the next day. He promised to keep in touch with me but he never did. I did not trust him and I was relieved when Mother said that she would not leave her home and move anywhere. I had taken photographs of a bungalow right opposite ours and said that if she wanted to, we could help move her to Spain and I could pop in every day and be on hand. She refused this offer as well. She became even more verbally abusive and things were so bad that I walked out on the third day, but thought better of it and returned and stayed for two more days. I promised to go home every three months to spend a few days with her, but later back in my own home in Spain, I regretted this and wrote to say I would come, but only if she promised to welcome me and not fight. She refused.

Yet again, I tried to put her out of my mind, but I kept in touch through a neighbour just to keep an eye on her. She was getting old and frail, and I had told her many times that if at all possible, I would not let her die alone.

A year later I was horrified to learn that my mother had been in hospital for three months. Why had no one told me? The neighbours, all of whom had fallen out with her, told me they did not want to get involved, even though they all had my contact numbers in Spain.

I booked a plane ticket and phoned the hospital to enquire how she was. They wanted to know who I was. I was her daughter.

"No," they said," she doesn't have any other relatives listed on her forms, only a son." I informed them she had a daughter, two granddaughters and by now, two great grandchildren. I phoned the girls, no they had not heard anything either.

When I approached the hospital bed I did not recognize my mother. She had aged beyond belief. She was very sleepy and I was not sure at first if she even recognized me. She drifted in and out of consciousness and I thought she was very near death. She rallied a little and in between bouts of dementia she praised Dick and reminded me of how rotten a daughter I was. For once, that sounded more normal, it was almost a relief! I stayed with her until they threw me out, but not before I had them amend the records for the rest of her family by blood.

Dana had told me that I was no longer the Executor in Mother's will, but Mother had told me the same often enough. All I had asked for was the family photos. I was assured that she would not leave me those either, but in all honestly I did not believe her. She could never be that mean could she?

I went back to the family home, and was alarmed to find that the back door was left open all day, to allow the dog to run in and out. In every room there was a note to contact Dick in case of any emergency, but there were no photos of me, nor the rest of the family. What was more alarming, none of the private papers I had helped her sort out were in the house.

I phoned Dick and asked him what was going on and his first words were "How did you find out?" I did not answer him. We agreed to meet the next day at the house and I asked for my mother's car keys as I could not afford to keep the hired car. In my panic I had taken out full excess, and it was costing a fortune. I was so upset, and I was terrified that I would have an accident.

A neighbour told me that when Mum had first fallen, before being taken to hospital three months earlier, she tried to phone me. Dick had told her I was in South Africa and given her a number that did not exist. She left a message for me to come, but of course I never received it. I guess she believed that I did not care.

The next day I spent the time scrubbing the floors while waiting for Dick. By now after three months on his own, the dog was both a basket case and incontinent. Dick did not turn up.

I went down to hospital to find him at my mother's bedside. He had all kinds of excuses as to why he had not let me know, and no, he didn't have the car keys or couldn't find them or some other excuse I can't remember what. He said that mother had just fallen asleep, but they had been chatting and doing the crossword together.

Taking a break outside, he informed me how useless my daughters were, they never visited, and their father was even worse. I tried to keep my counsel. We parted and I spent the rest of the day with Mother, but as I was about to leave, the lady in the next bed called out to me and said:

"It's such a shame that your brother came all this way and your mother did not say a single word to him." Proof enough for me that Dick told lies!

It was difficult staying at the house. The electricity was connected but there was no hot water and no heating either, even in August I was shivering. I spent the following day at the hospital which was a good deal warmer and Mother recovered enough to have a real go at me. I told her that she was being most unfair, as Granny had gone overseas when she married, Mother had left for Dublin when she married, and I had simply done the same with Jeremy. I stormed out, very angry.

I was still angry the following morning when I phoned a locksmith to open the garage. I thought if I could get to the car, then I could stay on and see my mother every day. The hospital said that she could not remain there much longer, they needed the bed. She should go into a home where she would get proper care. I decided to stay until she was settled in and check that she was going to be well looked after.

All my mother's papers were in the boot of her car, thrown in, in total disarray. I took them all back into the house and briefly checked a couple of bank accounts for signs of any large amounts going out in the last three months. Everything looked fine and then I did something I am very ashamed of, I read my mother's will. The temptation was just too much. I was not mentioned, no family photographs were left to me after all. Still it was my mother's choice if she did not want to acknowledge me, she could leave all her possessions to whoever she wanted. But it hurt, especially as I had never received my Granny's favourite brooch that she told me many, many times she wanted me to have.

I returned to the hospital and spent the rest of the day there. When I arrived my mother looked at me and said;

"I have been very cruel to you. I do love you but when you love people then you only get hurt." I agreed that she had been mean but it didn't matter anymore. It was the nearest she ever came to an apology or an explanation. I still treasure those few words. However, I did tell her that I knew she had disinherited me and yet I was still there. I had not come looking for her money. I wanted her to know that.

I tried to make myself useful by feeding Mum as they were short staffed, and I was there way outside visiting hours. Before I left, my cell phone rang. It was Dick's partner advising me that they had a warrant out for my arrest for breaking into the garage. They were driving up from the West Country and would see me at the house along with the police. In the background I could hear Dick swearing and cursing, bewailing the fact that he had wasted all his money sucking up to "the old bag" and now he might lose it all. If I'd thought he was just a fortune hunter before, I was sure of it now.

I had to leave, telling Mother the reason and I got in the car to drive back to the house.

At the top of the hill I stopped and phoned Dick, leaving a message to say that I had had the garage opened by a professional locksmith and I did not think that my mother would be too impressed if they involved the law. His partner phoned back almost immediately saying that it was all a misunderstanding and could we meet tomorrow for lunch and have a chat about everything? I agreed but I was not convinced. What was more I felt dirty. While family dramas had always been part of my life, this was more like a badly written soap opera of the worst kind. It was sleazy and I felt very uncomfortable.

To make matters worse I then had phone calls from the girls, asking about the police and how could I destroy Granny's property, and what did I think I was doing breaking the law, they had thought better of me. It was all too much, it didn't seem to matter to anyone what my motives were.

The next day neither Dick nor his partner arrived to go to lunch so I spent another day at Mum's bedside. She slept most of the time and hardly looked at the photo albums I showed, her hoping that she would remember the good times she had had on holiday with friends. It was quite difficult trying to remember any good times to talk about, there were so few of them.

Later I went to see her lawyer and asked if I could legally stay in the house. Apparently no, even though I had verbal permission from Mum in hospital to stay there and drive her car. I gave up and admitted defeat. They had told me that Mum was going to be interviewed by a psychologist and would most probably be sectioned. Then it would be Dick and my daughters as her executors who would handle everything.

I could stay no longer. The authorities refused to deal with me even though I was her next of kin, and there was little else I could do but return to Spain. I was devastated, somehow everything had gone wrong.

Over the next few weeks the girls occasionally contacted me with suggestions as to where they could find a home for Mum, and I searched the internet for suggestions. The whole situation was wrong, it felt as if my children had been put in charge of me. They were both busy working and had little time to spend sorting out Mum's affairs. None of them knew her as well as I did, my children had had limited contact with her and even less understanding.

They certainly chose a very nice home for her which cost a fortune, and a few weeks later I flew over again to see her. This time Michael came with me and we first went to one of his relative's 90th birthday celebrations and then drove down south. On the way I phoned Kylie who had agreed to meet us in London, to change plans and say that instead we would drive straight to Mum's house. Michael would stay one night and then leave for London the next day; where he was going to spend time with his children and grandchildren.

Kylie hit the roof and said that Granny would not want him to step foot in her house and as a result she was not sure if she would come down to see me after all. I felt as if the whole world was going mad, or was it just me? In any event she never came down from London at all and I had to get a taxi to and from the home to visit Mum.

Everyone was talking about how wonderful Mum was and how terribly I had behaved. Was this just because she was leaving them a large amount of money or had they been brainwashed since leaving South Africa? I could believe that neither my mother, nor Jeremy nor Dick would have a good word to say about me.

After spending a few days with Mum we left England, but by now I was in quite a state. Michael became very angry and was determined to tell the girls what he thought of their behaviour. I asked him not to, but this one time he was not about to listen. He wrote them a letter which made even me blanch and as a result his children broke off all contact with my daughters. I was in the middle and there was nothing I could do except to try to protect myself. I told the girls I was going to stay out of contact as I needed time to lick my wounds and get over the hurt. I left them to get on with everything.

I phoned Mum every week in the home and sometimes she was responsive and at other times not. I flew over again to see her twice more, staying at the cheapest bed and breakfasts I could find, and using coaches and taxis to keep the costs low. The expenses were eating into our meagre capital, but whatever had happened in the past, she was still my mother and I could never stop loving her, ever. Even after all this time I wanted to prove that I was a worthwhile daughter.

In all this, Michael was a real support, though I knew he had had quite enough of my dysfunctional family. His were all so normal, open, honest and friendly. He never had his son and daughter on the phone telling tales about each other and then swearing him to secrecy like mine had done. It was hard to remember what I was supposed to know and not know!

I admit to being curious and looked on the internet to see if the old family home was for sale. Kylie had intimated that the fees for the home were running out fast. It was a shock to see that it was already sold for an amount worth even more than I thought. It was a strange feeling to see my family home now belonged to someone else.

On my next visit to the home I met up with Kylie and she took me back to the house which looked as if a bomb had hit it. There was stuff everywhere, as they had spent only two days looking for anything they thought might be of value, and then just abandoned everything else. In the end they paid to have everything cleared out. I dread to think how much valuable stuff they missed and how much money they lost over the deal.

I had got to know the staff at the home and they phoned me when Mum was taken into hospital again. This time it sounded serious, so I flew over immediately. I think Mum recognized me for she squeezed my hand and I did not leave her side for the next three days, sleeping on the floor and being fed by the kind nursing staff. The girls knew by now she was very ill and made plans to join us.

In the end I was the only one with her when she passed away early one Friday morning. I closed her eyes and wept more than ever before. Now it was too late, now we could never make peace, there had been no Hollywood ending in her last few minutes on earth.

Kylie had been promising to drive down but only arrived some time later. As the nurse went to give me Mum's rings, I had noticed that she had been wearing her first engagement ring, the one from my father, I mentioned that I was not her executor, so she handed them to Kylie who put them in her handbag. Would it have hurt Kylie to give them to me?

Because we had lost all our precious mementos, I have no idea what Jeremy had done with all our precious stuff when he left Johannesburg in such a hurry. I now had no photographs of my mother, father, grandparents or of my girls before their late teens. Did Kylie understand this? Did she simply believe, as the girls so often told me, that my mother and I just hated each other? I just broke down and said how much I had needed Kylie, especially during that last long night. She just got angry with me.

Dana arrived with her children shortly afterwards and the three of us had a terrible row, especially when I saw them chatting to Dick outside the morgue. I couldn't believe they could be so friendly with him after all his lies and his deceit. He'd already sent a message to the hospital saying that he was too busy to drive up due to pressure of work, but sent his best wishes. I suspected that he didn't want to meet me. The girls assured me it was simply to keep good relations as he was a beneficiary as well, and they were sure he had my mother's best interests at heart.

I remember Dana exclaimed that obviously I thought I was the victim in all this, which quite frankly I felt I was. She couldn't see it. My daughters simply could not recognize that I felt it terribly disloyal to fraternize with Dick. I had flown over to England when they were worried about losing their inheritance, they wanted me to protect it. Now they were going to inherit everything, they were not going to rock the boat and risk losing all that money.

Feelings were still running high when Kylie dropped me off in the pouring rain to wait for my bus back to catch the plane. She said she needed to get back to London, but I was glad it was raining, it made my tears less obvious.

Back home I kept a low profile and was less than responsive to the odd phone call asking for advice. It was frustrating knowing that I could have handled affairs more efficiently and effectively, but both girls were well into their thirties and I guess we all have to learn sometime.

Kylie would send me loving messages on the phone, and I assured her that I loved her, but was too hurt to be in contact right now. I did ask her if I could see a copy of Mum's will, but she said they were bound by secrecy and if I wanted any information I would have to go through the solicitors.

Both girls assured me they were only carrying out their grandmother's wishes and as executors they could divulge nothing. They told me when the funeral was going to take place.

At the time, Christine was over in Spain and I told her that I did not have the courage to fly over. I was not sure how I would react to Dick and his partner, as I felt very bitter towards them. I was not on good terms with my daughters either and although Michael said he would go with me, that might have made things worse.

I asked the girls if they would request that Dick not attend the funeral, but they both agreed that it was important he go, as he was a beneficiary and he had told them that my mother had loved him as the son she had never had. I decided to stay away. If my mother had not wanted me to have even the family photos I doubt if she would have bothered if I went to the funeral. So Christine sat with me and was a great comfort as the day went past.

Kylie and Dana were horrified that I did not go. They thought I should have made the effort and that my absence only reinforced their belief that I never liked or loved my mother. They both said how much they enjoyed meeting Dick's son, why they had to tell me that I don't know.

But I was also amazed to hear that I had relatives living just a few miles away from my mother's house. I had not even known they were there and they would have been only too happy to have me stay at any time. I've since been in touch with them, yet another branch of the family that Mother was not talking to.

Back in England Christine was not pleased when she read the hysterical Facebook comments from Kylie about her grandmother's death, after all my daughter had only visited her grandmother a handful of times in the previous ten years. Christine replied to say that my mother had not been a nice person and had made many people unhappy in her life time. Kylie 'unfriended' her and also 'unfriended' me as well, so did Dana which was sad, as that was the only way I could look for pictures of my grandchildren.

Many people urged me to contest the will, and I thought long and hard about it. If I was honest, I didn't think I would win, there was too much hearsay involved, but even if I put in an application just to delay things and cause chaos, was it worth alienating my daughters permanently for money? Wasn't it better to retain my dignity and accept matters as they were? But it was hard to allow Dick to walk away with thousands and thousands of pounds.

26 THE ROAD TO DAMASCUS

No, I have never been to Damascus, but I did have that blinding moment of clarity, 'My Damascus Moment.' It was just a couple of weeks after Mother's funeral when Christine phoned me and suggested I tune in to *Talk Radio Europe* immediately. There was a discussion about personality disorders and she said they described my mother's behaviour exactly. I was on my way to see my counsellor and as I walked in she said "I have reached the conclusion that your mother was suffering from narcissistic personality disorder." Two people said the same thing to me within ten minutes of each other!

As soon as I got home I turned on the computer and looked it up. I'm not sure how I can even begin to explain my feelings as I read the various web sites. In all there are nine behavioural traits that indicate NPD, and if a person exhibits five of these then that is sufficient for a diagnosis. My mother had eight of them, and fell into the malignant category. Finally I really understood and believed that it was her and not me.

I experienced total euphoria as the more I read, the more the strands came together. Mother never had real empathy for anyone, she was quite unable to see things from anyone else's point of view. She exploited other people and caused them to be unhappy. She always felt she was entitled to more than she had, and expected people to admire her and believe everything she said. She was arrogant and was unwilling to share the limelight with anyone.

As I read further I could remember her saying things and behaving in the exact same ways as the characteristics described.

She refused to allow me to wear age appropriate clothes – the episode over the stockings. Every achievement I had she belittled and at the same time took credit for herself – "only because at great sacrifice I sent you to private school."

Yes, she constantly compared me unfavourably with other people, spoke about me as if I was not there, and denied any cruelty she inflicted. She told lies, another trait, this was a revelation too, and she was not honest with money, I had lost out on two inheritances and the money in my bank account. Because there was always a grain of truth in what my mother said, it was difficult to 'catch her out'. If I repeated what she had said to me, she would tell me that I was mistaken, or imagining things and that I was lying.

She was incredibly secretive about her behaviour - changing the moment the door bell rang - and I had already understood that she was very different from other people and insisted on total control.

The abuse is so subtle, so continuous and so insidious that few people see it. Even the child who experiences it finds it difficult to explain, especially to outsiders. On the surface, you have a mother who gives you adequate food, shelter, clothes and education, yet at the same time she is depriving you of self worth, confidence, and insists that you are totally worthless, and in my case just a ‘child of the devil’. Yet had I told anyone that, she would have said I was mistaken, I misheard, or I was lying yet again.

I’m not sure how long my euphoria lasted, then came the anger. Why did I not see this before? Why was my childhood such a living hell? I guess it was the ‘Why Me?’ syndrome. For a while I stifled the anger, trying very hard to forgive my mother. Her brain was wired differently, so she was mentally ill, so the least I could do was forgive her.

But then the thoughts would creep in as I remembered that she could turn her behaviour on and off like a tap. If she could do that, did she not realize that her behaviour was not acceptable? But for NPD mothers the rules other people live by, don’t apply to them, they are just too special.

For a long time I had believed, that had my father lived, and Mother had more children, then the whole scenario would have been different. I learned that this was not at all the case. Husbands and fathers either supported and enabled the behaviour, or they walked away.

Of the other brothers and sisters, usually one was the favourite or golden child, and there was always the scapegoat child, the one who suffered the abuse. In my case of course it was a one on one from the day I was born.

I joined an on-line forum and wrote a little about my experiences and was amazed by the replies from others who had had almost identical stories to tell. I can only describe it as standing in front of a board, and with each new discovery, jigsaw pieces come fluttering down and fall into place, each piece going to fill in the whole picture. My puzzle still has gaps, but the more I read, the more complete it becomes.

After the anger came the relief that I was not crazy, nor a misfit and I did deserve all those awards for my work, that I did achieve a worthwhile life. In fact the more I was trying to prove to Mother that I had done well, telling her of my successes, the worse I was making things, only I didn’t understand that at the time. I was in fact banging my head against a brick wall, and the only one I was hurting was myself.

As the euphoria, anger and relief drained away, I felt a deep grief. There was nothing I could have done, I wasted so much time. From the moment I was born, my mother was lost to me. I never had her in the first place! There is nothing anyone can do to change a person with this personality disorder, mainly because they do not see any wrong in what they do or say. It is the rest of the world that is at fault and you cannot persuade them differently.

The only action you can take is to cut off contact and concentrate on your own life. I think that my sanity was preserved as we lived overseas and far away from her and I could control the times I phoned home and fortify myself with a drink beforehand! But I could not divorce myself entirely, like a Pavlov dog, I was too well trained and indoctrinated. In my forties I was still apologizing to everyone for just about anything. It's hard believing that you are an OK person just like everyone else.

Maternal love is such an accepted belief that it is very difficult to explain to any outsider. You feel both shame and guilt, positive that they think that the problem is really you. Their mothers loved them, that's the natural way, so why on earth did your mother not love you? There must be something wrong with you.

Then the crux, am I also narcissistic too? Did I subject my children to the same upbringing? I was devastated to read that this syndrome, or disorder is thought to be over 60% hereditary. I combed the internet again and took every possible test, trying hard to be as truthful and honest as I could be. If my mother did not recognize it in herself, would I fail to recognize it too?

Then it struck me, if I was looking to see if I was similarly afflicted, that in itself suggested that I was just – normal! Perhaps I did deserve the good things that had happened to me after all. I could at long last take pride in my life.

The one underlying fact that all daughters of narcissistic mothers must face is that there is nothing, absolutely nothing you can ever, ever, do to change things. Yes, we can distance ourselves in order to protect ourselves, but we cannot change our mothers' behaviour, no matter what we do or say. She is as she is, and will never see anything wrong in herself and the way she relates to other people. Acceptance is the hardest lesson of all.

My mother died last year and although she has tried to rule from the grave by cutting me off completely and causing a rift between me and my children, I am fighting not to let that happen. I don't want to give her the satisfaction, but I see several of her traits in both my daughters, although not to the same degree.

This is so sad, but again I must understand that there is nothing I can do about their behaviour either. It does explain why I could never correct them, and why any criticism as they were growing up, let loose a huge wave of protest and overwhelming criticism of me in return. I let them get away with this, but in a lose/lose situation there is not a lot you can do.

Time heals and with repeated self affirmation many of us, once we have understood the scenario, can set out on the road to recovery. I'm still surprised when people phone to invite me for coffee or lunch. That's how this affects you. I am amazed when others laugh at my jokes or when I get paid a compliment. But there is a silver lining to every cloud, I do have a lot to thank my mother for.

I had a good education and this allowed me to earn a living. All those years I was walking over eggshells, being careful of everything I said, has enabled me to get the best from the people I employed. Years of listening intently so I could react in the least confrontational way, taught me to report interviews and record research accurately and concisely, it has been invaluable. All those conversations listening to and evaluating every word has served me well in my career, and more than one person has remarked that I have been the only reporter to interview them who has recorded the facts correctly. As a result, they have insisted that I was the only reporter they would talk to in the future.

Being very accurate in my research has meant fewer re-writes in my scripts. I find I listen to people and not only hear what they say, but I'm able to 'hear between the words', and identify the real issues.

I believe my mother also taught me to think of other people, although this initially was meant for me to think about her above all else, but the very characteristics that she lacked somehow have reversed in me. At the same time I have had to learn to be more assertive, sometimes to do what I want to do without feeling guilty or selfish. It took a long time to notice that everyone else around me was doing exactly that already! So many of us daughters of narcissistic mothers are easy to get on with, as we are so used to falling in with everyone else's wishes.

So it has taken nearly all my life to understand, and it has taken me years and years to grow up and stand on my own two feet. I've had to rely on myself to prove that I am just an ordinary person and undo all the abuse I suffered as a child. If I'd been born with a different, less sensitive nature, then probably I could have matured that much earlier, left home, broken all ties and become independent much sooner.

Yet I feel that a lot of potential has been wasted, what could I have really achieved had I had a supportive, loving background?

While a great deal has been written about physical abuse and sexual abuse, mental abuse can have a much more devastating effect on someone, especially if it starts in early childhood. Physical abuse usually stops when the victim grows up and can fight back. Mental abuse continues unabated. My stepfather Paul lived with this for several years. It affected him in his sixties and ultimately led to his death.

For years I blamed the upbringing my mother had, I simply didn't understand. I cannot say thank you enough to those web sites which opened my eyes and introduced me to over 27,000 other women worldwide, who have been through the same mill and who understand. They are there to listen and to share.

If the statistics are true that 9% of the population suffer from personality disorders, there are even more of us out there. I hope you find the answer like I did, that the most natural love of all, that of a mother for her child, is one we must always live without.

At the end of the day we are the survivors, for we have grown up without the support structures most people take for granted, and we are stronger and wiser as a result.

%%%%%%%%%%%%%%%%%%%%

ABOUT THE AUTHOR

Lucinda E Clarke - not her real name – has been a professional writer for the last 30 years, scripting for both radio and television. She has had numerous articles published in several magazines and currently writes a monthly column in a local publication. She once had her own newspaper column, until the newspaper closed down, but says this was not her fault!

She has won over 20 awards for scripting, directing, concept and producing, and had two educational text books published. Sadly these did not make her the fortune she dreamed of, to allow her to live in the manner to which she would like to be accustomed.

Lucinda has also worked on radio – on one occasion with a bayonet at her throat - appeared on television and met and interviewed some of the world's top leaders.

She set up and ran her own video production company, producing a variety of programmes from advertisements to corporate to drama documentaries on a vast range of subjects.

Altogether she has lived in 8 different countries, run the worst riding school in the world and cleaned toilets to bring in the money.

When she handled her own divorce, Lucinda made legal history in South Africa.

She gives occasional talks and lectures to special interest groups and finds retirement the most exhausting time of her life so far. There is still so much to see and do, she is worried she won't have time to fit it all in.

Her story, from a mentally abusive background to present day success, makes you want to laugh and cry, but above all, what sustained her was an unfailing sense of humour.

To my Readers

If you have enjoyed this book, or even if you didn't like it, please take a few minutes to write a review. Reviews are very important to authors and I would certainly value your feedback. Thank you.

Connect with Lucinda E Clarke on Facebook
https://www.facebook.com/lucindaeclarke.author
Or by email lucindaeclarke@gmail.com
Blog:- http://lucindaeclarke.wordpress.com
Twitter @LucindaEClarke

33789818R00131

Printed in Great Britain
by Amazon